DATELINE: STORNOWAY

A Newspaperman's
coverage of the
Western Isles
over the past
50 years

By

Bill Lucas

Leis Gach Durachd

Bill Lucas

ACKNOWLEDGEMENTS

This book is dedicated to my wife Anne
and our family
Sine, Donald and Fiona
and my grandchildren
Keir, Cameron, Heather, Rhiannon,
Daniel and Chloe

With thanks to all those friends, contacts, officials --
and their secretaries -- who have helped
me in covering the Western Isles
over these past decades

Thanks also to Shona of ShorePrint and Design
for her help

Copyright (C) Bill Lucas 2008

ISBN
978-0-9560393-0-9

All rights reserved. No part of this book may be reproduced in
any form without the express written permission of the publisher.

Email sales: **www.bethesdahospice.co.uk.**

Published by Hebridean Press Service

Second Printing

Printed by Gomer Press, Llandysul, Ceredigion, Wales

Contents

Foreword	6
Dateline Stornoway	8
Introduction	10
Stornoway	16
Back on the island	31
Characters and Personalities	42
The Courts	78
And Then there was Lochmaddy	101
Sea dramas	119
Air Affairs	146
The Inquiries -- including BCCI	176
Island Industries	242
The Miscellaneous Files	247
Civic Duties	273

Aerial view of Stornoway and harbour c. 1960's

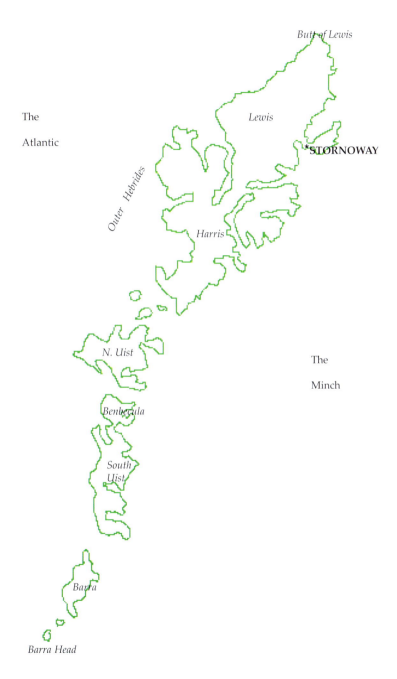

Foreword

For more than fifty years Bill Lucas has been an energetic and popular citizen of his adopted hometown of Stornoway.

It has never been easy for any journalist to meet the high and urgent demands of that profession in a small community where everyone knows everyone, where families are close knit with overlapping and sometimes unrecognised ties of kinship.

The appetite of the national and international media for hard news and the propensity for tabloid sub-editors to turn a local story into a headline grabbing expose of the 'quaint idiosyncrasies' of some small and remote community is not easily equated with the sensitivities and values of the community itself. Yet by sheer professionalism and a strongly disciplined objectivity Bill Lucas has achieved that balance to such an extent that he is locally regarded as a fair minded reporter and more importantly, as a respected pillar of the island community.

'Dateline :Stornoway', his engrossing account of the many events he has witnessed and reported on is written with that economy of words and immediacy of style which are the hallmark of good reportage. These delightful cameos of his life and times range from the Hamilton Advertiser, the Stornoway Gazette, The Scotsman in Edinburgh, and as a freelance from the Butt of Lewis to Barra and encompass courtroom characters, local worthies and events of human suffering, community loss and also moments of happiness and joyful hilarity.

In addition to his full life of journalism Bill has made a substantial personal contribution to the voluntary and public service sectors in the Hebrides. Stornoway Town Council (now of happy memory), Stornoway Pier and Harbour Commission, Ross and Cromarty County Council, and committees to attract industry and create sustainable development, have all benefited from his professional PR expertise and his wide range of influential contacts at every level of Scottish business and political life.

However perhaps out of modesty this rich seam of story and

anecdote remains untapped. We can but hope these will provide a second volume of memoirs of the life and times of Lewis as described in the words and camera of Bill Lucas.

'Dateline:Stornoway' is a must for the library of any booklover interested in the Hebridean scene in the second half of the Twentieth century. It will also prove a valuable source book for local historians and be an essential guide book for budding journalists.

Sandy Matheson
Lord Lieutenant of the Western Isles
July 2008

****

Other comments:

Brian Wilson: 'Bill has turned his reminiscences into an entertaining book.'

Murdo Morrison: 'In this book Bill Lucas gives us all a privileged insight into his many contacts with people and places ... the end result is a book which is readable and vastly entertaining.'

Rt Hon.George Reid, former Presiding Officer in the Scottish Parliament: 'It's an absolute joy -- informed, irreverant, and insightful.'

DATELINE : STORNOWAY

'You ain't even in Great Britain' came the tired and laconic reply from the American news bureau staffer in London. He had asked for a dateline for a story which I had filed and I had suggested Stornoway, the Western Isles, or even the Outer Hebrides.

The story concerned a young Norwegian who, along with his sister, was travelling on a cargo-passenger ship to America where their father was in the diplomatic corps. The young man had attempted suicide by slashing his wrists. The ship's captain decided to land him at Stornoway for hospital treatment -- the last hospital before hitting the Atlantic. The young man recovered.

In additon to sending the story to the UK national papers and the Press Association, I thought it would also be of interest to the United Press of America which had a bureau in London. The late night staffer telephoned back to ask: 'Is this guy gonna die?' I told him that if he read the last paragraph of the story he would see that the hospital spokesman had said that the patient's condition was now 'satisfactory.' Came the response: 'Listen bud, when I'm on nights everybody dies!'

This was followed by the query: 'Howma gonna dateline this?' and I offered the three options mentioned above. 'What about Inverness?' he queried. I told him no, we were not near Inverness. He then asked me to hold on and obviously went off to consult a map or a gazeteer. When he returned he informed me: 'Hey bud, you ain't even in Great Britain!'

It was all part of the joys of covering the 1200 square miles of the Western Isles as a newspaperman for 50 years.

Mind you some of the UK papers were not much better as far as geography was concerned. To them we were a dot on the map. On one occasion I filed a story on a Fleetwood trawler being in difficulties north of the Butt of Lewis and the Daily Telegraph telephoned back later to thank me for the copy but could I also cover a story concerning another trawler which was in trouble south of Barra Head.

Tongue in cheek I told him that I would have a bite to eat first and then go down on my bike to which he replied — as all the Fleet Street broadsheets did in those days — 'Many thanks old boy.' However I put him right by telling him that the trawler was probably just as near their Manchester office as it was near mine.

****

For the record the Western Isles -- or Outer Hebrides -- lie about 40 miles off the north west of Scotland: the next stop is New York!

I hope you enjoy this dip into the archives of The Hebridean Press Service, my news agency which was set up with the Gaelic motto 'Abair ach began is abair gu math e (Say little but say it well) although as some papers paid by lineage I did write more than I should on several occasions over the years!

The Encounter Magazine published an argument for brevity.
The Lord's Prayer 65 words
The 23rd Psalm 118 words
The Gettysburg Addresss 226 words
The 10 Commandments 297 words
US Department of Agriculture Order on the
price of cabbages: 15,629 words.

My survival as a news agency could not have been achieved without the patience and help of my beloved wife Anne who fielded the phone calls, helped phone the copy in the old days, and gave sound advice

Newspapers were always looking for fillers or newsbriefs to fill up a column. I have adopted the same idea. Any odd spaces at the end of chapters have items which have amused me over the years. Have a chuckle!

INTRODUCTION

The love affair with the Western Isles began in 1956. I had been a reporter on my home town paper - the Hamilton Advertiser -- for over 5 years, and there was two years National Service in the Royal Air Force.

After square-bashing at Hednesford in Staffordshire I was posted to Hereford and finally to Headquartes Bomber Command at High Wycombe. This was set out in the style of an English village in an attempt to fool 'the enemy.' The fire station had a tower to make it look like a church steeple, there were underground passages linking all the main buildings, and there were such exotic places as the 'Secret Registry.'

The underground corridors were my downfall. I liked a long lie and did without breakfast. I could travel from my accommodation block to the Administration site by the corridors and be in the staffing section without anyone knowing. This enabled me to miss the morning parade. I got caught on my last week of National Service which resulted in carrying out fatigue duties for seven days.

I was a shorthand typist in Air Staff Plans and some of my bosses were test pilots. At that time the aircraft about to come on stream were the 'V' force -- the Valiant, the Vulcan and the Victor nuclear bombers which were to replace the war-time Lancasters and Halifaxes. They were also testing the Martin Baker ejector seats.

In the ASP section there were giant photographs on the walls of the famous Dambusters raid on the Mohne dam in Germany by 617 Squadron when they used the bouncing bomb developed by Barnes Wallis.

Down the corridor was Air Chief Marshal Sir Hugh P Lloyd and one of my bosses was Wing Command the Hon. Derek Dowding, son of Air Chief Marsal Hugh P Dowding, former AOC Fighter Command when the Battle of Britain took place. My regret was that I did not take up the offer of a posting to SHAPE headquarters in Paris for the last six months of my National Service.

However there was an opportunity for sport and at week-ends and I filled in as scrum half for one of the Old Wycombensians teams. There was the occasional visit to London to take in some of the west end shows -- at that time Mary Martin (the mother of JR of Dallas fame) was in South Pacific, and also a visit to Sadler's Wells opera to see what it was all about. There were also visits to the Centre Court at Wimbledon and to the Henley Regatta.

On return from National Service I had this desire to work in the Highlands -- with an eye on Inverness. An advertisement then appeared in the World Press News for a reporter for the Stornoway Gazette. A friend in the tennis club got me a copy of the Gazette at Glasgow Central Station and having read it from cover to cover I decided to apply for the job. I also thought it had a sense of humour -- on the back page in the Situations Vacant column it stated: 'In loving memory of my dear husband...'

Being full of the vanity of youth I wrote off to the editor-proprietor James Shaw Grant telling him that I had a nose for news, otherwise I was quite good looking! I got the job and arrived in July 1956, just three weeks before the Royal Visit by the Queen, Prince Philip, Prince Charles and Princess Anne. They arrived on the Royal Yacht Britannia during their annual cruise through the Western Isles.

This experience taught me to be careful about who you were speaking about in the isles -- everybody knew everyone else or was related to them. When I arrived back at my digs following the Royal Visit the landlady asked me all about it. I told her that one of the Councillors -- in the excitement of being presented to Her Majesty -- had actually curtsied instead of the traditional bow. When I told her who it was she said: 'That's my brother!'

The training on the Hamilton Advertiser stood me in good stead for covering the isles. There had been a thorough grounding in all kinds of general reporting, local authority coverage, the courts, cattle shows, sports, and even covering Hamilton Park races, Motherwell speedway, and the pony trotting at Steppes.

My mentors at the HA were Editor Tom Murray, and Chief Reporter Alex McCormack Thomson, along with Tom Williamson and Claud Thomson, later a well-known staff man on the Herald.

The photographers during my time at the HA were Chick Bain, then Harry Benson, who later became an internationally recognised lensman. His photograph of The Beatles' pillow fight in their New York Hotel bedroom has been used worldwide and he was described by one publication as 'the man who shot the presidents' as he has photographed all the US presidents from Dwight D Eisenhower onwards as well as the most powerful men and the most beautiful women. He was also only a few feet away when Robert Kennedy was assasinated. I remember Harry telling me once that when he was sent to take a photograph of Lord Beaverbrook on his birthday -- he was in a sun lounger at his home -- the Beaver told him:'Only one shot.'

The other Advertiser photographer in my day was Jack Hill who left for the Evening Citizen. He made a name for himself when he caputured a remarkable photograph of a gunman who had held up a post office in Glasgow. As Jack pointed the camera at him from the car the gunman then seized a passing woman as a hostage to use as a shield. The gunman was arrested by two police officers. The Evening Citzen printed a special edition that night.

Among my first jobs as a cub reporter was to telephone the butler at Lauder Ha' early afternoon every Friday -- just before the paper went to press -- to find out the latest condition of Sir Harry Lauder, who was on his death bed at the time.

There were three courts to cover -- Sheriff, Burgh Police and JP. There were also licensing courts to be covered as well as Council and District Council meetings. You were also allocated districts and it was your job to glean news from these areas. In my time there I covered Blantyre, Bellshill and Shotts. One of the big stories during my time with the Advertiser was a £3000 bank robbery from the Clydesdale Bank. Ravenscraig in Motherwell was about to mushroom and become the centre for the steel industry in Scotland.

It was demolished in 1992 and now a £29 million sports facility is to be built there. The village of East Kilbride was about to blossom as a new town.

The Advertiser, which had the largest circulation for a weekly newspaper in Scotland (45,000) was located in a former church in Campbell Street. Formerly it had been the Ebenzer Chapel where the missionary-explorer David Livingstone and his parents had previously worshipped.

At the HA I learned all about the composing room with 10 noisy Linotype machines where the operators produced lines of leaded type from the news copy supplied by the editorial staff.

When it was placed in galleys it was forbidden for journalists to touch type: you had to point out any corrections to the page make-up man. However you did learn to read type upside down as it lay in the galleys. You also learned all about the proper correction marks to make when checking column or page proofs.

There was a Reading Room where column proofs were compared with the original copy for accuracy. In those hot metal days each newspaper had a style book for journalists, lino operators, and the proof readers which had to be rigidly adhered to.

There was also the process room where half-tone blocks were made from the photographs.

The corrected type and photograhic blocks were then put into a steel forme. In the sterotyping department a papier mache or replica of the metal page was produced. This was then used to create a semi-circular curved metal plate which was then placed on the rotary printing press situated in the machine room in the basement. When it started late on a Friday afternoon it could be heard throughout the building. For stop press news, there was also a fudge box.

I had to check the galley proofs for the death notices in case some worthy had passed away, and to check the public notices so that entries could be made in the news or photographic diaries.

Decades later we had progressed to computers and on-screen make up for pages, but there was more glamour and excitement in the old 'hot metal' days and the smell of printers' ink.

From the editorial department in the Advertiser you could see the bookies' runners on the street corner scattering for cover if there was a police raid. Street betting was an illegal practice at that time and betting shops had not come into existence..

In 1956 -- the Centenary of the Hamilton Advertiser, -- it was time for me to 'Go West young man'.

****

Aged 77, Archibald MacLeish, one of America's most distinguished men of letters, and winner of Pulitzer Prizes for both poetry and drama, accompanied his son Kenneth and photographer Tom Nebbia on their assignment to cover the Western Isles for the National Geographic magazine in 1969.

Later he wrote: "To me, the great importance of the Western Isles is not to the understanding of the past - not to myth, or to curiosity or to the traveller's itch -- but to our lives now. We inhabit (we do not *live* in it) a deteriorating society which is falling apart because it is ceasing to be a society and becoming an economic arrangement held together by a romantic awe of technology. If we are to recover our lives we must recover our sense of society; and how are we to recover our sense of society unless we have a touchstone - an example - to show us what a society should be in human terms if we were to achieve it? The only touchstone I have seen in this century is here in these islands."

THE APOSTLE
(The Bill Lucas Two-Step)

Ian Crichton

Bill - a Journalist from Hamilton - was given the nickname 'The Apostle' by a well known local character when, over 30 years ago, he came to the Island to work for the Stornoway Gazette.
A few years later Bill set up his own News Agency. He settled in Stornoway, where he lives with his wife and family.

© COPYRIGHT 1992

STORNOWAY

On arrival at the Stornoway Gazette my colleague was Bill Carrocher who went on to become a Press Officer in the Scottish Office, then the Commonwealth Office -- where part of his duties was to organise Royal Visits -- and he then became PA to the head of the BBC.

During my first week Bill introduced me to old Dan Macgregor the chief librarian who called in to get his copy of the paper every Wednesday (there were two editions on those days).

When he heard the name Lucas, he said: 'We'll call you The Apostle (the Gaelic for Luke). That stuck and many years later my good friend Iain Crichton composed a lively two step of that name. (See previous page).

During his Gazette time Bill Carrocher was the author of a humourous column entitled 'The Bodach as a Rubha.' It was a happy office and the girls -- Jean Anne, Beitha, Katag, Mog, Joan, and Ishbel --always seemed to be singing. Ishbel Macaskill became a well-known Gaelic singer.

I had been doing a bit of reading about the Western Isles and one which took my fancy was 'Highland Journey' or 'Suil air Ais' by Colin Macdonald, a North of Scotland Board of Agriculture adivsor in the Hebrides. His closing words captured so admirably and vividly the charm of the Outer Hebrdes.

'And then? And then! Behold the Hebrides! Enchanted islands of the west! Sanctuary of the soul-rest and heart-healing where time is properly regarded as the infinite thing it is; whose spell once cast is ever potent. Islands of bent grass and seaweed, of salmon and sea trout; of wild wheeling greylag, of curlew and teal; of song and of story; of Gaelic and homespun, of peat fires so radiant, of hearts warm and leal.'

In 1956 you still had to be acquainted with the local lingo -- and I don't mean Gaelic but the patois of Stornoway, a town inhabited by coves (males) and blones (females) One of the first things you learned was the specific three-note Stornoway whistle or the Stornoway Wire, which was easily identified by SY coves. It could stop a Stornowegian in his tracks not only in SY but in Glasgow, Sydney, Hong Kong or Singapore.

I'm indebted to Norrie Macgregor of the Stornoway Historical Society who took the trouble to compile a list of these words and phrases. There was the Opera House (a public toilet) renowned for Gaelic singing when someone had a half-bottle. Bachells were boots: a bluebird the Mitchell bus: the cob was the cockle ebb: the Burma Road was the lower end of Smith Avenue: Colditz was the Cearns housing scheme. The greeting 'What's fresh'? meant 'What's new?' Down the vile was to go down the town. Gissa was give me. A greepan was a cheeky youngster, and a meppan was a brat. The gut house was the fish processing factory. The hoil was the harbour. A slope was a policeman and to be arrested was to Kennethed, as the police station was in Kenneth Street at the time. An ollack was a stone and the ocroch was the town tip. To identify someone you asked 'What's his ear markings?' a reference to the tags on sheep or cattle.

Lazy corner was the corner of the Inner Harbour where the pier lawyers gathered to sort out the world affairs and discuss the latest gossip.

The country cousins were described either as a Maw or as a Scorp and were usually referred to as belonging to the other side of the cattle grids which were on the roads leading into town.

A person in his cups was referred to as being scutt (plastered) or well oiled (drunk): or having a list to port, or a full cargo on board.

A meek was a half-penny and a wing was a penny. The residents from the Battery were known as Crotans, and the people from Newton were crabs. When the new Council offices were built it naturally became known as the White House.

I was given an early introduction to the laid back attitude to life in the isles. An elderly crofter arrived at the office to tell about his tattie shaws which were 9ft long. After taking the usual details I asked him when he lifted the potatoes and was told: 'About 9 months ago.' He had been saving up this titbit until his next visit to town!

There was the other one about the Lewis crofter who was seeking a subsidy for his cow which meant that the cow's ear would have to be tagged. He wrote off to the Department to enquire 'if it was the right ear when looking at the cow or with the cow?'

Of course on an agricultural level I learned all about the common grazings and the souming which governed how many sheep or cattle a crofter was allowed to have on the common grazings.

When I set off to cover my first island cattle show at Barvas I asked Bill Carrocher if it was just the usual as far as the prizewinners were concerned -- the sire and dam. He told me: 'If you ask who the sire is you'll be told it was the Department of Agriculture Bull!

Here's two examples of the timelessness in the islands. The humorous Business Hours notice in the loom shed of my friend Donald John Mackay of Luskentyre -- who became famous when he received an order for Harris Tweed from the international shoe company Nike -- stated:

'Open most days around 9 or 10
Occasionally as early as 7, but some days
as late as 12 or 1
We close about 5.30pm or 6pm
Occasionally about 4 or 5 but
sometimes as late as 11 or 12.
Some days or afternoons we aren't here at all
And lately I've been here just about all the time
Except when I'm someplace else.
But I should be here then too.'

There was also a sign in Ivor's engineering workshop which stated: 'The only man who ever got a job done by Friday was Robinson Crusoe.'

****

The Gazette suppled news to the national papers. The editor took two thirds of the the lineage money, and the remaining third was split between myself and Bill Carrocher.

At that time we used Press telegrams for sending news stories to the national papers. These came in packs and there was a special Press rate of 3s. for each 60 words or less handed in between 9am and 6pm (day rate) and 3s. for each 80 words or less handed in between 6pm and 9am (night rate)

The telegrams were taken to the Post Offices with the list of newspapers who were to receive them

However that changed to phoning the stories to each newspaper where it would be taken down in shorthand and then typed, or it was typed directly. Some of these copy-takers became journalists.

The Royal Visit to the Western Isles began just three weeks after I arrived at the Gazette so it was a busy time supplying news copy to the national papers on the places they were to visit and the people they were to meet.

The Queen met a character known as Cailleach Gray - a fish gutter, who presented Her Majesty with a golden cutag, the knife used by these ladies for gutting the herring. Because of a superstition that it was bad luck to give someone a knife it was the custom to present a coin to the giver and Cailleach Gray received a gold sovereign from the Queen.

Over 200 island servicemen were lost on New Year's Day in 1919 when the Iolaire sank at Holm and tragedy also struck in January 1957 when the Fishery Cruiser Vaila ran aground and five crew members were drowned. More of this in a later chapter.

The 'Vaila' ran aground at around 5.30am in poor visibility, and as she settled further onto the rocks, the Captain gave the order to abandon ship. Two lifeboats were launched safely, but a third became fouled and capsized, and the remaining men, including the captain, were thrown into the sea. The captain was later rescued by one of the other boats, but despite valiant attempts to find the missing men none were found alive.

The sinking and tragic loss of life resulted in a fatal accident inquiry being held in February that year at Stornoway Sheriff Court. The inquiry found that no negligence was involved on the part of the captain or crew, and that all steps had been taken to safeguard life.

Also breaking at that time was the story of the proposed Rocket Range for Uist which will be referred to later.

There was also the tale of the mission house at Lemreway being burned down because of a dispute.

On the Gazette I was the main man for sending the news stories to the national newspapers -- it was one way to augment my salary -- and I became well-known to the various newsdesks.

Then one day I got a phone call from Max MacAusland, News Editor of The Scotsman, asking me down for an interview in Glasgow and we had to meet at the One-O-One for dinner. Max by the way was the young Daily Record reporter who broke the story of Nazi Rudolph Hess landing in Scotland.

On the night of May 10th 1941, Hitler's deputy, Rudolf Hess, bailed out of his aircraft, a Messerschmitt 110, after a 5 hour 900 mile flight and parachuted into a field at Floors farm, near the village of Eaglesham on Fenwick Moor.

On surrendering to a ploughman he told him in English, "I have an important message for the Duke of Hamilton". He was taken into custody by the local Home Guard.

There was a claim that Hess intended to arrive at the small landing strip at Dungavel Mansion, home of the Duke of Hamilton, near

Strathaven. Some believe that he was on a mission to meet the Duke, whom he had met at the 1936 Berlin Olympics, to negotiate a treaty that would allow Germany to concentrate on the invasion of Russia.

Alasdair Dunnett had been the Editor of the Record and when he moved to The Scotsman he took Max with him.

When he offered me a job in the head office in Edinburgh I accepted although I explained to him I was really wanting to work in the Highlands. Max said that Roy Thomson, proprietor of The Scotsman, had plans to buy up weekly papers in the north and the central publishing area would be Inverness. He said they would need a journalist there to oversee the whole set up. The prospects looked good so I set off for Edinburgh.

They say it's Capital punishment to work there but I did enjoy my time in Edinburgh with the opportunity to cover a wide range of stories and to travel first-class throughout Scotland.

The shifts played havoc with your social life and at that time you worked a different shift each day, the last one being from 8pm to 3 am. The staff car took you to Leith Docks to check on the shipping arrivals and departures, and to the Royal Infirmary to check on any casualties. There was a book at the gate with the name of the patient admitted, his address, his condition and what type of accident. Even the ward to contact for an update. A far cry from today!

The Scotsman office was a beautiful building and when Roy Thomson (later Lord Thomson) bought it he remarked that the real estate alone was worth £1 milliion. (It is now a luxury hotel)

There was a marble staircase leading from the editorial department upstairs but we were not allowed to use it -- it was roped off and used only for visiting VIP's. We had to use the lift.

Shortly after joining I was covering a book launch by a famous author at which my editor Alastair Dunnett was present. We left the George Hotel together along with an Edinburgh dignitary and I always remember that Alastair introduced me as his colleague, not some young reporter.

Because of my experience in covering cattle shows I was seconded to the Agricultural Editor Bob Urquhart for the Royal Highlands Shows which were held in various parts in those days. It was Bob who put forward the idea of having a permanent Royal Highland Show based at Ingliston. At the time of writing there is now a proposal to move to a new site nearby to make way for an extension to Edinburgh Airport.

There was also the opportunity to cover a large number of dinners to which The Scotsman was invited, This entitled you to claim one guinea for cleaning your dinner suit!.

Expenses were reasonable and when they were paid each week it was an opportunity to dine at one of the better restaurants. When a new young reporter joined the staff and submitted his first expense sheet he was obviously letting the side down. Max sent him over to my desk so that I could show him how to be more creative in filling in an expense form!

My time there also involved covering General Elections and I remember that the Tory candidate in the constituency I covered was the late Earl of Dalkeith. I had been given the address of one of his committee rooms in Wemyss Place and told the taxi driver to take me there. He pulled up outside an exclusive shop for ladies underwear.

Nothing daunted I went in and said: 'This may sound crazy but I'm looking for the Earl of Dalkeith .' She directed me through the back to where the Duke was waiting to be interviewed in front of a roaring fire. It gave me an introduction for my story. 'One man running his election campaign on a sure foundation....'

His Labour opponent at that time was Advocate Ronald King Murray and the last time I had interviewed him I had to cross the whole length of Sutherland to do so.

There were many yarns about The Scotsman journalists in the old days. Rumour had it that one occasion the golf had taken rather too long and the Leader had not been written. Apparently the editor asked for a copy of that day's Times, cut out their leader, and wrote at the top: 'We entirely disagree with the views expressed in this Times' leader.'

There was the journalist who had been sent through to cover the launching of the Queen Mary and was rather late getting back to the office in Edinburgh as the champagne had been flowing. No copy had arrived and the sub-edtiors were getting a bit anxious. The journalist could not be seen at his desk but the waste paper basket was overflowing with copy paper, each one commencing with the words: 'Yesterday was the day....' but it never got any further. He was later found under the desk.

There was also the one about the young fellow who had just left university and who was to start as a sub-editor. He turned up at 7pm in a dinner suit. When someone asked him if he had been somewhere or was going somewhere later on, he replied that he thought they would be adjourning for dinner at 8pm! He was disabused of the idea as most subs and late shift journalists had to suffer the canteen.

One of my colleagues there was on the late shift when it was discovered that an Edinburgh worthy had died. As first edition time was approaching he headed for the morgue file where information on such people was kept in alphabetical order. He grabbed the background info to write the obituary but unfortunately his eye missed one of the lines and it appeared that the gentleman had ....'served in the Royal Company of Archers (the Queen's Bodyguard for Scotland) during the Second World War.' Bows and arrows would have been the secret weapon against Hitler!

Another colleague was Philip Stalker who always covered the General Assembly of the Church of Scotland. He was also an elder and a commissioner to the Assembly and caused no small stir when he stood up in the Press box to vote on certain issues.

Also there was another character, Ronald 'Bingo' Mavor, the drama crtic of The Scotsman.

Another little money spinner while on The Scotsman was providing stories for Scottish Television and putting in Saturday shifts for some of the Sunday papers in the Thomson Group - such as the Sunday Times and others. The result was you could be paid for three shifts for a single Saturday. This meant giving up the rugby, tennis or golf every so often.

When they were short staffed in the Glasgow office I was usually sent through there because I knew the area and could speak Parliamoglesca.

The Edinburgh Festival was a busy time for the editorial staff each summer. However we did get the opportunity to travel around the country and we enjoyed several 'out of town' assignments as they were known to staff journalists.

I had heard from sources that the first Corporal missile was to be fired shortly from the Rocket Range in South Uist and photographer Dennis Straughan and myself were despatched to the islands.

Our first call was to see Father John Morrison, known to the Press as 'the 'Rocket Range priest.' His famous quote on the compensation being offered to crofters for the loss of land was 'not enough to buy a cow's tail.'

Anyway there was also a ritual when you visited Father John. No sooner were you seated than the housemaid arrived with a silver tray with glasses, a bottle of whisky and water. On one occasion he was perplexed that he had no whisky but only gin, and he had nothing to give us to mix with the gin except sherry. It was an unusual cocktail.

He confirmed that so far as he knew the firing of the first Corporal rocket was to be very soon. We headed for firing range and no one seemed to flag us down or ask what we were doing there. We saw a Corporal missile on a trolley and Dennis took a few photographs. For some reason I had a camera with me as well and I took a few shots.

As we were getting back into the hired car we saw an officer coming across the machair at a great rate of knots and looking very irate. Dennis hid his camera in the back seat under a coat and said:'Give me your camera.'

It started off with 'What do you think you are doing here?' and we told him we were from The Scotsman doing a story about the rocket range. He threatened all sorts of things and then Dennis told him: 'We're only doing our job but to make you happy I'll give you the film.' He then opened my camera, took out the spool and exposed the film to daylight.

The officer was profuse in his thanks and told us that any time we were back he would be glad to see us. He wasn't as chuffed when the photograph was used on the front page of The Scotsman. That day Alasdair Dunnet the Editor came through to ask us what we had been up to as the MOD had been on the phone threating us with a Shedule D notice or something like that. We explained the background and he went away smiling.

At that time the Free Church Synod of Glenelg -- which covered Lewis, Harris, the Uists, Skye and the Western seaboard -- sent a resolution to the Prime Minister, the Minister of Defence, and the Secretary of State for Scotland, expressing fear that the Government intended to make the Outer Hebrides the 'guinea-pig of the Western Powers' by turning the islands into a special defence area because of concerns about a NATO base for Stornoway Airport.

I also headed to Inverness in 1959 to cover what was known as the 'Waters Tribunal' The inquiry was ordered by Parliament -- there had been a campaign by the Independent MP for Caithness and Sutherland, and the Daily Sketch.

The inquiry was ordered after allegations that 16 year old grocer boy, John Waters, had been assaulted by PC George Harper and PC

Robert Gunn in an alley near the Bay Cafe in Thurso (known locally as Cardosi's) on December 7, 1957. It was also to look into what action Caithness police had taken in connection with the matter. The incident had been sparked apparently by the boy making pig grunts at them in the cafe.

Lord Sorn presided accompanied by Sir James Robertson and Mr J N Dandie. All the top legal luminaries of the day were there to represent the various parties. Senior Counsel to the tribunal was Mr C J D Shaw, QC, Dean of the Faculty of Advocates, and Junior Counsel was Mr David Y Abbey, advocate. Mr J O M Hunter, QC assisted by Mr R A Bennet, advocate, represented the Waters family. The Police Constables were represented by Mr Manuel Kissen QC, assisted by Mr Ewan Stewart., advocate. Mr Harald Leslie QC and Mr J S Mowat, advocate, appeared on behalf of the Chief Constable.

Some considered that the tribunal might have been a 'ministerial error of judgement.' It was estimated to have cost £20,000.

The inquiry opened on March 17, 1959. and lasted for a week. My colleague Bert Porter and I were filing about 10,000 words per day as The Scotsman decided to give it a really big coverage spread over many columns. For the three PA staff - headed by Jimmy McGuire, a former Hamilton Advertiser man -- it meant they could cover the evidence by doing 10 minute 'takes'.

However for us it meant starting off with a 15 minute take, and by the time that was telephoned back to Edinburgh, it meant your colleague had covered a 30- minute spell. There was an open line to the office all day. Each take kept getting longer. We gave up typing and dictated direct from our shorthand notes.

On the final day we were nearly all asleep when Harald Leslie QC, got to his feet and lambasted the whole procedure. He said: 'It is a most extraordinary thing, even at this late stage, that after a protracted week, I do not know why we are still here. It would be comic if it were not tragic.'

Mr Hunter QC said it was not the form of inquiry which commended itself to some members of the legal profession in Scotland, and Manuel Kissen QC, claimed that the boy had been 'playing the little hero' in front of his friends in the cafe.

Half way through there was a memo from the office that my daily expenses were running at £5 a day and I had to explain that all these top class Counsel only drank large whiskies!

In the evenings, at either the Station Hotel or the Caledonian Hotel, the legal eagles put pen to paper and composed bardic epics on the case. I'm probably the only one left with a copy as I typed it for them. The language during the tribunal had been extremely blue so I'll quote a few expurgated verses:

> The winter wind in Thurso streets
> Blew cranreach cauld and rude
> But Cardosi's caff was one big laff
> With sentiments somewhat lewd
>
> Out of the wintry weather
> Two constables sauntered in sight
> Now wern't they nosey to go to Cardosi
> On such an inclement night.
>
> Close by the top of the alley
> In a boudoir, recherche, chichi
> Manicuring his toes, prior to repose
> was ensconced Mr Andrew Macphee.
>
> Startled by all the commotion
> He gasped with anxiety
> Whoever they blame for this dark deed of shame
> They surely won't pin it on me
>
> He rushed down the stairs in his shirt tails
> I'll false allegations forestall
> And found his wife quaking, uneasily making
> A statement to Mr Dowdall*
>
> Thus ends the true story of Rattles
> Harper, Gunn, pig grunts and jeers
> But if you fell equal, you'll soon hear the sequel,
> In the good old House of Peers.

* A well-known Glasgow criminal lawyer

The Tribunal, which made its report to the House of Lords and the House of Commons in April 1959, concluded : 'Constable Gunn did assault Waters , but had the constables been prosecuted there would probably not have been a conviction. Under Scottish law no person can be convicted upon the uncorroborated testimony of a single witness and this rule is extended to cover a proof of a major fact such as identification. Had the case gone to a court of law the two constables could not have been called to the witness box and could have remained silent without prejudice to their defence.'

Regarding the second part of the report the Tribunal found that the action taken by the police to have been all that it should have been.

Strange enough in 2006 the Waters tribunal cropped up again in the Scottish Parliament when Alex Neil, the Scottish Nationalist MSP, asked who had set up the inquiry and what its terms of reference had been. This was in relation to another celebrated inquiry concerning Detective Sheila MacNee.

I was also sent to cover the largest ever Gathering of the Clans since the ill-fated one at Culloden in 1746. This took place at Bught Park in Inverness in 1960 and was held in conjunction with the World Pipe Band Championships. For the fourth year in succession the winner was the famous Shotts and Dykehead Caledonian Pipe Band.

As I wrote at the time lest dirks be drawn there had been a draw to allocate the tents for each clan - and the Macdonalds and the Campbells were at each end of the park! I checked up to see if they had visited each other. The Campbells said they would wait for the Macdonalds to make the first move.

Macdonald of Clananald was cautious enough to say that he might visit the Campbells but added: 'After all, we've buried the hatchet.' At this juncture a man standing next to me told the Chief: 'Well you must have buried it in me, because my name is John Campbell Macdonald!'

During my Scotsman days there was also a bit of discreet freelancing by providing diary items for the Scottish Daily Express and the Scottish Daily Mail, items which would have been of no interest to my employer.

One one occasion Stuart Lindsay of the Herald and myself were travelling to Fort William by train to cover the Scottish Land Court and in the First Class compartment with us was an elderly gentlemen who quizzed us all the way north. Imagine our surprise when we discovered he was Lord Gibson who was presiding over the case which involved the Lochaber Crofters versus the Secretary of State for Scotland. The Foresty Commisison wanted to plant trees in a certain area on low lying land but the crofters wanted them up on the hill away from the good grazing land.

The solicitor for the Scottish Office did not have much of a chance when his Lordship (who happened to be an FP of my old school) said at the outset: 'So here we have this mighty man, the Secretary of State for Scotland, against these poor humble crofters.'

Stuart and I felt the same so before retiring that night we booked an early call for the solicitor --at 4am!

The last big story I covered for The Scotsman before leaving was the arrival of the US Polaris submarine the Patrick Henry -- motto 'Liberty or Death' -- to the Holy Loch in March 1961. It sailed into British territorial waters for the first time and tied up beside the depot ship Proteus. It had 16 missiles on board. By staying submerged for 66 days and 22 hours, the submarine had set up a new patrol record after covering 11,000 miles.

The Patrick Henry was named after a Governor of Virgina, whose father, John Henry, came from Aberdeen. A leading spokesman in the cause of self-government for the American colonies, his speeches became famous. It was from one of his quotations that the submarine took its motto. 'I know not what course others may take, but as for me , give me liberty or give me death.'

There were of course anti-Polaris protestors, one of them in a canoe who was stopped by Naval frogmen. He was swimming towards the Patrick Henry after his canoe had been intercepted.

When Roy Thomson bought the Kemsley group of newpapers -- including the Press and Journal which had a large staff in Inverness -- it became apparent that my transfer to the Highland capital was not going to take place.

So it was time to heed the call of the Hebrides and cross the Minch once more.

I knew at this time that the news stories which should have been coming out of the Western Isles were not being sent and during those long night shifts I began to plan the Hebridean Press Service, a freelance agency which would provide news, features and photographic coverage from all over the isles.

I touted the idea around a few newsdesks and they agreed that there was a need for a good freelance service.

My Scotsman colleagues thought it was a daft idea and told me I would starve. They seemed to think I would be sending my copy by a trained seagull. However when I handed in my resignation to Alastair Dunnett he wished me every success and said that if he was my age he would try it himself! Later when he came on a National Trust for Scotland cruise to Stornoway I was able to entertain him in our home.

****

A one liner which has nothing to do with the Lewis Pipe Band.

'Hey buddy, how late does the pipe band play?'

'Oh, about half a beat behind the dummer.'

BACK ON THE ISLAND

On arrival in Stornoway I took up residence in the Lewis Hotel and also found office accommodation initially in a former fish office on No. 1 quay known as the Dardanelles. Eventually I moved into the Maritime Buildings and from my office I could see vessels arriving on either side of the pier. It was a great source of news with the fish market close by, lorries coming from all parts of the island to pick up goods on the quay, and in the evening it was usually thronged with people who came to meet friends off the ferry. Nearby were the Customs and Excise offices and the Fishery Office.

Regular residents at the Lewis Hotel were the Traffic Examiners and they had some wonderful tales. Here's a few of them.

The senior examiner had been fortifying himself the night before because his first candidate in the morning was to be one of the tinkers. After breakfast he popped a couple of peppermints in his mouth to take away the smell of the whisky.

To make matters worse the van was an old banger (long before the days of an MOT) and it was not doing Jack's stomach any good at all. He tells the driver to draw into the kerb and then take off again. When the tinker executes this move he forgets to take off the handbrake which results in a very strong burning smell permeating the vehicle.

As he could not tell him what he had done wrong during the test he finally asked him: 'Can you smell anything?' After a sniff or two the tinker replies: 'Peppermints, boy, peppermints.'

Before the Narrows in Cromwell Street became a pedestrian precinct, a Minister was going through his driving test. It was in the days when you still had to give hand signals even if the vehicle had indicators. As the car approached the junction to turn right into Point Street he duly stuck his right hand out the window . As the vehicle slowed down at the junction. a woman coming out of the chemist's at the corner stepped forward and shook his hand.

An elderly chemist was told to turn right and go up Church Street but he refused telling the examiner that he never went up that way!

There was also the other boddach who settled into his seat, put on the seat belt, checked wing and rear view mirrors. The Examiner then told him to drive off. Just before doing so and to make himself more comfortable for the task ahead he took off his bunnet and hung it on the rear view mirror!

However once the L plates had been torn up the islanders resorted to their own 'Code of the West,' an island version of the Highway Code as I recorded in a feature article for The Scotsman. The single track roads -- really floating roads built on peat -- at that time had plenty of lay bys.

The article followed the introduction of MacBrayne's new car ferries to the isles. Motorists were cautioned to ignore competely the remarks made by Lord Craighton who told delegates from the Western Isles not to pine for dual-carriageways. 'Your single track roads will give the tourists time to enjoy your wonderful scenery,' he claimed. On the islands, however, we knew different. Take your eys off the road for a few seconds and you'll find yourself five feet down in the peat.

On the narrow twisting roads there were no traffic lights, and strangely enough we had a fly-over in Carloway. To cross at road junctions in Stornoway was - and stiill is -- a deadly dangerous business and is often achieved by a blast of the horn, and a burst of speed.

At other times the patience of the motorist was rewarded especially when two vehicles stopped alongside on a narrow road to have a chat. The fact that they were blocking the highway had no significance: you had to bear in mind that they might be second cousins who had not seen each other since the New Year or the last family wedding or funeral. It was on these occasions you could enjoy the surrounding scenery.

Parking on street corners was another favourite pastime and made life exciting. The other was to turn right or left without any hand or indicator signals. The tourists' ignorance was no excuse. He should have known that that particular lorry always turned left at that junction and that the Co-op van always turned right there.

Driving experiences on the island reminds me of my old friend the late John Morrison of Northton in Harris. He also owned the local bus which plied its way between Harris and Stornoway.

John was a cheery character and knew everyone. When driving he was also looking to the left and right to see what was going on and how the sheep were doing.

There was a cailleach sitting next to him in the front seat of the old bus going up the Clisham road (the Clisham is the highest mountain in the Outer Hebrides) and it meant a great deal of changing of gears because of the character of the engines in those days.

The old woman was getting a bit perturbed with all the activity and all the gear changing and told him: 'John, you just keep your eyes on the road and I'll stir the petrol for you!'

****

The story is told of a new minister who had just been inducted. The first week he preached an acceptable sermon which lasted 45 minutes. The next week it was only 20 minutes, and the third week one hour and 20 minutes.

A concerned senior elder explained that they were enjoying his preaching but wondered if there was any particular reason for the different length of sermons.

Explained the new minister: 'The first week I had my own teeth, but then I lost them and borrowed my father's which were not a very good fit. The third week I borrowed my wife's teeth!

One aspect which has changed over the years is the ability to get around the islands and to file news copy and send pictures. My territory covered 1200 square miles , all the way from the Butt of Lewis to Barra. Before the North Ford causeway was opened I had travelled in a tractor from North Uist to Benbecula when the tide was out, and come back by a small boat when the tide was in. Covering Lochmaddy Sherirff Court in North Uist meant a flight to Benbecula, a hired car and usually two nights in the Lochmaddy Hotel. Later the inter-island air services made a big difference, then the causeways. I suppose I was one of the few freelance journalists who used scheduled air services to cover my patch.

Getting the news stories out usually meant phoning and making transferred calls to each newspaper or radio and television station. When telephone exchanges were manned you could give them a list of numbers at the start and as soon as you finished one call they put you through to the next one. Then came the Telex 15 with the punched tape, and then the Telex 23 which had a screen. Next was the Tandy, the standard tool for most journalists for a while, until we moved on to the various laptop computers.

Prior to the BBC moving into a studio in Stornoway I was equipped with a 'black box' which was attached to the telephone and gave a better quality when transmmitting interviews or doing voice pieces.

Way back in the 1960s I suppose I was among the first multi-media journalists. I've set out for stories not only with the notebook and pen, but with a BBC Uher tape- recorder, a Beaulieu cine camera with a zoom lens, as well as my still camera. It was sore on the neck.

At the beginning of the 1990s the Graphic union agreed to licence me (a member of the National Union of Journalists) to be able to send pictures by wire machine. This could transmit a black and white print in about 7 or 8 minutes, but if it was colour it took about 20 minutes. Now that we've moved to digital photography there 's no darkroom and we can transmit pictures in a matter of seconds.

HA Editorial staff in the 1950's: David Martin is in front (later a BBC producer) behind is Brenda Patterson, on the left is David Steel, and in the cormer Alex McCormack Thomson, chief reporter, who later became editor. Top right is the author and in front of him Tom Williamson, senior reporter.

Myself and Bill Carrocher with the ' blones' in the Gazette

Linotype operators at work in the HA composing room

*Assembling type, photos and advertisiing blocks
into a final page*

*Completing a forme of two pages before stereotyping.
Left :a forme on a mangle to make a stereotype matrix. Below:
The printing plate being placed on cylinder of rotary press*

Smith's Shoe Shop in days of yore was the real Press Association and centre for island news. It was the last ceilidh shop in Stornoway and therefore all kinds of information filtered through it and so it was a great place for tip-offs. Of course you had to check out all such information not once but twice - and sometimes three times - just in case they were setting you up!

In the phoograph above are (l to r) D L and brother John Alex (known as Put) and George F. In the background Jan and Angie Smith.. Since then the waistlines have all increased.

Their business also expanded into clothing and other items. A Hearrach arrived one day and commented: 'Och it's just like Harrods,' "Oh, I wouldn't say that ' said DL in all modesty. 'I was talking about the prices!' said the Hearrach.

This was the venue for the parliament of local worthies and first call for any exiles. DL assured me that I was the last person to get two pairs of shoes repaired there before they closed. He said he had only one sole left and was waiting for a one-legged man! 'Just bad ordering' commented his brother George F. Ah the repartee was good.

Put's son, Kendon, who became a celebrity chef in his adoopted Colombia, died suddenly of a heart attack aged 48 in February 2008. A friend of Presidents, he was a columnist, author and TV chef.

The old fish mart and the narrow lane beside it known as the Dardanelles where I had my first office. Note the green Iron Man (the public toilet) beside the telephone kiosk. The old Coast Line buildings can be seen beside the ship and Lews Castle in the background. Below: The Maritime Buildings where HPS later operated. My office was beside the ladder - ideal for keeping an eye on what was happening in the harbour. The building has now been demolished.

The Loch Portain car ferry at Leverburgh in Harris which made inter-island travel so much easier

The jolly traffic examiners - Archie, Jack and Fred - with a tale to tell

As we are writing this during an election campaign it reminds me of what some people think of politicians.

The Jerusalem Post recorded that a Michael Kinsley once described a gaffe as when a politician accidentally tells the truth.

That is akin to the obversation by a former Lewis District Councillor, Donald John Mackay of Caversta in South Lochs, who opined: 'The only time politicians are telling the truth is when they are calling each other liars.'

****

Old Colin Scott Mackenzie, former Procurator Fiscal, was at one time a member of the Board of Management of Craig Dunain Hospital in Inverness, where many patients with mental problems were treated. As he was going to a Board meeting one day he was walking up the drive when he espied King Cole, a Stornoway worthy, who regularly appeared before the Court on various offences usually involving drink. He was digging away in a plot of ground and sweating in the warm summer weather. Colin stopped to speak to him and gave him half a crown.

After the meeting he was coming back down the path and again encountered King Cole who was still digging away. Feeling perhaps he had been a bit mean he gave him another half dollar.

A few weeks later he met him in Cromwell Street in Stornoway and said: 'So they let you out then? 'What do you mean, let me out, I was over there working as a gardener.' 'Oh, said the Fiscal, 'I thought you were a patient.' Said King Cole: 'I thought you were one, especially when you gave me the second half dollar!'

****

CHARACTERS AND PERSONALITIES

The islands produced a wealth of characters and personalities.

One of the well-known ones was 'Ganga' Slater and the following is a tribute I wrote shortly after his death.

> "God grant me the Serenity to accept the things I cannot change;
>
> 'Courage to change the things I can;
>
> 'And wisdom to know the difference."

'It was the comfort of those words which helped to sustain — in his last few years — one of Stornoway's most colourful and likeable characters, Angus Alexander Slater, affectionately known to everyone as 'Ganga.

This belated tribute has been inspired by the excellent photograph reproduced above - taken by his wife Chrissie — and taken at a most appropriate location, Stornoway's Inner Harbour.

This was the area Ganga knew best and the one he relished most. It was where he grew up, where he rescued at least 19 people from drowning, where he enjoyed an early morning walk at week-ends when he could listen to the subdued chatter of the seagulls and the cries of the birds in the Castle Gounds

It was here he earned his living, once as a fish cadger and latterly as a fisherman, although there had been other jobs in between. It was from the harbour that he set out on many a mercy mission to give a hand when boats went aground or were adrift.

He lived life to the full until the end of last year when illness took him on his last voyage at the early age of 53 years.

The rolling seaman's gait (he served in the Royal Navy during the war), the big grin, and the croaky voice all belonged to the Ganga we knew. His suitably laced repartee was a joy to listen to and to those of his friends and acquaintances it was the 'in thing' to know the latest Ganga-ism. He disliked pomp and was quick to prick it, irrespective of the person's station in life.

Like most he had his share of youthful peccadilloes, but his had added wit and charm. This is not the place to catalogue them but some easily spring to mind. There was the famous occasion when he returned from Harris and the van he was driving finished up on the parapet of the bridge with a 40 ft drop on the driver's side.

Who else could have established legal history as to the definition of a 'fry' of fish from a visiting trawler — '16 boxes M'Lord.'

When officialdom was finally embarrassed enough by the number of rescues he had made from the harbour and decided to recommend that his humanitarian services be recognised, who else but Ganga could tell them so succintly regarding the disposal of any testimonial.

His tales of school life were a joy to listen to, particularly the Friday afternoon quizes when the reward for a correct answer was a goodie (a sweet).

Examples: 'Who fed the children of Israel?' — Ganga's reply: 'Calum Ross' (the slaughterman). Where do the green men come from? — Marybank (at that time the home ground for tinkers). 'Who invented the bagpipes?' — Doyle (one of the Pipe Band members).

Ganga was warm hearted and generous. He loved children and disposed money freely to any toddler. It's an old fashioned phrase but he was the type who would have taken the shirt off his back to give it to you. His close friends will tell you that he would even have taken it off someone else's back if necessary!

Although Ganga decided to follow other paths in the last few years the change in his lifestyle did not affect his cheerful outlook and general good nature. He had in fact become a different person from the one we knew.

We're going to miss you cove — both of you.'

A number of years after writing this his widow Chrissie told me that one of their pieces of furniture was from the wreck of the famous 'Politician' featured in the book and film known as 'Whisky Galore. It had been 'liberated' from the ship at the time.

In 1999 a commemorative seat marking his many rescues was installed at the harbour by the Stornoway Pier and Harbour Commission.

****

Remember there's only 60 seconds in a minute - except when prefaced by just a....

CALLA

Another seat commemorated at the same time was for another local hero. He was Malcolm Macdonald, who for 40 years served on the Stornoway Lifeboat, 20 of them as Cox, during which time he saved 227 lives.

Calla, as he was known, held the RNLI silver and bronze medals and was also awarded the MBE. He was made a Freeman of the Burgh of Stornoway. He died in 1992.

Calla had many exploits to his credit. In December in 1964 the Daily Record had commissioned me to do a feature profile on Calum for their 'Man of the Week' which was carried on Page 2 along with the famous cartoons, Andy Capp and Angus Og!

The by-lined feature was headed: 'Cool Calum - Hero on a Mercy Mission,' and read as follows: "He showed the most amazing common sense and coolness of judgement'.... These words referred to 55 year old Malcolm Macdonald, coxswain of the Stornoway Lifeboat for the past 12 years, and the only holder of the RNLI's silver medal in the history of he Stornoway station .

However, it is only when you meet this unassuming man with the greying hair and the twinkling steel-blue eyes in the weatherbeaten face that you begin to realise the meaning of the words used by Lord Saltoun, chairman of the Scottish Lifeboat Council, when he presented the silver medal to Calum Macdonald two years ago.

He received his award (his second) for rescuing a man and a woman from the fishing boat 'Maimi' during a full winter gale on a treacherous shore near Stornoway.

Ten years before he had been awarded the bronze medal when he rescued Guga hunters who were marooned on Suilisgeir 40 miles north of the Butt of Lewis.

Calum admits he 'just drifted into the lifeboat crew.' 'I didn't really have any ambition to become cox of the Stornoway lifeboat,' he said. 'But my uncle was the cox for many years, and I was always interested in the sea and boats'

He has a boat of his own and is one of the pilots at the port who guides in the many foreign vessels which call at Stornoway.

Although slow to talk about himself, Calum is quick to praise his crew. He said: 'They really deserve a lot of credit. You need steady and reliable men, and I was fortunate to have a good crew around me.

'We have a 52-foot boat, one of the largest types now on service in Britain but we do get exceptional pastings at times. She can do nine knots irrespective of the weather, and we have been out in winds of 100 miles per hour.

'Since the present lifeboat - the "James and Margaret Boyd " was launched in 1955, she has had 77 calls and rescued 32 lives from ships, although she has picked up many others from islands and isolated stretches of coast.'

During his 30 years' service he had voluntarily risked his life on hundreds of missions in the Minch and the Atlantic.

The Stornwoway lifeboat covers about 500 miles of coastline — the largest patrol area for any lifeboat in Britain.

In recent years there has been an average of ten calls each year, although in the past three weeks the lifeboat has been called out three times — and two of these were false alarms within 24 hours of each other. 'These calls have to be answered like any other - but it does sicken the crew quite a bit,' says the cox.

But whether false alarms or genuine distress calls when the maroons go off the quite spoken men who crew the lifeboats never fail to turn out on their missions of mercy.

In December 1964 the maroons did go off and the Stornoway lifeboat was called out in hurricane force winds to a ship in Loch Torridon.

I had filed the feature and photographs of Calla earlier in the week and I knew that it was to be carried in the Record on Saturday. The weather was bad that week and on the Firday the lifeboat was launched in winds gusting to 90 mh.

I told the Daily Record that the news story would go well with the feature and they carried the rescue misison on the front page with a photograph of Calum. The heading read: LIFEBOAT IN GALE DRAMA - Bid to Reach SOS Ship in 90 mph Fury.'

The introduction read: 'A lifeboat set out on a fantastic against-the-odds race last night to reach a boat in distress.

'Winds were gusting to 90mph and lashing rain made visibillity "almost impossible" as the Stornoway lifeboat knifed through the seas.

'It was the second time in 48 hours it had made the terror 30 mile trip across the Minch towards the mainland... As the lifeboat, coxed by 55 year old Malcolm Macdonald, ploughed into the teeth of the storm, Coastguards reported: "The boat in trouble has been sighted as is listing badly. The weather conditions are terrible."

Calum was one of the last people to be made an Honorary Freeman of the Burgh of Stornoway before local government re-organisation was introduced.
During his 29 years as cox the lifeboat saved 180 lives. His involvement had been part of a family tradition with about a dozen of his relatives involved with the RNLI station. At one time Calum and his two brothers were in the crew and his wife and sister were involed in the Ladies Lifeboat Guild.

The family tradition was carried on when his nephew, also Calum Macdonald, became cox and mechanic. He hit the headlines in September 1980 when he was involved in the rescue of 29 men from the Hull tawler Junella, which ran aground off Skye in a force 8/9 gale. The lifeboat was rising 8 to 12 ft in the swell while alongside the Junella.

The official report by the RNLI Inpector for Northern Scotland stated: 'The coxswain displayed seamanship and courage of the highest order in manoeuvring the lifeboat alongside the casualty.'

Calum receivd the RLI silver medal and also the Maud Smith Award for the most outstanding act by a lifeboatman in 1980.

A worthy successor to his uncle.

****

DOMHNULL THOE

Another character you would meet at the Lazy Corner — the meeting point at the inner habour for the 'pier lawyers' who could put the Council, the Harbour Commission, the Stornoway Trust and the world to right all within five minutes — was Domhnull Thoe (Donald Macdonald)

Big Dan, as he was sometimes known, was the Burgh lamplighter for many years. He was a verbal historian who could regale you with tales of Sober Island in the harbour, worthies who used to frequent the town, or his POW experiences during the Second World War.

If you met him on his walk over the golf course you would never get your round finished as he would tell you how the Ranol hole got its name, how it used to be a viable crofting township before the people moved down to Sandwick to make way for the golf course.

He had many an ecclesiastical tale to tell too. My favourite — told to his father by the late Rev Kenneth Macrae who was minister of Stornoway Free Church for 34 years — was the one about the elder from the Highlands who was attending the General Assembly in Edinburgh in days of yore.

Perhaps not very elegantly dressed and wearing what was fashionable on at that time - a Kilmarnock bonnet — and sporting a long white beard, he was surveying the scene at the bottom of the Mound when he became the butt of three Divinity students approaching him. One was overhead to say: 'Do you think that's Abraham?' 'No' said his companion, 'It's Moses.' 'You're both wrong,' said the third, 'Its Elijah.' As they came abreast the elder — who had overheard their banter — he looked them in the eye and used 1 Samuel 9 as a text. He told them: 'I am neither Abraham, Moses, nor Elijah. I am the servant of Kish, the son of Saul, and I am looking for my master's three asses, and behold I have found them!* A fine example of verbal karate.

****

MAJOR

Another personality loved by many generations in the island and further afield was Duncan 'Major' Morison, MBE, well known international pianist.

Duncan's father, a carpenter, worked at Lews Castle in Stornoway which had been built by Sir James Matheson of Matheson and Jardine fame. It was owned by Major Duncan Matheson when Duncan's father was there. When Duncan was born he was baptised as Duncan Matheson Morison, after his father's employer. Thereafter he was called 'little major' by the Matheson family.

Duncan kept up his connection with the Mathesons. He had attended the wedding in 1967 of Katharine van de Werff . Her daughter Claudia -- whose great-grandmother grew up in Lews Castle -- unveiled the refurbished Lady Matheson monument in the Castle Grounds in 2006.

It was in 1933 that Duncan won an An Comunn Gaidhealach scholarship which took him to London and thereafter became a protege of the Marchioness of Londonderry and remained a firm family friend until the end of his life and visited them for holidays.

In 1935 he dedicated his collection and arrangements of Lewis songs — entitled 'Ceol Mara' — to the Queen Mother when she was Duchess of York. They remained life-long friends and always exchanged Christmas cards.

His outstanding musical talents resulted in him travelling all over the world. Before the Second World War he was a concert pianist and was an accompanist to the celebrated singer Father Sydney McEwan on his tours of Australia and New Zealand. He also carried out concert tours with the singer Robert King. They were planning a tour to North America when war broke out.

Before the war he also played before Herman Goering, Chancellor of Nazi Germany. Duncan told me: 'He wanted us to meet Hitler, but fortunately we had a prior engagement to play for the Rev

Donald Caskie, who later became known as the 'Tartan Pimpernel.' He was in charge of the Scots Kirk in Paris and helped many Allied troops — including some from the Hebrides — to escape.

Duncan returned to his native Lewis in 1949 and became an itinerant school music teacher. In those days there were no pianos in the schools and he carried around a small xylophone. He was a popular music teacher to generations of Lewis children and he prepared them for solo singing and choral work for the local and National Mods.

He was in great demand at all prestigious occasions, as well as at concerts and ceilidhs. For 30 years he was organist in Martin's Memorial Church in Stornoway. He was also honoured for his work for An Comunn Gaidhealach.

His family home in Ness was renovated and became an arts and music centre known as Taigh Dhonnchaidh and his home in Stornoway - Seminary House -- is to be used as a centre for young musicians, a project which would have been dear to Duncan's heart.

****

A sympathy card read: 'As time passes gradually we move toward the day when the comfort of our memories is greater than the sorrow of our loss.'

CHATELAINE OF THE ISLES

Mrs Elizabeth Perrins arrived in Lewis in style complete with millionaire husband — Captain Neil Perrins the sauce magnate — a French chef and a butler, to take up residence in their newly purchased 12 bedroomed fishing lodge on the 12,000 acre Garynahine Estate on the west side of the island.

She was a colourful character: a former Schiaparell model, Parisian society girl, actress, nurse and then a police sergeant in the Liverpool docks area during the Second World War. (Her uncle, Lord Royden was a former chairman of Cunard, which was started by a Lewis family).

During her time on the island she was seldom out of the news because of her outspoken views on many subjects — particularly the absentee landlords of other estates. She was never afraid to enter the lists with anyone in authority.

With a name like Perrins it was usually fairly easy to place stories about her - especially Diary pieces for the Hickey column in the Daily Express and the the Charles Greville column in the Daily Mail. She enjoyed the publicity.

However to start at the beginning. She was born in Spittle in Cheshire but brought up in the Haute Provence region of France with her twin sister. In France she became a freelance model but worked mainly for Schiaparelli. This inevitabley led to her being a Parisien society girl.

In 1932 she returned to England and then joined the Liverpool Playhouse and was on the stage for a short time but found it did not satisfy her.

She then decided to take up nursing as a career. It was during this period that she met her first husband, an American orthopaedic surgeon, and they married in 1936 and settled in Liverpool.

She told me: 'From then until 1939 I just enjoyed myself. When war broke out I decided to join the Liverpool Police force, worked in the dock area and rose to the dizzy rank of sergeant.' After that she and her husband ran a large private nursing home in North Wales and then moved to London in 1950.

They had four children — two boys and two girls. During her time in Lewis her daughter Mary, a model, was married to the Hon. Patrick Howard, a brother of the Earl of Suffolk and Berkshire. Her sister Sally was married to Peter Hennessey of the cognac family. (Mrs Perrins confessed it was the one brandy she did not like!).

However, in her own words she then 'bolted' with sauce magnate Captain Neil Perrins of Lea and Perrins fame. He was also involved with the renowned ceramics company Royal Worcester. He himself had two children by a former marriage, Andrew and Gail. She met the Captain (a former Welsh Guards officer) in 1954 and they married after her divorce in 1956 and settled in Norfolk.

Her third great romance started in 1960 when she and Captain Perrins decided to come to the Hebridean Isle of Lewis and she became the Chatelaine of Garynahine Lodge.

They had a lot in common. Her interests were horse riding and sailing and the Captain was keen on shooting and fishing. However their decision to move to the Hebrides was taken independently. Unknown to each other both of them had noticed an advertisement in The Field for the 12,000 acre Garynahine Estate, well-known for its Red River salmon fishing.

He thought 'Puss' (his favourite nickname for her) would never go to Lewis to live. She also saw the advertisement, marked it and left it on his desk. He told her: 'You're' a bloody wily woman Puss. That is the best hint I have ever had!'

For Captain Perrins it was like a homecoming because on both sides his ancestors came from the Western Isles. His paternal grandmother was a Macdonald from Lochboisdale in South Uist, and his maternal great grandfather was a Macneill from Barra.

Shortly after their arrival on Lewis there was the famous story about the 'Ghost of Garynahine.' RAF personnel making their way home on the 'passion wagon' from a dance in Stornoway to the camp at Aird, Uig, claimed they had seen a white apparition near the Red River at Garyhanine.

All was revealed when Mrs P admitted that she was the lady in white. At that time they always dressed for dinner. She had been in the habit of going for a stroll after dinner wearing a white dinner gown. She claimed that the poaching on the river had almost stopped. Later she made a guest 'ghost' appearance at the Stornoway Agri-Horticultural Show in the Castle Grounds in Stornoway when she arrived wearing a white mask on a white horse and wearing the same dinner gown with which she had scared off the poachers.

Her escorts were young teenage friends of her daughters who were are Heathfield, Ascot, the school which Princess Alexandra attended. They all wore white masks and berets for the occasion.

The well-known racing driver Innes Ireland and his wife were also among the guests at the lodge. He was the agent for the Sno-track, which the Perrins wanted to use to take their guests across the moor to the fishing lochs.

In 1961 she and her husband decided to purchase a local firm — Maclennan and Maclennan — which produced Ceemo Tweeds. Captain Perrins became the chairman and Mrs Perrins the managing director, vice-chairman and designer.

She shook the islanders when she announced that she would be breaking away from the 'traditional hairy Harris Tweed' and would be concentrating on a Lewis Tweed — a high fashion ligtweight cloth incorporating made-man fibres such as lurex. It was marked under the name of Ceemo Fabrics.

In her usual forthright manner she said at that time that she was prepared to help the islanders if they were prepared to help themselves, but she wanted her tweed on time and she wanted them flawless. She even threatened: 'If I do not get my tweeds on time to meet the markets then I am prepared to go round the villages and townships with a loud speaker van telling them - in Gaelic if necessary - that it will not do.'

It quickly achieved success and three years running —between 1963 and 1965 — she won eight gold medals at the International Textile Exposition at Sacramento in California. Even Jackie Kennedy wore the cloth. Although there were plenty of orders on hand — she spent a great deal on marketing — and the firm was heading into financial trouble.

At that time she claimed: 'Success has overtaken us far more quickly than we anticipated and we have a shortage of working capital.' The result was that decrees for more than £5000 were granted at Stornoway Sheriff Court against the firm.

She pleaded with the Treasury officials in the Scottish Office to give a £7500 temporary loan through the Highland Fund but they refused. The firm went into voluntary liquidation owing £75,000 but some critics said that it was more like £250,000 which had been invested and lost, partly due to the expensive advertising campaigns, lavish Press receptions in London's Savoy Hotel, and agents dotted all over the world.

At the liquidation proceedings in Stornoway Sheriff Court Captain Perrins, the true gentleman, went round to shake hands personally with each creditor. When entertaining at Garynahine Lodge, his favourite expression when pouring a second large dram was: 'A bird can't fly on one wing.'

Neil died shortly afterwards while they were on board their motor sail yacht 'The Gail and Mary' at Tarbert in Harris. They were on their way to Dublin. Mrs Perrins decided to sell the neighbouring Scaliscro Lodge Hotel — which had become the first hotel outside the town of Stornoway to get a licence to sell alcohol.

In 1968 she decided to turn landlady to save the estate when she was crippled by death duties following the Captain's death. She turned Garynahine Lodge into a sporting estate for paying guests during the fishing season at £128 per week - a stiff price in the 1960s. She catered for the incredibly rich who wanted a break from the harshness of life.

Being the daughter of a millionaire as well as a widow of one, they were given a taste of the gracious living that was found in the the country houses of the Thirties.

On one occasion she offered an old-fashioned Christmas in the lap of luxury for 20 guineas a day. It was a pre-1914 Christmas holdiay for a small number of adult guests which she said would be a 'bumper Christmas and a whopper of a Scots New Year.'

They came from all over the world to the plushest boarding house on the island and the driveway and roadway were lined with Rolls Royces, Bentleys and Daimlers. Indeed she even made headlines in one of the Sunday newspapers because she had the only bidet in the Hebrides.

During this period two incidents come to mind. My mother was on holiday on the island and I took her for a spin as I was going to interview a German woman who had escaped from East Berlin and who had written a book about The Beatles.

When Mrs P learned that my mother was in the car she insisted on entertaining her in the lodge while I carried out the interview in another room.

On the way home my mother explained that Mrs Perrins had given her a triple sherry. Not knowing what to do with it and not finding a suitable pot plant, she told me she had poured into into a bowl beside her chair. I burst out laughing: it was the bowl used for the dogs' drinking water.

On another occasion when I called she told me just to come into the kitchen and talk there as she was preparing a meal for her paying guests. As she turned from the cooker the monkey gland steaks went skiting over the floor. She told the maid: 'Just put them on the plates, by this time they'll be well into the wine and won't notice anything.'

Mrs P claimed in all modesty that she was 'the best bloody non-professional cook in Britain.' This she attributed to her French upbringing. Unlike other estates she allowed her guests to keep all the fish they caught on the river.

While all this was going on she was electedas a member of Ross and Comarty County Council which necessitated flying from Stornoway to Inverness for the meetings in Dingwall.

She led the first modern day protest march on the island because of the County Council's refusal to bring the Pentland Road up to standard.

Led by a piper, about 200 banner-carrying men and women took part in the march through the streets of Stornoway to the Post Office where a petition was posted to the Secretary of State for Scotland, Willie Ross, demanding a public inquiry into why the County Council had persistently refused to repair the road.

The marchers were the rebel ratepayers who were refusing to pay their rates because of the Council's 'shameful neglect' of the Pentland Road. They claimed the road would save up to 12 miles on the round trip between Stornoway and Carloway. When Sheriff Officers began serving them with a summons, Councillor Perrins told them to pay up and leave the fight to herself.

Then there was the campaign to rehouse six elderly spinsters who lived at Garenin, in the last street of 'black houses' in the Isle of Lewis. These were the traditional bee-hived shaped thatched houses. While the Council had agreed to build 12 houses at Garenin the Scottish Development Department had turned down the proposal because they said the site was not suitable.

Mrs Perrins declared: 'This is 1971 and it is disgraceful that elderly people, crippled with arthritis, should be living in unfit houses with outside water and outside sanitation. These black houses were fine in their day but these ladies are now too old and infirm to look after them. The situation is now urgent.'

Another success was the forestry scheme on the estate at Garynahine.

Island parents also smarted after a 'get with it' rocket from Mrs Perrins who accused them of being 'too pious and not understanding the needs of their teenagers.'

Shooting from the hip she said: 'I have seen some kids going for walks across the moor in their high heels shoes. Well chums, don't tell me they're just going for a country walk. It is a darned sight better for them to be dancing in a youth club. You have got to guide the kids.'

She later re-entered the textile trade again when she invested in a company known as Garry Weavers Geocrab Ltd. She became a director and designer in the firm. The Harris factory was actually built by the first Lord Leverhulme who at one time owned Lewis and Harris. One of the main advantages of the Harris factory at Geocrab was that it had its own free electricity because there was a water-powered turbine and generator. It was to produce power woven 60- inch width cloth for high fashion women's garments and also furnishing fabrics.

Mrs Perrins planned to display some of her furnishing fabrics in her new £21,000 early Georgian-style home built on the estate a short distance from the lodge which she was then planning to sell. It had four double bedrooms, three bathrooms, a circular Queen Anne staircase, library, drawing room and dining room.

'What better way to show off a new range of fabrics?' she asked when I went to interview her. 'Indeed the house will become our showroom.'

In the venture with her was managing director of the firm, Garry Maclean, who had been her manager in the old Ceemo firm. Referring to her designs, he described her as the most 'successful colourist I know.'

Mrs Perrins took up painting and within a matter of months had an exhibition of her landscapes and seascapes at the St James Gallery in Dinnet.

She made her enemies on the island, some calling her a 'saucy bitch' (because of her marriage to sauce magnate Captain Perrins), the Ghost of Garynahine, and also the 'willowy witch' — she was 5ft 10 inches tall and scrawny compared to most island women.

Neither was she the darling of the other estate owners in the isles — most of of them absentee landlords. They felt she was a traitor to her class.

She accused them of using Lewis as 'Louise XVI did the bed of Marie Antoinette: a playground.' At one time she threatened a sit-in at Sir Hereward Wake's Amhuinnsuidhe Castle in Harris and on occasions paid the defence expenses for poachers caught on neighbouring estates.

In 1973 when she was approaching 60, she decided to leave the island an return to La Belle France. She had been living on her own for the past eight years since the Captain died.

She told me at the time: 'Sixty is the time the Government wish women to retire, so I'm just doing it 18 months early and making myself redundant.

'However, what really changed my mind was a little dirty yellow envelope which arrived with my surtax in it. This is the first time for many years, because of various business ventures, that I have been hit with a naked tax. I just cannot afford to live here any longer and I think you need more money to be comfortable as you get older.'

It was the end of a colourful era in the island's history, as colourful as her language at times. She had a choice vocabulary which was no doubt honed to perfection when she was a police sergeant in the Liverpool docks during the war.

She had arrived in style 14 years previously and she left in style in August 1973 in a chartered plane, accompanied by her personal physician, a veterinary surgeon, and her four dogs — two pugs and two whippets.

She was heading for the South of France to live among the carnation farmers in Provence, the same area where she had been brought up. Bearing in mind the Common Market she had organised an Italian maid, a Spanish gardner, and a 'tame Belgian taxi driver.'

Mrs Perrins died six years later and the former controversial estate owner was laid to rest beside her husband in her beloved Lewis on the hill known as Cnoc Glas in Kintulavig Park, which overlooked their former home at Garynahine Lodge, the Blackwater Salmon River and East Loch Roag.

When the Captain died in 1965 special permission had to be sought from the Secretary of State for Scotland because Cnoc Glas was not a recognised cemetery.

At her funeral Pipe Major Angus Macleod played a selection of her favourite pipe tunes — including The Battle's O'er, and the Flowers of the Forest-- which she had specially requested in a letter written some time before.

Among the mourners who flew in on a chartered aircraft were her daughter Sally and her husband, Mr and Mrs Peter Hennessey: Her daughter Mary and her husband, the Hon. Patrick and Mrs Howard (her father-in-law is he Earl of Suffolk and Berkshire):   her niece, Mrs Maldwin Drummond: her sister Mrs Anthony Bevan: and Lord Kinross, the family lawyer and friend of the late Captain Perrins.

Her daughter Mary said after the service that although it was supposed to have been a family funeral she was very pleased indeed that so many of her mother's friends from the village had turned up to attend.

****

THE MELBOST BARD

Murdo Macfarlane, the man known throughout the length and breadth of Gaeldom as 'The Melbost Bard,' died in the home of a relative at Tong in Lewis in November 1982. Aged 82 years, he had been in ill health for some time.

Up until a few years previously Murdo was a fit and healthy man which he used to attribute to his year round swimming in Broad Bay at the foot of his croft in Melbost. It was there too that he gained much of his inspiration for his poems and songs.

Murdo was as much a philosopher as a poet, and the theme of his songs ranged from the nostalgia of the exile to songs of humour, love and war.

Born in 1901 he was deeply affected by both world wars, the loss of the Iolaire with 200 island servicemen, and the mass emigrations of the 1920s, which inspired some of his best known songs.

In his younger days — with a horse and cart — he worked for Lord Leverhulme who owned the island in the 1920s. When the work schemes collapsed Murdo, like many others, emigrated to Canada. It was as a result of that experience that he wrote one of the golden favourites of Gaeldom, 'Faili horo.'

A great admirer of Robert Burns, Murdo himself was once described as the 'Cole Porter of Gaeldom.' While his work was well known in Lewis for many years, it was some time before it became recognised further afield, and then he was besieged to take part in television documentaries and other programmes and visiting journalists beat a steady path to his doorstep where they were always given a warm reception.

On his 72nd birthday a book containing a collection of his songs, entitled 'An Toi Neamh Dionhair,' or 'Private Thoughts' was published and was widely acclaimed. The foreword stated: 'There's none alive today with Gaelic more pure nor with greater power in it than Murdo Macfarlane, the Bard of Melbost.'

Many of his songs reflected a hankering for the old days and he felt that 'fourpence of delight then could not be purchased now with a ton of gold.' One other thing made him sad. He said that when his father and mother died they had left their world behind them, but when he died his world would have already gone.

Despite this viewpoint, however, it was modern technology in the shape of the tape recorder which helped him to put to music some of his compositions. Unable to write music himself, he would hum a tune and tape record it, and then a friend would provide the musical notation.

As a result of this he became well known for some of his Gaelic 'pop' songs with a lively beat. One of these was 'A Mhorag' which won the Pan Celtic Folk Festival top award for the group Na-h-oganaich.

Murdo loved the Gaelic language and was always willing to give talks to young school children and playgroups. An active campaigner on behalf of the Gaelic language, he wrote 'Canan nan Gaidheal (The Language of the Gael) which almost became the unofficial anthem of Gaelic.

He was an active and prominent member of the community and was highly visible during the 1979 devolution referendum, and just before his death he was actively involved in the Keep NATO out campaign of the early 80s.

The life and work of Murdo Macfarlane was remembered in an exhibition at An Lanntair Gallery in Stornoway Town Hall in 2002 and a television documentary about his life and work was also screened.

****

DOLAN — THE CO-OP MISSONARY

Dolan Kay, alias Donald M Mackay, a Stornoway Free Church elder, was regarded as a missionary in the Co-op supermarket near his home in the Battery in Stornoway.

I enjoyed his friendship, his advice and the hospitality of his home over many years.

He was a regular in the Camerons for several years and saw service overseas — including Palestine and Egypt — before returning to Lewis after the Second World War when he was converted and became a Soldier for Christ.

Dolan was an elder in Stornoway Free Church for 20 years and was an excellent example of that oft quoted phrase 'True Christians are the Bible other men read.' He lived up to his ordination vows of discharging his duties 'faithfully, diligently and cheerfully.'

His sense of humour and missionary zeal endeared him to everyone he met. A Harris Tweed weaver, working on the old Hattersley loom, his weaving shed was his sanctuary where he was able to meditate and pray before heading out into town with a Gospel message.

He had 'a word in season' not only for his brothers and sisters in Christ, but for those who had no saving knowledge of his Saviour. He met them in the streets, in the shops, and for a period it seemed he was the missionary to the Co-op staff and customers.

Dolan had a great affection for the young people and those who had started following the Lord. He was instrumental in starting the outreach in the Community Centre at the Cearns, on the outskirts of Stornoway, the largest housing scheme in the Western Isles.

It was there, on a Saturday night — and sometimes at fellowship meetings on a Sunday after the church service — that he was in true form as the 'Principal' of the Cearns School of Theology.

Where else could you hear such classics as: 'The Devil doesn't wear squeaky boots.'

On the evils of the material things of life: 'I've never yet seen a shroud with pockets in it.'

There were others: 'Our troubles are like policemen, they arrest you.' 'Sin, like the swine of Genessaret make you always in a hurry.' And he was always reminding us of the 'I' in sin.

Dolan was also regularly used as a speaker at congregational fellowships and as a supply preacher throughout the Presbytery.

He was a year round swimmer in the sea near his home at the bottom of Miller Road until his health broke down.

He will also be remembered for his generosity — most of it unseen — but mainly for the dispensing of bachelor buttons (peppermints) when he met people arriving for church services. His wink was famous and even in hospital, when verbal communication became impossible, there was always a wink of recognition.

He and his wife Annie celebrated their golden wedding in 1993. Before his death in 2001 he spent the last year of his life in the Western Isles Hospital.

****

JOCK OF THE RODEL HOTEL

The genial mine host at the Rodel Hotel in the southern end of Harris was Jock McCallum, proprietor of Rodel Estate as well as the hotel owner.

The hotel was famous because it was the only licensed premises in Scotland where you could buy the deluxe tipple, Royal Household Whisky. When looking for a deluxe brand when he owned the Club Bar in Stornoway he was able to get a quota of RH from Black and White, which was only supplied to the Royal houshold.

The story goes that when the former Prince of Wales came ashore from a naval vessel at Stornoway he visited the Club Bar and was delighted to know they stocked Royal Household. As a result Jock was able to continue to get a supply when he bought the Rodel Hotel in 1934. (The present Prince of Wales hit the headlines when he asked for a cherry brandy in the Crown Hotel in Stornoway many years later.).

Because of EEC regulations prohibting discrimination on the open market the company took Royal Household off the market in the 1980's. However there is still a bottle on the shelf for viewing purposes only at Rodel.

The Rodel Hotel was a Category 'B' listed building. It was built around 1820 and was originally a shooting lodge on the Dunmore Estate.

Little had been done to it over the years but it was the haunt of the shooting and fishing fraternity who used to dress for dinner. However sawdust on the floor in the public bar round the back of the hotel would have been a luxury!

On a seagoing trip with my friend Harris Mackenzie (these escapades would have made Para Handy laugh) I foolishly asked for water to go with the whisky and Jock leaned over the counter to enquire: 'Who fainted?' The water was produced in an old battered kettle.

and when Harris suggested it was time he modernised the reply came back that he was going to get an electric one!

The toilet facility outside the door was merely an L-shaped wall covered in verdigris. When a tourist asked on one occasion where the toilet was he was informed: 'Out that door and anywhere between there and Stornoway.'

On another occasion when a summer tourist asked for ice for his drink he was told to 'come back in December.'

In 1956 the Queen called at Rodel during her cruise through the Western Isles and there is a plaque on the hotel commemorating the occasion stating that 'HM the Queen landed here in 1956.'

However the plaque is 15 ft high on the wall, which caused one local wag to comment: 'She must have been very athletic!'

But the food and the banter were good. Jock was also an Inverness County Councillor and also at one time chairman of the Western Isles Tourist Organisation.

Plans in 1984 to upgrade the hotel did not get off the ground - one of the objections from the Georgian Society was anorthosite dry dash render would 'stand in permanent contrast to the main house and to the landscape.'

However the surrounding area was covered with anorthosite and it had been Jock's ambition to see such a quarry developed only a mile up the road at Lingerbay. But more of that later.

One of the permanent guests at Rodel was one Oliver Cohen, whose brother was at one time the Lord Mayor of London. He had been farmed out by the family but once a year he headed south for the cricket at Lords and could rattle off bowling and batting averages of the top players of the day.

Jock died aged 90. The hotel was eventually upgraded and extended after his death by his two grandsons, Donnie and John.

A place well worth a visit to hear more of the yarns.

THE AMBASSADORS

Two ambassadors for the Island of Lewis and the town were two 'Stornoway boyes' -- the Denver cowboy, alias Johnny Cannut Macdonald, and his inseparable buddy, Eddie Macmillan Glennie (the Knottie Scottie as he described himself).

They made various trips home, usually coinciding with Royal National Mods, especially if the venue was Stornoway. They invariably came bearing gifts, whether it was key rings or other momentoes.

However in 1997 they arrived with a beautiful framed photograph of the liner Metagama. The ship played an important part in the history of Lewis when it sailed direct from Stornoway to take 300 men and women to Canada in 1923. The painting was a gift to Stornoway Pier and Harbour Commission and it now hangs in the new Ferry Terminal Building.

After roaming the world Eddie threw down his anchor in Vancouver, and Johnny -- whose waist band was a big as his cigars -- settled in Denver. When they were around the craic was good.

Eddie worked in the docks in Vancouver as a longshoreman supervisor and died in 2004 as a result of cancer. He was 74. He is survived by his wife, and a stepson and stepdaughter. His remains were cremated, with one half being buried in Vancouver and the other half flown home to Stornoway for burial.

After a major operation in 1997 he wrote an open thank you letter to the local paper to keep all his friends up to date with his medical progress. Full of nautical terminology, it was a classic:

'Launched February 22, 1930 at Keith Street, Stornoway. Plied the local waters until 1947, then from '47 to '52 all waters far and wide, finally dropping my hook in Vancouver's beautiful bay.

"Of course several trips back to the launching pad to bunker up at the local fuelling berths with the pals and gals and a refresher course in Ganga's Gaelic.'

However after years of 'haphazard maintenance and neglect ' he was advised that the old hulk had to be surveyed and to renew the certificate of efficiency. This, he says, resulted in him being drydocked and after being examined by the rudder inspector a major overhaul was in the works.

He recalls: 'There they proceeded to remove some irreplaceable parts, a patch here, a seal there, relocate the stern gland, redirect some flexible tubing, seam rivetted and caulked with archangel tar and oakum. Six days later, all sense of shyness and modesty shot to hell, a flotilla of uniformed female nurse under-graduates came to review this reconditioned SY hulk, prod, peep, flip and feel.'

He says he was discharged with a temporary certificate of efficiency, shallow water only.

He recalled that the unofficial director and advisor of this major overhaul was none other than the Right Honourable Johnnie Cannut Macdonald, his lifelong pal and partner from Denver, Colorado, in conjunction with Sandra, his Chief Officer and Pilot, conspirators of the highest degree.

He adds: 'As of February 25, 1997, a Certificate of Competence and Efficiency was issued to this drifter, with an advisory note to treat the refurbished hulk with a little more concern about its new lease.'

It was Eddie's way of thanking everyone who had been concerned for him and the letter was signed: 'Eddie Glennie, the Hebridean Vagabond.'

****

THE COUNT

My friend Comte Robin de la Lanne Mirrlees, the eccentric French-born Laird of Great Bernera in Lewis, is another character who has adorned the island landscape for over 45 years.

He's had a rich and colourful life. He was born in Paris in 1925 of French and American ancestry, but he is extrememly proud of a thin red line of Scottish blood.

Oxford was a happy experience for him as it was an opportunity to broaden his mind and meet people who were, later in their careers, to become members of the government or even prime ministers, and also people who were to reach the top in commerce and banking.

During the Second World War he volunteered and served in the artillery, in an Indian regiment, and came to have the deepest feelings of respect and admiration for the Indian people. He saw active service in Arakan in Burma. He was on the general staff and had the good luck to know General Auchinleck, the Commander-in-Chief, and General Wavell, the Viceroy, and through them made friends with some of the Indian leaders, including Mr Jawaharlal Nehru.

He left Delhi with regret when he was promoted to be attache in the British Embassay in Tokyo.

He recalls that after the war he had the good fortune to become one of Her Majesty's Heralds, and enjoyed the work immensely as it involved the organising and taking part in Royal ceremonies such as the Opening of Parliment, and also the compilation of archives from all over the Commonweatlh with some contacts in America. His superior at that time was the Earl Marshal of England, the Duke of Norfolk, and he says that he had the good luck to be invited to a ball at Buckingham Palace attended by all the Commonwealth leaders. The Count told me that during that time he was reading to the blind and travelling extensively. He donated two scholarships for children from the Iron Curtain countries to study for six months at a time in Britain.

He said he also contributed as best he could to foreign charities such as Ethiopa, Bangladesh and others. Later, however, he began to feel that this was counter productive, and quotes a Confucian proverb: "If you see a hungry man don't give him a fish, but teach him how to fish.'

When he retired he bought the Island of Bernera (pop 350) which extended to 6000 acres. He contributed to the expansion of the salmon fisheries there.

He points out that his grandfather created an engineering empire, which was amalgamated with Hawker Siddeley. One of the Mirrlees engines is on display in the Science Museum in London.

His great uncle George Grinnell invented a type of firefighting equipment and with the considerable proceeds built Grinnell University in the USA. He says his mother's great-grandfather barely escaped from the French revolution with his life, and later founded and owned 14 textile companies in the USA and supported innumerable charitable organisations. He later had the rank of Ambassador to Prague, Rome and Paris.

His grandmother came from a well-known Quaker family and together with his great uncle paid for the support, education and employment of nearly 200 orphans. His uncle helped create the Tongaat Hewlet sugar and industrial combine which flourishes in South Africa and was part of the Tate and Lyle conglomorate.

The Count told me: 'Therefore in a small way I have tried my best to follow my family's example -- to be creative, give employment, and contribute to society. I could equally well have lived tax free in Switzerland and enjoyed a quiet life of leisure. I have two granddaughters and I am trying to inculcate the same ideals in them.

One of his happiest memories he says was his good fortune to be invited to the Hapsburg-Thyssen wedding, where he says he had the time of his life.

He recalls: 'A small group of us, including the Chief of the Campbells, and my godson, flew from Scotland to Vienna where fresh snow had fallen in the morning, and we proceeded in the direction of Maria Zell, climbing into the hills up winding roads and passing miniature villages with baroque churches, sprinkled with white snow which put Christmas cards to shame.

'An entire monastery had been borrowed for the ball where 600 lucky guests from the bluest blood and the dizziest heights of industry and banking were foregathered in all their finery of glittering orders and Paris dresses with stupendous jewellery, myself having the good luck to meet a particularly charming person.

'We had been given a strict command to wear kilts and I found myself, rather to my surprise, trying to teach Scottish reels to some of the Austrian beauties there.

'Never easy to impress, I was nevertheless impressed by the warmth, outgoingness, and total lack of pomp of Archduke Otto, the Emperor, as he is still viewed ever after so many years, by so many of his devoted followers.

'On our walk up to the Cathedral at Maria Zell (incidentally it's one of the pleasing traditions in Austria that numerous villages incorporate her name) we passed between ranks of superb officers in their resplendent uniforms of the Hapsburg army - shakos, sabretaches, pelisses, and drawn sabres, all a dazzle in the new white snow, and the golden winter sunshine.

'On my way, keeping of course a respectful distance from the drawn sabres, I remarked to one of the dashing officers concerning the imposing appearance of a brass canon and asked: "Does it fire" My silly question naturally elicited no response.

The imperial party were preceded into the Cathedral by the most magnificient officer of all bearing aloft the golden flag of the Hapsburg Empire ensigned with the double-headed eagle, which he slowly and majestically waved from side to side.'

The Count continued: 'All during the wedding ceremony the serenity and radiant beauty of the bride held all our attention, while the voices of the unseen Salzburg Mozart choir, specially invited, could be heard singing the Mass, voices -- need I say -- that with their far away echoes up in the decorated roof, were of an ethereal beauty which we can never forget.

'The High Mass presided over by the Cardinal had to be translated into several languages of the Empire, including Hungarian, and was therefore of a long duration. The cold outside the Cathedral was Arctic, but we had been warned, and the distinguished lady beside me was wrapped in stunning ankle length sables, with hat to match. At intervals she threw herself on her knees, and not wanting to be outdone, I too descended on the knee, only to be told later on by her that her main motive had been to save her hat from the attentions of the great eagle flag!

'At last the rings were exchanged by the bride and groom and His Eminence pronounced the young couple man and wife.

'Instantly the artillery officer's withering glance was made plain to me as a 21-gun salute detonated outside from the very brass canon which I had so rashly remarked on, and rattle the saints in the stained glass windows.

'It was not long before the huge crowd outside could see their new Archduchess and her husband coming down the steps of the church, while we lesser mortals hastened out a side door to warm ourselves with life-saving hot Austrian wine.'

Referring to foreign monarchies, the Count observed that they did not adpot the "don't touch me' approach. He said Archduke Otto and his wife and heir mingled with their people in the most loving and affectionate way, as a father with his family.

He said everyone was welcomed and he was totally accessible, and people could call him by his name and crack a joke. He added: 'It was no surprise to see people on their knees in the snow trying to kiss his hand or the coat of the Emperor, weeping and calling on him not to depart. The Imperial family being so well beloved are apparently discouraged by the government -- with its lingering Marxist undertones -- from living permanently in Austria.'

While it was good for him to reflect on the good times, he was hit financially in the mid-1990s when Lloyds of London faced liqidation following a string of natural disasters such as the Alpha Piper oilrig fire and the Exxon oil spill which resulted in £8 billion of losses.

Count Mirrlees, who is also the titular Prince of Coronata, was a Lloyds name, suffered as a result of the financial nightmare. He managed to clear his debts by selling Ratzenegg Castle in Austria, and his mother's home in Le Touquet in France, and a house in Hatton Gardens -- quoted in Vogue mazaine as one of the best houses in London. He also sold off antiques, paintings and silver to pay off his £2 million debts.

In an article I wrote for the Sunday Times at the time he mused that: 'Perhaps I should look for a rich widow.'

The life-style of the car-less Count was curtailed because of his financial losses. He used to go abroad to America, France and Austria every year.

However his financial situation halted any plans he had for developing his beloved Bernera.

In 2004 he had a stroke in London and was taken to the Hammersmith Hospital where he contracted MRSA. He was later transferred to the Western Isles Hospital in Stornoway where he spent 15 months and received tender loving care from all the nurses. He now resides in the care unit at Bernera.

****

Ganga

Domhnull Thoe

Major

Johnny and Eddie with framed Metagama

The Count outside his home on Great Bernera: Lodge is rather grandiose for a croft house!

The Ghost of Garynahine

Captain Neil and Mrs Perrins

Mrs P with pugs and whippet

Dolan

Melbost Bard

Jock McCallum of Rodel

Calla with Freedom casket in shape of a lifeboat

THE COURTS

When I arrived on the island in 1956 the resident Sheriff was Sheriff Campbell Ross, who was delighted after a refurbishing of the premises to have the Ross Coat of Arms on the front of the bench. I think he had been in the Colonial Service because he prided himself on having a knowledge of Urdu. When a well known Pakistani was in front of him one day and he was asked for his name he replied Sher Mohammed. This was an opportunity for His Lordship to show off his linguistic skillls and he enquired of the Procurator Fiscal if he knew that Sher meant Lion. 'Yes, lying ...' muttered the Fiscal. 'What was that?' asked the Sheriff. 'Nothing my Lord, nothing,' came the reply.

Campbell Ross was followed by Sheriff John Allan, then there was Maclean, followed by Hamilton Lyons, who introduced the 'flying sheriff service,' whereby His Lordship flew in twice a month to sit at Stornoway and once a month at Lochmaddy in North Uist.

His successor, Sheriff Scott Robinson, reflecting on the flying sheriff service at the time of his retiral in 1983, said that within the limits which wind and weather prescribed for the Western Isles, the service had been a success. The number of occasions when they had failed to sit within the previous 10 years had been very few.

Regarding pressure for a resident sheriff he said that he felt that there should be a review of shriveal duties not only in the Western Isles but in the Highlands area generally. However, in his opinion, there was insufficient work between Stornoway and Lochmaddy court to jutify the apppointment of a full time sheriff.

He recalled that one of the most interesting aspects of his judicial experience in the Western Isles during his time were the many unusual cases which came before him. He could also remember one sitting at Lochmaddy Sheriff Court which went on until 4am and seeing the dawn come up through the window of the Court House. He had then caught the 6am ferry to Skye to sit at Portree Sheriff Court at 10 am!

Among the other Sheriffs who graced the bench in my time were Bill Fulton, Donald Booker Millburn, Ian Cameron, and the present incumbent David Sutherland. Filling in on occasions were James Fraser and Colin Scott Mackenzie.

Court cases at Stornoway and at Lochmaddy Sheriff Court in North Uist provided avid reading, and none more so that those involving police raids on licenced premises and the bothans or drinking clubs. In March 1963 Sheriff Principal D M Campbell declared the bothans illegal when three men from Ness were fined a total of £99. They were found guilty after trial of trafficking in exciseable liquor at South Dell bothan on March 30 without holding a certificate: and keeping a quantitiy of excisebale liquor in excess of one gallon on the unlicensed premises for the purposes of trafficking.

There were about 10 bothans in Lewis at the time and the trial was looked upon as a test case by the islanders.

Details of how they operated were revealed during the trial by one of the accused. He told the court that the South Dell bothan was made of concrete blocks and lighted by Calor gas, and had been erected in 1961. There were 29 shareholders, although the number changed occasionally, because some of the men left the village to work on the mainland. He admitted that exciseable liqour was kept and consumed on the premises, but denied that anyone paid for a drink when it was served.

He went on: 'We collect money before we go to Stornoway for the supplies. For the first lot we collected £2 5s each from 25 men. We collected 10 containers and brought them over in a van. We go for supplies about every six weeks. The 11 gallon container would last three or four nights. No one had more than four or five pints each night but there was no check kept. We were prepared to trust each other.'

Asked about the £6 found on the premises he said that the shareholders also contributed a shilling per week each for coal and gas and any breakages. Any losers at darts also put 3d into the box. There was also a collection of 2s 6d each from over 20 members for the football pool.

Asked by Mr Douglas Kesting, the solicitor for the accused, if any visitor to the bothan would ever be required to pay for a drink, he replied: 'No.'

'How would he get a drink?' — 'He would know somebody inside. He would be treated to a glass of beer.'

Earlier police witnesses gave evidence that they had raided the premises about 12.20 am on the morning of March 20. They had found seven men inside, and the three accused had pints of beer beside them. When charged one of them had replied: 'It is not being trafficked in.' Two others said: 'There was no sale.'

The police officers also said that there was no record of the building on the Valuation Roll and inquiries had shown that the bothan was not being assessed for rates.

Chief Inspector John Mackenzie, who had obtained the warrant to raid the premises, said that when he had asked who owned them or who was in charge, he was told that no one owned them and no one was in charge.

Mr George Maclennan, clerk to the Stornoway District Licensing Board, said that nobody in the Parish of Barvas. which included South Dell, held a certificate for the sale of intoxicating liquor.

The owner of a public house in Stornoway told the court that he supplied the South Dell men with ten 11-gallon containers of beer about every five weeks. Each container was sold for £5 10s. He had been supplying them for about 18 months. He was always paid in cash.

Sheriff Principal Campbell said that after hearing the evidence he was satisfied that there had been a deliberate breach of the Licensing Act. He added: 'These premises were like a public house, although perhaps not a very luxurious one. There was a sum of money found in what was obviously a till. There was a whisky bottle with a nip measure in it.'

After the Court Chief Inspector Mackenzie revealed why he had made the raid. He said: 'I decided to take action after receving numerous complaints from parents who were worried about the welfare of their sons frequenting these bothans. The South Dell bothan was convenient for the purpose of a raid. Following the Sheriff's decision, which proves that these places are illegal, we will be keeping our eyes on the situation.'

****

It was the late Colin Scott Mackenzie, Procurator Fiscal at the time, who coined the apt name 'bothaneers' to describe those who operated the illegal drinking clubs.

The perpetrators usally employed the legal skills of my friend the late Laurence Dowdall, the doyen of crimal lawyers, and the late Willie Dunn, who had Ness connections. The bothans were mostly located in the 'dry' parish of Barvas, although there was one in Shawbost. At that time it meant that anyone wanting a legal pint or a dram had to make a round trip of over 50 miles to Stornoway. It was in the days when newspapers used verbatim reporting and liked to carry the cut and thrust of court room dramas.

In addition to the courts which sat at Stornoway and Lochmaddy in North Uist, I have also covered courts held at unusual locations. One was at a croft house in Balallan, where the elderly lady witness was not well enough to come to court and the Sheriff heard her evidence in her living room. Others locations were the Western Isles Hospital and also in an office at the terminal building at Stornoway Airport.

Here follows a flavour of what the readers enjoyed.

July 5, 1967:

Six bothaneers -- men form the 'dry' Ness area on the Island of Lewis, charged with trafficking in exciseable liquor in a bothan or illegal drinking club, were found not guilty yesterday at Stornoway Sheriff Court.

As they left the building after being acquitted by Sheriff Hanilton Lyons, the bothaneers declared: 'We will be celebrating tonight.'

The island courtroom was packed to capacity when the trial began. Extra seats had to be brought in and even the jury benches were used for the public. The well of the court was stacked with cartons containing cans of beer and whisky bottles, which were productions in the case.

The men, all weavers, denied trafficking in exciseable liqour without a certificate in the premises known as the bothan, Europie, Ness, on February 9, 1967: keeping or using unlicensed premises where liquor of a quantity exceeding one gallon was kept for the purposes of trafficking.

A charge of bartering or selling whisky in the unlicensed premises without holding a certificate was dropped by the fiscal, Mr Colin Scott Mackenzie. Similar charges against another man, concerning the bothan at Adabrock, were also dropped.

Sergeant John Wood (36) who was in charge of the party of police who raided the bothan, told the court that they arrived about 10 minutes to midnight. He said there had been letters of complaint about the bothan sent to the local police officer in Ness.

When he knocked on the door of the bothan someone had called to him to come in. When he went inside seven people were sitting on a bench going round three sides of the wall. Another man was sitting in front of the stove and others had glasses beside them.

There were three full bottles of whisky and one half full bottle with an optic measure, and they found 108 cans of beer stacked on a bench. Two of the men were sitting with glasses in their hand and the others had glasses beside them. An adjoining compartment was stacked with empty beer cans and bottles.

Sergeant Wood told the hushed courtroom that when he asked who was in charge of the premises or the contents he got no reply from the men, and no one admitted to being the owner of the bothan.

Cross-examined by Mr Laurence Dowdall, who appeared for the weavers, Sergeant Wood said: 'There were thousands of empty beer cans and dozens of empty bottles,' and then added: 'It was just like a drinking club.'

The witness agreed with Mr Dowdall that there were only two licensed premises in Lewis outside of Stornoway, and that people in the Ness area would have had to come to Stornoway (about 25 miles) if they wanted a drink.

Questioned about the £6 6s 8d found in a tin on the premises, the Sergeant said: 'I never saw any money being taken or people being supplied with drink.'

Mr Dowdall: 'In fact this money could have been a collection for indigent ladies or the Propagation of the Faith?' -- 'It could have been' said the Sergeant.

The Sheriff: 'Or the darts stakes.'

Mr Dowdall: 'What are these bothans for Sergeant?' -- 'For illicit drinking.'

'Surely all the good people of Ness have other things on their minds besides drinking. They could be there for communal use? '

'They could,' replied the witness.

Mr Dowdall: 'They could be there for use as a bottle party?' 'Yes'.

'The bothans do supply a social amenity? 'Yes.'

Other police officers who gave evidence suggested that there were at least 2000 empty cans of beer in the storage compartment and one admitted that he did not hear any conversation when they arrived at the bothan. He said they could have been discussing the problems of the Middle East as far as he knew.

In his summing up Mr Dowdall told his Lordship that there was no evidence that the building at Europie was a reputed shebeen, and that there was no evidence of trafficking.

He added: 'Normally the police send in a stooge who can later give evidence that he bought a drink or was served a drink, or they send someone with a marked pound note.'

Sheriff Lyon said: 'There is evidence to the effect that a certain amount of drinking was taking place in these premises at the time of the police visitation, but there is no evidence of bartering or selling or anyone dealing or trading or anyone exposing or offering liquor for sale by retail, which is the meaning of trafficking according to the Act.

'Since I am unable to hold that there was trafficking I find the charges are not proven but I feel I ought to dispose of it by recording a finding of not guilty.'

After the trial Mr Dowdall said he would be writing to the Fiscal on behalf of his clients for the return of the beer and whisky which was confiscated by the police!

****

In February 15, 1977, some bothaneers were not so fortunate: Read on.

A packed island court was told yesterday of the night 10 policemen raided a bothan -- an illegal drinking club -- and found 26 people inside, as well as 11- gallon kegs of beer, 415 cans of beer, whisky and rum.

During the trial at Stornoway one witness was detained in custody after receiving repeated warnings from Sheriff Scott Robinson about his failure to tell the truth.

There were four men in the dock, and a warrant was issued for the arrest of a fifth who was understood to be at sea.

They denied trafficking in exciseable liquor in the Europie bothan, Ness, on October 23, 1976, and other days unknown: not having a certificate for the premises: and occupying or using unlicensed premises where there was a quantity of exciseable liquor in excess of one gallon which was used for the purpose of trafficking.

Chief Inspector Allan Macleod, who headed a team of nine officers, led the police raid. He described a bothan as a small shed used as a meeting place and in common use as a drinking place.

He told the court they had received anonymous letters complaining about people drinking in the bothan to 8 o'clock in the morning. They had obtained a warrant to enter the bothan. He said that they had found £8 pounds in coins in a box in the corner and another £5 nearby. They never found any notes.

He said there were 26 people in the bothan -- 22 men and four women -- drinking beer and spirits. There were four full 11-gallon canisters of beer, five empty ones, and one part full. There were 415 cans of pale ale and lager, and 22 partly-filled cans, and 68 empty cans. There were several dozen beer and spirit glasses.

Said the Inspector (in true Sherlock Homes style): 'I came to the conclusion that this was a place used for drinking!'

Sergeant Murdo Maciver said there were 1133 beer can rings -- he knew because he had had to count them.

Detective Sergeant Colin Macdonald said that above a cupboard on the wall was a Gaelic sign stating 'Ceud Failte' - A Hundred Welcomes.

The Sheriff remarked that in Inverness it was normally 'Ceud Mile Failte' - a hundred thousand welcomes.

'Yes,' replied the sergeant, 'but you cannot get so many into a bothan!'

The first civilian Crown witness, a 64-year-old man from Europie, when asked what a bothan was, replied: 'According to the Gaelic Bible it is a sheltering place.'

Asked if there was a more modern meaning, he replied: 'No.' After prodding by the Proucator Fiscal, however, he admitted that one could obtain strong drink in a bothan. He himself went about once a forthnight to the one in Europie. He was then warned both by the Fiscal and the Sheriff about prevarication. He said that no one owned the bothan, and he did not know who were the organisers. On the occasions he had been at the bothan he had never seen anyone buying liquor. He had consumed alcohol inside the bothan but they had brought it from Stornoway.

He then received another warning from the Sheirff who told him that he was satisfied that the witness was lying. He repeated that he had never bought liquor in the bothan and stated that he had never seen any of the four accused selling liquor. He had not paid for the drink before he got it in the building.

The Sheriff then ordered that the witness be detained in custody until the end of the proceedings.

Another Europie witness, aged 52, also stated that he did not know who organised the bothan.

'Is it a secret society?' asked the Fiscal. 'Is it the Cosa Nostra of Europie?'

Replied the witness: 'The bothan is everybody's responsibility. He explained that the normal procedure was for a number of men to get together to buy a supply of drink in Stornoway. They then got carriers to take it over to the bothan.

A young Swainbost man said he had been in the bothan on the night it was raided. When he arrived after a concert in Ness Hall he had put 40 pence into a box for two cans of lager. He showed the money to two of the accused who were sitting on either side of a box. He helped himself to two cans from a box under the seat. He too said he did not know who was in charge of the bothan.

He burst out laughing when he was shown some football sweep stake cards which had 'Brownie's Benevolent Fund' printed on the top. He told the court that that was the nickname of one of the accused.

Another witness said he had just been there to play darts.

Willie Dunn, who was defending, suggested to one witness that the money in the box was raffle money.

The outcome was that two of the accused were found guilty of all three charges and were each fined £105. The two others were found not guilty.

Sheriff Scott Robinson also ordered forfeiture of all the liquor and the equipment.

****

Even licensed premises were raided, and the Borve House Hotel in Barvas was raided twice within two years.

In 1973 a dissertation on the sandwich was dispensed at Stornoway Sheriff Court by Sheriff Douglas Donald during the trial of the hotelier.

He denied that being the holder of a restricted hotel licence he had sold drink other than for consumption with a meal to four men (three of whom were deceased): and employing a 13 year old schoolgirl to sell or supply drinks on June 8.

The young girl told the court that she was not employed at the hotel but helped out in the kitchen at week-ends because she was related to the hotel proprietor's wife. On the night in question the proprietor had gone to attend to her young daughter who was ill and she had left a tray of drinks and sandwiches for four customers. The girl said she had taken the tray to the men.

A police constable gave evidence that as a result of a car accident in which two of the accused had died, he had charged the hotel proprietor. A third witness had died since the accident after giving him a statement.

Mr Laurence Dowdall, defending, who had an objection upheld against the Fiscal leading evidence of a precognition taken from one of the deceased, claimed that a sandwich was a meal under the terms of the Act. The Crown witnesses had made it clear that both hot and cold sandwiches were served with drinks in the hotel

Sheriff Donald said that the sandwich had a long history as it had started before the potato. When people went into an inn and ordered a round of beef it was served on a round of bread to soak up the gravy. That was why people now referred to a round of sandwiches.

He found both charges not proven.

****

In February 1975 there was also a trial at Stornoway following a police raid on the same hotel ....

Stornoway Sheriff Court yesterday heard that when police raided an island hotel with a restricted certificate on a Saturday night, they found 33 men inside drinking.

In the dock was the proprietor of the Borve House Hotel in Barvas, who pleaded not guilty to supplying 33 men with exciseable liqour other than as an ancilliary to a meal on November 23, 1974.

Chief Inspector Norman Macdonald told the court that when he went inside the premises about 9 pm he found 33 men seated at tables and drinking beer and spirits. There was a plate with sandwiches on some of the tables, although he did not see them eating any of the sandwiches. Quantities of beer and spirits continued to be served while he was there and he did not see any food being supplied with them. Underneath the counter there was a frozen chicken and an uncooked mutton gigot. There was also a bone with some meat left on it which could have made a few sandwiches.

He told the court that a restricted hotel certificate was granted so that alcoholic drink could be served with main meals in the afternoon and evening, and it could be served as an ancilliary to these meals.

Mr Laurence Dowdall, defence agent, asked if he was saying that refreshments could only be supplied with main meals. 'No, I am quoting chapter and verse of the Act,' he replied. He agreed the word meal was not described.

Said Mr Dowdall: 'You know that case law states that a sandwich is a meal. A very eminent judge (Sheriff Douglas Donald who was hearing the case) has stated that the sandwich had a very long history and had started before the potato.'

The Chief Inspector said he was not certain whether he had looked in all the cupboards in the kitchen. When asked how many men he had with him he replied: 'The Inspector, a sergeant and six men.'

'Were you expecting a mass escape?' aksed Mr Dowdall.

'No, I was making sure I had plenty of officers to do what I wanted them to do.'

Following a question about whether it was all males that were found on the premises, the Chief Inspector replied: 'It's difficult to tell the difference nowadays.'

Procurator Fiscal Jack Skene remarked: 'The classic way is to examine the jeans.'

Mr Dowdall: 'Could you spell that please.'

Referring to photographs taken when the police were there, Mr Dowdall asked about the 'jolly gendarmes' who were smiling in some of the photographs and the witness said he liked his men to be pleasant in carrying out their duties. He agreed that the premises did not open on a Sunday and that it was quite normal to allow stocks of food to run down on a Saturday.

Mr Roderick Maclean, clerk to the Stornoway District Licensing Court, agreed that the restricted hotel certificate meant that there would be no 'vertical drinking' at the serving hatch. However you could stay at the bar provided a meal was served there - a pub snack.

Fiscal: 'I take it there should be no horizontal drinking either?'

Several of the customers in the premises that night said in the witnesss box that they had to order sandwiches with their drinks. They claimed it was not possible to get a drink without getting sandwiches.

One witness denied that to a stranger it could just look like a public house.

In summing up Mr Skene said that rightly or wrongly the accused's position was that if he served sandwiches - a sandwich being a meal - that that was sufficient to bring him within the ambit of the law. He submitted that this was an erroneous view.

He claimed the order for a sandwich was a subterfuge to get a drink and get round the law. In this case the meal was ancillary to the drink. He asked the Sheriff to find the accused guilty because they had been breaking the law with impunity.

Mr Dowdall for the defence said that it was deplorable that in this 'dry' area of Barvas where a hotel with a restricted hotel certificate was subject to police supervision, that it was possible for people to drink until 2 and 3 in the morning in the bothans (the illegal drinking clubs in the north end of the Parish of Barvas).

He submitted that his client had been acting within the law, had sufficient food in cupboards which the police had apparently not examined, and suggested to His Lordship that it would be unsafe in a case like this to arrive at a verdict of guilty.

Sheriff Donald reserved judgement until March 4 when he ruled that sandwiches being served in the hotel with a table licence were the 'open sesame' for the consumption of drink.

In his judgement Sheriff Donald said that there was a whole body of opinion that the licensing laws were in a state of confusion and disconsonant with the conditions of contemporary life. The present case might well be taken as symtomatic of that opinion.

Referring to the somewhat 'massive raid by a strong force of police' who had discovered liquor being served to 33 men in the lounge of the hotel which was subject to a restricted licence, he said they were all seated and eating at tables on which were sandwiches and drinks. He added: 'The guests were all male and in a jovial mood and well behaved and neither their enjoyment or decorum was at all affected by the presence of a considerable number of police constables and high-ranking officers.'

Some 20 of the patrons seated at the tables had given evidence so that the Court was enabled to get a very clear picture of what was happening.

He said the witnesses were very frank and were indeed clearly firm believers in the legend of the sandwich being a meal and so were completely free from inhibition. It became quite clear that they were all regular patrons of the establishment on Saturday nights. It was part of their lifestyle and it was an inexorable rule of the establishment that no drink could be served without there also being included an order for sandwiches.

He continued: 'Their purpose indeed of going to the hotel was unanimously said to have been to have a pleasant social evening with their friends and there can be no doubt that they formed one large social party. It was however maintained that it is a human condition or failing that social bonhomie was only fully attainable by the provision and consumption of a certain amount of liquor so that it was fair to infer that some consumption of liquor was an ancillary to the success of their social gathering.'

He said that the attitude of the staff who gave evidence was that provided the first order from a table accompanied by an order for sandwiches, orders for further drink could be unrestricted.

Sheriff Donald concluded: 'From the whole bulk of evidence there could be no possible doubt that the sandwiches ordered and consumed were entirely ancillary to the consumtion of drink and not vice versa and this state of affairs ought to have been self evident to the licensee unless he too had blinded himself to the plain purpose of the present Act by subscribing to the legend of the simple sandwich forming an open sesame to the consumption of drink for purposes quite other than ancillary to a main meal.'

He accordingly found the accused guilty as libelled.

A letter was read from defence agent Mr Laurence Dowdall -- who was unable to be present because of illness -- stating that his client had been in the trade for 50 years and had spent £26,000 on improvements to the hotel. The court had heard that witnesses had gone there not for a drink but for a ceilidh and his client had thought he was within the law.

Mr Dowdall also said that they had heard that if there was no hotel at Borve they would have had to travel 18 miles for a drink or frequent the bothans (the illegal drinkings clubs in the 'dry' Parish of Barvas). He asked His Lordship for an absolute discharge.

Procurator Fiscal Mr Jack Skene told the Sheriff: 'I can only hope that the police will take some action against these bothans. It seems a great pity they were operating against licence holders.'

Sheriff Donald gave Robertson an absolute discharge after he received an assurance from the licensee that the practice would stop.

After the Court the hotelier said he was asking for a stated case (an appeal). He added: 'While the absolute discharge is a favourable decision so far as I am concerned, I feel I must appeal because it will draw attention to the need for changes in the licensing law and for the implementation of the Clayson Committee proposals.'

****

The reference to the Clayson Committee reminds me of my time on The Scotsman when I did shifts on a Saturday for various Sunday newspapers within the Thomson Group.

The Sunday Times had asked for reaction to the licensing changes proposed by the Clayson Committee, one of which was the extension of the licensing hours. The story was duly filed.

However the following week while on holiday in Stornoway I was in the Golf Club with two well-known worthies -- Charlie and Bertie. They were known to visit several licensed premises during their morning constitutional around town -- long before the premises officially opened to the public at 11 am.

When Charlie asked Bertie what he thought of the new proposals for extending the drinking hours we were aghast when Bertie said he was totally against them.

He then explained: 'Let's face it Charlie, it would give us no privacy!'

It would have been a great quote for the Sunday Times article.

****

Following a request from the Fiscal to have the bothans demolished a report said that it was a matter for the Fiscal as trafficking in exciseable liqor was not a 'material consideration' within the Town and Country Planning Act.

In a facetious report John Marshall the Planning Officer felt that the demolition of the one at Habost - in a traditional thatched 'black house' -- should be deferred until it had been established as to whether it should be listed as a building of 'architectural and historical interest!'

Then in 1964 there was the case of the mobile bothan.

A Shawbost weaver thought he would do a good turn for the lads in the village so he used his Bedford van as a bothan.

He was fined a total of £45 by Sheriff John Allan when he pleaded guilty to bartering or selling whisky by retail without holding a licence in a Bedford van parked beside a peat road at Loch Raoinabhat, 350 yards south east of the Shawbost-Carloway Road: and keeping or using the van for the purposes of trafficking in liquor.

The Sheriff ordered forfeiture of the exciseable liquor found in the van as well as a £1 note which the accused had in his hand when the police raided the van.

Enjoying a dram in a Stornoway pub after the court case the accused told me: 'I was really only trying to do a good turn for the lads in the village. It was the May holiday week-end and they wanted supplies of whisky and beer. The lads are working all day and can't get a drink unless they go into Stornoway 16 miles away.'

He added: 'I don't think they'll ever stamp out the bothans in the 'dry' areas until they provide a licensed hotel or pub. Until that time the bothans will continue to flourish under cover, although I myself have learned my lesson. In addition to the £45 fine I have lost about £15 worth of liquor which was confiscated by the court.'

****

When the police raided a Stornoway public house on a Saturday morning they found 9 members of the Skye Pipe Band in full regalia, two locals, and a Pakistani pedlar all drinking.

This was revealed at Stornoway Sheriff Court in October 1974 when the publican pleaded guilty to supplying drink - through the hands of his servant, the head barman -- to 12 people outwith the permitted hours.

The Procurator Fiscal, Mr Colin Scott Mackenzie, said that Chief Inspector Norman Macdonald, accompanied by a sergeant and two constables, went to the bar after receiving confidential information.

The two constables went to the back door and the Inspector and the sergeant to the front. The rear door was open and when the constables went inside the 12 people mentioned in the complaint were in the public bar leaning against the counter or sitting at tables with drinks. With the exception of three they were all members of the Skye Pipe Band and were in full band regalia.

The police did not see any monetary transactions. The Band members had been taken there by one of the local men. The licensee himself was not on the premises at the time.

There was a tongue in cheek submission by the defence solicitor, Mr Kenneth Macdonald, who said that the Skye Pipe Band were over in Stornoway for their annual visit and he hoped that the whole matter had not fractured inter-island relations too much.

He explained that the band was due to parade through Stornoway at 11 am -- before the pubs opened -- and as most pipers liked to wet their throats before starting on parade, they had been taken to the bar by a local piper. They had entered the premises through a back door. They had not paid for any drinks as they had been treated to refreshments.

Mr Macdonald continued: 'It says much for their courage that they went on with their parade and their playing was not affected by their nerve-wracking experience. I feel there are mitigating factors.'

He pointed out that there were 9 employed in the bar and if the licence was revoked they would lose their jobs and his client's family would lose their livelihood. His client had taken precautions to ensure that this would never happen again.

Mr Macdonald said that while many Far Eastern countries had a reputation for producing pipe bands, he could give no explanation as to why the Pakistani had been on the premises as he was not connected with the Skye Pipe Band but lived locally.

Sheriff Douglas Donald said: 'This sort of thing ought not to happen. I do not think this is the proper court to consider the licence. The fine will be £3 for each person on the premises, a total of £36.'

(There was a follow up to this because certain members of the Pakistani community pointed out that the pedlar was not a Pakistani but was a Sikh. It was also Ramadan and no Pakistani would be on licensed premises at such a time).

****

Ken, our flying solicitor who uses his plane to fly down for the court at Lochmaddy, once had a sticker on his car which stated: 'Money isn't everything: but it sure keeps the kids in touch.'

****

There have been many eloquent lawyers in the courts. John Morrison of New Tolsta, a former Dep. Assistant Commissioner with the Met (he died in October 2008) used to recall that when he attended the 'Black Panther' trial as head of the Yard's murder squad, the accused Donald Nielsen was defended by Gilbert Gray QC. As he addressed the jury, the junior prosecuting Counsel slipped a note to John which stated: "Every line a headline, every phrase a gem, at the going down of the sun, and in the morning, the jury will remember them."

The Stornoway court also heard the tale of how a 20 year old had hindered the police in the execution of their duty by swallowing a ignition key.

An agent for the accused objected when the Crown produced an X-ray plate showing the key lodged in the man's stomach stating that no search warrant had been obtained.

The young man and his co-accused had pleaded not guilty that while acting together they had taken away a pick-up truck without the consent of the owner. The young man also denied stealing the ignition key or alternatively swallowing it when the driver was requested to give a sample of breath for a breathalyser test.

The court heard how a schoolteacher had borrowed the truck and left it in the car park. When he returned he found three men at the bonnet who were 'well oiled.' They claimed the truck was theirs. When the police arrived the teacher told them he had left the ignition key in the truck but the police could not find it.

A police officer told the trial that when he asked one of the accused to remove what was in his mouth he had made a forced swallow. He told him that he would be taken to the hospital the following morning for an X-ray.

When the X-ray was produced solicitor John C Young objected claiming that it had been improperly obtaind. 'Clearly it was done without the benefit of a search warrant,' he said.

Sheriff Scott Robinson agreed. He said he was not entirely satisfied that consent for the X-ray had been properly obtained - what the English would have called 'an invasion of privacy.' He found him not guilty of stealing the key or swallowing it.

However he found the accused guilty of taking away the vehicle without consent and imposed fines and driving bans.

Afterwards the accused said: 'I found the key a bit hard to swallow.'

ISLAND JUSTICE

One of the finest judgements ever dispensed at Stornoway Sheriff Court was by the late -- and controversial -- Sheriff Ewan Stewart. Confronting him was a young miscreant who admitted to stealing two charity boxes - one for the RNLI and one for a cancer organisation.

The trouble with such thefts is that no one really knows how much money is in a charity box when it gets stolen.

The youth was therefore taken aback when His Lordship asked him 'Do you know I have the second sight?' The youngster was not sure whether this was a trick question and remained silent.

The Sheriff then enlightend him: 'Well I have the second sight and I happen to know how much was in each of those charity boxes. There was £60 in the Lifeboat one and £50 in the cancer one, and you will pay compensation for those amounts to those two charities.'

****

The other concerned one of the tinkers who made regular appearances at the Burgh Police Court, usually on a minor breach of the peace or drunk charge. He was fined £3 by John the Barber, one of the Police Judges appointed by Stornoway Town Council.

After the court the Clerk -- Murdoch Macleod -- remonstrated with him pointing out that the same tinker had been fined £3 for a breach at the last court and that this time it should at least have been a fiver.

But John had his answer. He told him. 'You see every time he gets fined he comes down to the shop to sub the money from me and I knew I only had £3 in the till.'

Thatched Bothan at Cross, Ness, with beer kegs at the entrance

Procurator Fiscal Colin Scott Mackenzie sen   *Laurence Dowdall, solicitor*

AND THEN THERE WAS LOCHMADDY.....

The installatiion in May 2003 of Stornoway Procurator Fiscal David Teale as Fiscal at Lochmaddy Sheriff Court -- he was referrred to as 'tenacious' by Sheriff David Sutherland -- reminded me of a trip to Lochmaddy many years previously with the then Stornoway Fiscal, Colin Scott Mackenzie, who was also responsible for the North Uist court.

I was to be there as the official court shorthand writer for a Fatal Accident Inquiry - a duty I carried out for many years before such work was put out to contract by the Crown Office. (How this saved the public purse I have yet to fathom out because on one occasion at Stornoway the shorthand writer came from the Isle of Man!).

I had flown down from Stornoway with Colin, Sheriff Scott Robinson, and the pathologist who was to be a witness.

Colin had hired a car from the Maclennan Brothers' garage at Balivanich. However just near Langass the Rover packed up with steam coming from the radiator and we had to push it into a lay-by.

We then thumbd a lift and the first vehicle to come along was a MacBrayne cattle truck. Remembering the dignity of the Court the Sheriff and the Fiscal went into cabin with the driver, and the pathologist and myself stood in the back among the poo.

However the saga did not end there. Colin had been told by the garage that a similar car had been delivered to the court. At the end of the proceedings -- it was dark -- Colin threw his gear into the Rover parked at the court house door, and then went back inside.

When he came out again to head for the hotel it was just in time to see the car disappearing. A nearby policeman was told to follow the car. When he was telling the Police Sergeant what had happened and how his car had been stolen with his gear in it, the Sergeant told him: 'I don't think so, your car is over there!'

However one motorist driving his own Rover must have been a bit alarmed when he saw the blue lights flashing behind him.

****

It was a custom at Lochmaddy that the Sheriff, the lawyers and myself would dine together in the evening at the Lochmaddy Hotel. Normally the Sheriff paid for the wine on the first night and then one or other of the lawyers on the second night. Myself and others would supply the liquers with the coffee in the residents' lounge.

One such visit co-incided with the cattle sales and one young high-spirited auctioneer from Perth had aready let the white parrot out of the cage in the lounge. I was returning from the dining room along the corridor with a Glasgow lawyer from Hughes Dowdall when we saw the auctioneer undo the fire hose, switch out the light in the lounge, and then hose the only occupant -- Sheriff Bill Fulton. We decided to disappear into the bar out of the way.

However Bill Fulton -- he would have made an excellent Scottish rugby forward -- just rose, went upstairs, changed his clothing, and came back down to the lounge. The auctioneer's wife was rapidly on the scene to explain that her husband had recently sustained a head injury in a car crash and that he was really not responsible for his actions. She apologised for his behaviour and it was gracefully accepted by the Sheirff. However we know of other Sheriffs who would have had a different viewpoint.

These are only some of the examples of what could happen at Lochmaddy. The court cases you are about to read were varied and sometimes the court sat until way after midnight.

****

THE GIANT

In the sixites one character seemed to dominate the court cases at Lochmaddy and despite his slim build and 5ft 5ins height, he was known throughout the isles as The Giant -- alias John Macintyre. His exploits were like something from the wild west.

At one time he escaped from custody and was on the run for four days and then began to phone the police making conditions if he was going to give himself up to the authorities. He once explained to an avid Press corps that he got his nickname because he was very small as a boy and then started to grow.

My report on January 19, 1965, read:

A handcuffed prisoner who escaped from a police car in South Uist and remained at large for four days was sentenced to a total of three months imprisonmnet at Lochmaddy Sheriff Court last night.

He was 23 year old unemployed labourer, John Macintyre from South Uist, who pleaded guilty to five charges of careless driving, drunk driving, assaulting two police officers, escaping while in custody, and breaking and entering while at large.

After sentence was passed by Sheriff John Allan slim dark-haired Macintyre was immediately handcuffed with his hands behind his back and led from the court.

Dr Alastair Maclean (46) of Daliburgh, South Uist, told the court how he arrived seconds after Macintyre's car went off the road into a ditch on the night of November 13. He saw a man lying underneath a wheel and then saw Macintyre's buttocks breaking the surface of a loch beside a ditch.

'If I had not arrived Macintyre would probably have drowned' said the doctor. 'When he came to he was using foul language. The man with Macntyre, John Walsh, was unconscious and was also injured. Two soldiers arrived in a Land Rover. Macintyre and Walsh were taken to the Sacred Heart Hospital in Daliburgh.'

At the hospital Macintyre said he wanted to be examined for drunk driving. He refused to take off his wet clothing and then disappeared.

Asked if he thought Macintyre was fit to drive the doctor said that he thought he could and added: 'He had had his stomach washed out which is just the normal treatment for an alcoholic.'

Two nuns at the Sacred Heart Hospital, Redepta Pilkington (58) the Mother Superior, and Mary Justina (28) also gave evidence of Macintyre's condition at the hospital and how he suddenly disappeared.

Burly Corporal Raymond Morgan (30) one of the soldiers who drove Macintyre and his friend to the hospital, said that in the Land Rover Macintrye had 'challenged both of us to fight: he must have been drunk.'

A minister, the Rev Kenneth Macleod of Daliburgh, told how he had been visiting the hospital and how his car had been stolen from the car park. It was later found near Macintyre's home.

The Procurator Fiscal, Mr David Shaw, in his summing up, said that there was a great deal of circumstantial evidence showing that Macintrye was the man responsible for the theft of the minister's car and the other offences concerned with it.

Sheriff Allan found that there was insufficient evidence to convict the accused on the five charges involving the theft of the minister's car.

Referring to the charges to which Macintyre had pleaded guilty Fiscal David Shaw said that when police went to arrest Macintyre at his home for a drunk driving offence he had tried to escape and had violently resisted arrest.

He had had to be over-powered and put on the floor to get the handcuffs on him. He had butted Sergeant Donald Fraser on the face, and also violently asaulted PC Donald Nicolson.

Mr Shaw said that while Macintyre was in custody in the police patrol car they were on the way to the doctor's house to have him certified as being incapable of driving because of drink. The police car had gone into a ditch on the driveway leading to the surgery and dwelling house occupied by Dr Jeddle at Griminish. Sergeant Fraser had had to get out and push the car out of the ditch. As soon as it was on the driveway again Macintyre had thrown open the rear door and ran off making his escape. It was dark and the police had lost sight of him immediately

He said road blocks had been set up and the police force had been increased by two officers from Inverness and two from Skye. The search had continued for four days in the worst possible conditions with high winds and torrential rain. Eventually police officers surrounded Macintyre's house and he was re-arrested.

Mr Shaw said that while Macintyre was at large he had broken into a house used only as a summer residence and had stolen a hacksaw blade.

Mr R R Macewan, who appeared for Macintyre, said he did not find it easy to address his Lordship at all as to how his client should be dealt with and he thought a sentence of imprisonment was most likely. He said all the offences seemed to take place after his client had taken a certain amount of alcohol. He had been involved in a tragic accident which he said had affected him ever since.

The sentences imposed on Macintyre were as follows: Careless driving a £20 fine or 30 days imprisonment, and his licence endorsed: drink driving £30 or one month, and banned from driving for two years: 3 months imprisonment for assaulting the policemen: 60 days for escaping from custody: and 60 days for breaking and entering. It was a total of 3 months imprisonmnt.

In November 1967 there was an even more bizarre case involving the Giant when he had a half bottle of whisky in the dock, the lights went out, and when the court resumed he was nowhere to be found: he was down in the hotel bar. As the saga continued at court that night I kept phoning in update introductions to the story and was told by one night news editor: 'I think you're making them up!'

November 23, 1967: John 'The Giant' Macintyre was reprimanded at Lochmaddy Sheriff Court last night for trying to pass back a half bottle of whisky from the dock to a friend in the public benches. Sheriff Clerk Peter Corcoran spotted it and Police Sergeant Robert Gordon of Lochmaddy intercepted it. When Sheriff Hamilton Lyons asked: 'Where did that come from?' Macintyre replied: 'It fell out of my pocket and was causing an obstruction in the dock.'

Sheriff Lyons told the sergeant to take it away but Macintyre tried to interrupt. Sheriff Lyons said: 'Macintyre, who is doing the talking?' 'My lawyer and you sir, but I want justice here today.'

His sternest warning came after he was noticed making threatening gestures to a witness, making faces and clenching his fist. A 19 year old domestic help was giving evidence at the time and later had to be helped from the witness box. Macintryre had been hiding behind the Fiscal as he was questioning the girl.

The Sheriff ordered Macintrye to stand up and told him: 'If this behaviour continues you will be committed for contempt of court for a period vastly in excess of anything which might result from the case presently before me.'

Later when the electricity generator unit broke down the court was plunged into darkness and the trial had to be adjourned for half an hour. Sheriff Lyons said it would be better to adjourn because it would not be possible to take notes or to see the demeanour of the witnesses.

However when it was decided to resume by the light of two Tilley lamps the accused could not be found. The Fiscal told the Sheriff that instructions had been issued to the police to arrest Macintyre but he arrrived back in the courtroom just as the police were going out to look for him. He had gone to the bar in the Lochmaddy Hotel

Macintyre, who was facing eight charges ranging from assault to drunk driving, was jailed for six months after the 12 hour trial which had concluded several hours earlier at 12.40 am. Immediately after his appearance he was driven in a police car to Benbecula Airport and then flown by BEA to Inverness to carry out his prison sentence.

****

THE LOBSTER CASE

March 5, 1979:

A North Uist lobster fisherman left the witness box at Lochmaddy Sheriff Court to give a demonstration of a left-handed single half-hitch knot. He was showing Sheriff Scott Robinson how he knew that the lobster creels he had set off Manish Point the previous year had been tampered with because they had been closed with a right-handed knot.

In the dock was Alasdair Macdonald (34) fisherman, and Angus Ferguson (26) fisherman, both from Houghharry, North Uist. They denied that while acting together they stole two lobsters from creels set off Manish Point on July 31 last year, and also attempting to steal lobsters from 14 creels at the same location. The creels belonged to Gillespie and Donald Macdonald of 12 Sollas, North Uist.

Mr Ken Macdonald of Stornoway appeared on behalf of Alasdair Macdonald, and Donald Ferguson of Portree acted on behalf of Angus Ferguson.

'You are both appearing for members of your own clan I notice,' remarked his Lordship.

The island courtroom was packed to capacity when the trial began. Gillespie Macdonald (37) told how he and his brother -- partners in the lobster boat 'Violet' -- began to be suspicious last June about a drop in their catches.

On investigation he found that the lobster creels which he had closed had been tampered with. He knew this because the knot had been tied in a different way. He then stepped from the witness box to demonstrate on a creel that he tied the half-hitch in an anti-clockwise direction, because he was left-handed. He had found that some of the creels had been opened and then closed with a right-handed half-hitch. He reported the matter to the police.

Police Sergeant John McFadzean told the court how he and another constable had kept watch from a concealed position on Manish Point on July 31 and had seen the accused Macdonald's boat lift two of the Violet's creels and take out two lobsters. He said there was no question of the creels belonging to the accused and those belonging to the Violet being entangled because they were about 25 yards apart.

In a statement under caution to the police Ferguson had stated: 'I only started fishing with Alasdair Macdonald at the beginning of the season this year. When we go out he tells me what creels to lift. I know that some of the creels that we lift do not belong to him but he is my boss. I do as he tells me.'

Before the evidence concluded both accused decided to change their pleas to guilty and they were each fined £300. Their plea of not guilty to a second charge was accepted by the Crown.

****

THE £ SYMBOL

June 20, 1979

The lack of a £ symbol on an American typewriter stolen from the 46th Chief of the Clan Macneil, resulted yesterday in an island electrician being fined £75 at Lochmaddy Sherff Court for theft.

John Archibald Maclean (27) of Castlebay, Barra, pleaded guilty to stealing a Smith Corona typewriter, valued at £50, from Kismuil Castle, Barra, between August 1975 and May 1977.

Kismuil Castle is the island home of Iain Roderick Macneil, the Clan Chief, who lives in Ithaca, New York, but normally spends the summer months at the clan seat on the Hebridean Isle of Barra.

One of the post-prandial customs associated with the castle when his ancestors lived there was for a trumpeter to sound a fanfare from the battlements and then proclaim: 'Hear, O ye people, and listen, O ye nations. The Great Macneil of Barra, having finished his meal, the Princes of the earth may dine.'

The court was told yesterday that when the Chief was at the castle in 1975 he got in touch with the accused to carry out some work for him. He gave him two keys to the castle. The chief did not return until May 1977 when he discovered that some items, including a typewriter, were missing, and he reported the matter to the police

In August 1977 after he had again returned to New York he began to receive typed letters and bills from the accused. The typeface looked familiar and he also noticed that everytime a £ sign was required, it had been written instead of typed. The typewriter which had been stolen did not have a £ symbol but only a $ symbol.

A typewriting expert had established that the letters from the accused had been typed on the chief's typewriter and the information was passed to the police. When the accused was charged he said that while working in the castle he had found a typewriter in an attic. He had used it for a few months before selling it at the Barras in Glasgow.

****

BLOOD THEFT

April 1991

Lochmaddy Sheriff Court heard how a man who had previously been charged with drunk driving had broken into the police station to steal his blood sample. He then set fire to the items he had stolen - but missed his own blood specimen.

Twenty eight year old roof felter Thomas Walsh, of Rigside, Lanark, whose sentence had been deferred for a social inquiry report, was fined a total of £1275 and banned from driving for 18 months.

He had pleaded guilty to driving with an excess of alcohol (156mg) on March 12 near Torlum, Benbecula: being the holder of a provisional licence driving without a supervisor: driving without 'L' plates: and on March 13 breaking into the police station at Balivanich in Benbecula and stealing two files containing copies of police reports, a quantity of blood and urine kits, a desk diary and a plastic litter bin.

He then removed these items from the police station and set fire to them in a field in Balivanich with intent to destroy the blood sample obtained from him and with intent to avoid prosecution and to pervert the course of justice.

Procurator Fiscal Mr Colin McClory told the court that after being processed at the police station at Balivanich for drunk driving and other road offences a blood sample had been securely lodged.

The police station had been locked up and secured about half past midnight However when officers came on duty the following morning they found a window open and various items missing. Suspicion fell on the accused and he admitted everything in a statement to the police.

He had opened the police window with a shovel which he found outside. Anything lying about he put inside a plastic bin. He hoped his blood sample was among the items. He then walked across a field and set the items alight and destroyed them. He hoped he had destroyed any evidence against himself. He was very drunk at the time.

The Fiscal said however that Walsh had walked six miles from the hotel and six miles back and must have known what he was doing. He gave a very detailed account of his actions to the police and was able to show them where he had set fire to the items.

Fortunately, however, the accused's blood sample had been stored elsewhere in the police station.

Stornoway solicitor Mr Ken Macdonald, who appeared for the accused, said that his client had four previous convictions but none for dishonesty. On the night in question he had received a loan of a van and was stopped by the police. His actions after that were totally ridiculous because the loss of a licence would not have affected him at all. He did not even need a licence.

He said that when his client went back to the hotel he got very drunk and then got it into his head to get his blood sample back. He removed various items but did not get his own blood sample so at the end justice had not been interfered with in any way.

Mr Macdonald told Sheriff Ewan Stewart: 'It was a futile, stupid, incompetent and drunken act.' He asked his Lordship to impose a monetary penalty

Sheriff Stewart imposed a fine of £400 and an 18 month driving ban on the first charge: £50 on the second: £25 on the third: and £800 on the fourth.

****

BLUE PETER

October 11, 1978

When a civilian working at the Rocket Range in the Hebrides failed to receive a bonus offer of £5 worth of pornographic books after taking out a subscription for similar publications, he took his complaint to the Consumer Protection Department in Stornoway.

They investigated his complaint but were 'shocked and appalled' when they saw the type of magazines, so they reported the matter to the police.

Yesterday the sequel was heard at Lochmaddy Sheriff Court in North Uist when the mail order company concerned, Figcrest Ltd of 228 Green Street, Forest Gate, London, was fined £80 for sending pornographic material through the post.

The company pleaded guilty to sending three postal packages each containing one copy of the magazine 'Playbirds,' which were indecent and obscene, to Peter Jenner (49) of the Barrack Services Depot at the Royal Artillery Rocket Range in Benbecula, contrary to the Post Office Act. The magazines were sent between October 1977 and March 10 this year.

The Procurator Fiscal, Mr Colin Scott Mackenzie, told the court that the witness Jenner had completed an order form requesting certain magazines, 'Playbirds,' and 'New MS.'

On the order form it had indicated that if someone ordered two or more subscriptions they would send them £5 worth of books of a similar nature free of charge. The accused had sent £19 but did not receive the magazine 'New MS' or other books. He then complained to the Council's Consumer Protection Department at Stornoway.

Remarked Sheriff Scott Robinson: 'It would be an unusal task for the Consumer Protection Department.'

The Fiscal agreed. He said that the Department official concerned, Mr Robert Middleton, had requested Mr Jenner to provide all the relevant documents and the magazines received. The Fiscal then added: 'On looking at the magazines Mr Middleton, who was not brought up in the sheltered and cloistered atmosphere of the Western Isles, but who comes from the North of England, was appalled and shocked by the magazines and rather angry that his Department should be used to follow up this matter.' He had formed the opinion that the magazines were obscene and had reported the matter to the police because they had been sent through the post.

The police too had formed the opinion that the magazine 'Playbird' was obscene and decided to try and intercept one of them. 'Such interceptions are not made lightly,' said Mr Mackenzie. 'One of the magazines was seen going through the post and a warrant was obtained for the police to seize one. Included in the mail for Mr Jenner was the magazine 'Playbird' No. 23. I would ask your Lordship to order the destruction of the magazines.'

He added that when one of the company was informed that they were to be charged he had said that he thought intercepting the mail was a 'diabolical liberty.'

In a plea of mitigation by letter the company said that they were a mail order concern in the field of adult books and magazines. At their premises in London a quarter of a million orders were processed and despatched each year. All members of the staff were instructed not to send any book or magazine through the post if it was deemed indecent. A commercial carrier was the standard method of delivery.

When imposing sentence the Sheriff said that such matters should be discouraged in the Western Isles.

Yesterday Mr Jenner, a civilian employed at the RAOC Barrack Services Depot of the Rocket Range, said he was pretty annoyed at the Consumer Protection Department going to the police without consulting him. He added: 'It's been an expensive business. I won't be continuing my subscription for the magazines. My wife does not even know about it yet.'

(A popular member of the Range Sea Angling Club, he was thereafter known as 'Blue Peter.'

****

There's a yarn about an Irish man who decided to take elocution lessons. He finished up with a posh voice and his teacher said it was now time to put it into practice.

The next day he goes into a shop and asks very politely for a copy of The Times, half a dozen Cuban cigars, and a box of Belgian chocolates.

The fellow behind the counter says to him: 'Are you Irish?'

'However did you know? he asks.

Came the reply: 'Because this is a butcher's shop.'

HERCULES THE BEAR

When Hercules, the 8ft high 40 stone TV commercial bear went missing while on location in the Hebrides, it resulted in his owner Andy Robbins facing charges.

Hercules disappeared on August 1, 1980, after going for a swim near Petersport in the South East corner of Benbecula. He was last sighted on the Island of Wiay which lies off Petersport. There was a massive land, sea and air search following his disappearance and he was AWOL for three weeks.

Andy, a former Commonwealth wrestling champion, who lived at the Sheriffmuir Inn in Stirlingshire, bought Hercules as a cub from the Highland Wildlife Park. He took part in TV commercials for Kleenex and beer. The bear was finally sighted near Cleatraval. Although Andy was in hot pursuit Hercules seemed reluctant to give up his new found freedom. He was finally shot with a tranquillizer dart.

After he fell asleep he was put into a large net and air-lifted to Lochmaddy Playing Fields in North Uist where he was then transferred to his specially built £30,000 cage-come- travelling home.

A delighted Andy and his wife (who belongs to Grimsay in North Uist) then went into the cage and fed Hercules on prawns.

But the tale did not end there. Andy was charged with keeping a wild animal without a local authority licence contrary to the 1976 Dangerous Wild Animals Act.

When the case was called at Lochmaddy Sheriff Court a letter was submitted from Mr Joe Beltrami, the well-known Glasgow lawyer, pleading not guilty to the offence and the trial was fixed for July 14. The maximum penalty for such an offence was £400.

Andy had denied that on August 20 and 21, 1980, and September 13 and 14, 1980, at Petersport, Benbecula, the Island of Wiay, and the Island of North Uist, that he kept a dangerous animal, namely a European Brown Bear of the family Ursidae, without a local authority licence.

Andy had planned to bring the bear to the trial as a 'silent witness,' in his new £65,000 coach, built for him in Belgium.

However on May 7, 1981, the Procurator Fiscal, Mr Colin Scott Mackenzie, dropped the charge, and explained: 'I had informed Mr Beltrami that if Mr Robbins could obtain a proper licence under the Dangerous Wild Animals Act of 1976 from Stirling District Council, then I would consider that the public interest had been served and that the public would then be protected. I now understand that the District Council has granted the necessary licence.'

Mr Mackenzie also revealed that since Mr Robbins had been charged last January that he had receieved pleas from 'diminutive citizens' urging 'hands off Hercules.' He said: 'I assured them individually that I was not going to do anything to Hercules and that it was his owner I was dealing with. Now that the licence has been granted he is no longer in jeopardy from the authorities.'

One man who was disappointed was George Peat of the Lochmaddy Hotel in North Uist. His hotel had been fully booked by Press representatives and TV crews who had planned to cover the 'Hercules trial'.

Andy said: 'I am delighted with the decision to drop the charge as it clears Hercules name for the future. He can now work anywhere in the UK. He is the only bear in the world with two licences -- one for a performing animal and one for a dangerous animal. We plan to present a Hercules swimming trophy for competition among the Uist schools.'

The £1000 reward for information leading to the capture of Hercules was shared by two Balmartin crofters.

BERNIE THE BULL

In 1988 there was the case of three island men being found not guilty at Lochmaddy Sheriff Court of causing the death of a £1400 Aberdeen Angus bull.

The Department of Agriculture bull -- appropriately named Ty-Isha Entertainer -- was being towed across the 300 yard Sound of Vatersay on its way to service 40 cows in the township of Caolais on Vatersay. (However, as is their wont, the Press corps covering the case decided to stick to alliteration and call him Bernie the Bull).

Defence solicitors argued that there was no case to answer. There had been no intention of causing the animal unnecessary suffering. It was an honest endeavour which had gone wrong.

The three crofters from Vatersay denied a contravention of the Protection of Animals (Scotland) Act on April 15, 1987. The charge alleged that the accused forced the Aberdeen Angus bull to swim across the Sound of Vatersay -- between the mainland of Barra and the Island of Vatersay -- while attached by rope to a rowing boat and that it was overcome by water under-currents and suffered death by drowning.

One of them also denied failing to bury the carcase but the Procurator Fiscal decided to drop this charge.

Sheriff James Fraser said there was insufficient evidence to show that the traditional method of swimming cattle across the Sound was cruel.

The accused felt it was a great result and vowed to drink a toast to the Sheriff -- or maybe more. They also said they would continue the tradition by swimming their own cattle across the Sound.

(A £4 million causeway was opened in 1991).

SEA DRAMAS

The Vaila

Covering sea stories -- many of them tragic -- was part and parcel of providing a service to newspapers, radio and television.

The anniversaries of some of these events meant that news items and features were also required over the years. There were therefore recurring stories on the Whisky Galore ship The Politician, the Iolaire disaster in which 205 men lost their lives at the entrance to their home port, and the Flannan Isles Lighthouse mystery.

As mentioned earlier the first major sea story I covered shortly after arriving on the island was the sinking of the Fishery Cruiser Valia after she ran aground on Eilean Iubhard at the mouth of Loch Shell, 14 miles south of Stornoway.

The crew abandoned ship. Although the launch and one lifeboat got away safely the second lifeboat became entangled in the davits when the ship lurched suddenly. Two men were thrown into the sea and the six others had to jump. In the dark five men were swept away to their deaths, but the captain, who had a torch which he was flashing on and off, and two seamen near him, were picked up by the the crew of the launch. It was described as the 'worst shipping disaster in Lewis waters in peacetime since the Iolaire.'

When the Stornoway lifeboat arrived on the scene they took the first lifeboat in tow and picked up the body of one of the drowned men, but there was no sign of the launch which had run out of fuel and drifted aground at Lemreway.

There the survivors were taken into homes, fed and clothed, and a message was sent to Stornoway that nine crew members were safe. Once the lifeboat arrived at Lemreway the survivors were taken on board and transported to Stornoway.

Eight of the crew were local men and, as news of the disaster spread through the town, a large crowd gathered at the harbour to watch the lifeboat come in and the survivors come ashore.

Providentially all eight local men were saved, but all the crew were well known in the town. The Lewis Hotel provided refreshments for the men before they were taken to the Seamen's Mission.

The sinking and tragic loss of life resulted in a Fatal Accident Inquiry being held in February that year at Stornoway Sheriff Court. The inquiry found that no negligence was involved on the part of the captain or crew, and that all steps had been taken to safeguard life.

One of the survivors opened up a public house on the outskirts of Edinburgh and I met him years later when I was on The Scotsman.

****

Another Fishery Cruiser, the Norna, was blown aground in Loch Shell where she had been anchored on Friday, September 25, 1964. Because of the heavy weather it was decided to send the Stornoway Lifeboat to stand by in case a dangerous situation developed at the ebb tide.

The Stornoway Life Saving Apparatus Crew were also called out. (The LSA later became known as the Coastal Rescue Equipment Company and are now known as Coastal Rescue Officers).

However the weather did not moderate and on the Saturday the lifeboat passed tow lines on board. The FC Minna and the FC Ulva anchored to seaward of the stranded vessel. Attempts to tow off the Norna were unsuccessful.

A salvage vessel, the Swen, then arrived from Loch Ewe and the Norna was towed off at 23.00 hours on the Saturday, and escorted by the salvage vessel to Stornoway on the Sunday.

****

THE POLLY - WHISKY GALORE

One of the favourite stories which keeps resurfacing concerns the sinking of the SS Politician which sank off Eriskay on February 4, 1941, with 250,000 bottles of whisky.

It resulted in the famous book by Sir Compton Mackenzie, 'Whisky Galore' and also the Ealing film. The whisky, which had been liberated by the thirsty islanders was stashed away in all sorts of unsual places and bottles were being found over the years. There were also diving expeditions on the wreck in the Sound of Eriskay, and the anniversaries of the sinking always brought demands for stories.

A Stornoway man, Willie John (Bucach) Macleod of Newton Street, who was 83 when I interviewed him in 2005, is the last man alive who was part of the salvage crew on the Politician.

He was a young 18 year old joiner when he became part of the salvage team. He was employed by Ducan Maciver of Stornoway as a diver's mate. He told me the puffer, which had been used as a tender boat to take materials and personnel to and from the wreck, had come up from Lochboisdale to pick him up along with some other men. These included Joe Beaton -- who later became a well-known Stornoway docker. He was there as a labourer.

There was also Donald Macdonald from Maryhill, Tom 'Buzzard' Macdonald, old Roddy Wedger Mackay, a blacksmith. Murdo Morrison from Tolsta worked the pumps for the diver. Roddy Macleod from Back was a winchman. They were all employed by Duncan Maciver, the local salvage agent in Stornoway.

Willie says they were there for about three months and they lived with a family in Eriskay but the bosses lived in Lochboisdale.

He recalls: ' In addtion to the thousands of cases of whisky of all kinds, there were also baths, toilets and wash-hand basins, bicycles and spare parts for bicylces. There was also plenty of money. I left before she floated because my work was finished. I left the tender at Lochboisdale where I then got the ferry 'Lochmor'.

'I remember an argument on board the Politician at the time. Duncan Maciver was all for the boat going to Lochboisdale once it was afloat. There was a right barney going on because he felt it would be fatal for the boat if she was put on a sandbank. He felt the suction of the sand would hold her down. I remember him making his way aft on the ship. I left for London. It was not until after the war that I learned that she had been towed into the Sound of Eriskay and sunk there.'

Willie reflected: 'It was an interesting period. I was making wooden frames for the diver for patching the ship. They were then caulked and sealed to make her watertight. The whole deck of the ship was about 8 or 9 whisky cases high. There were several brands of whisky. One day a diver sent up two hogsheads which we thought would be beer, but it turned out to be pure raw whisky. We were going ashore with buckets of it:.It was some do! There were bottles of whisky everywhere.

'One of the men in the digs with me was Old Bob, an Irishman, who was in charge of the Irish workers down there. He asked me one day if I would like to go fishing with him so I agreed but I did not see any fishing gear. He then took two sticks of dynamite from his jacket, ignited them and threw them in the water. We had fish galore.

'We saw the Customs boat one day heading for Eriskay. They went to four boats, picked up the moorings, and there were a few cases of whisky on each of them.

'We rescued a bath, wash basin and a toilet for our landlord on Eriksay. We had a job getting the bath up from the shore to the croft house. There was a stream running past the house and the boddach (the old man) told us just to leave it beside the stream because there was no running water on the island at that time.

'I went back 30 years later in my own boat and called in at Eriksay and made enquiries about the family. The daughter worked in a local shop and when I told her about the bath she said: "It's still there, come up to the house and I'll show it to you." She told me they had many a bath in it.'

How did Willie get his nickname? He explained that as a young boy he used to go to his uncle's house in Lower Sandwick. There was a man there named Ivor Murray who made little rafts. Willie stood on one of them and there was an offshore wind and he was carried out to sea on it. It took him out to Holm. A Buckie boat picked him up and took him into Stornoway and he got a hiding when he got back to his uncle's house. From that time on he was known as Willie Bucach.

The Customs have a system for accounting for Wrecks which belong to the Crown. A former Customs Officer friend told me that in remote parts of the realm -- such as the magical and mysterious Hebrides -- they employed Civilian Deputy Receivers.

They were given a bundle of officially addressed envelopes and some Wreck forms on which to record and advise the Receiver of Wrecks in Stornoway of what had been washed ashore. (The most regular was bales of raw rubber - they couldn't think what do with them). The Receiver would then arrange a sale and pay the CDR a reward from the proceeds. In those days the CDR also had an honorarium of about £5 per annum.

He told me that he seemed to remember that when the Politician went aground the first thing the Lochboisidale CDR did was to send his letter of resignation to Stornoway. 'He wisnae daft,' he adds. He recalls that the offical report was hilarious.

About 40 people, mainly from South Uist, appeared on whisky theft charges, and 19 were given jail sentences.

In a BBC programme on the 'Polly' in December 2005 various people were interviewed. Iain Smith (96) recalled the bales of cotton, the bikes and the whisky on board. Mary Macinnes (89) remembered taking the whisky and putting it in the peat banks and down by the shore under the rocks. 'The peat stacks became bigger' she said.

Another remembered the parties all over the island which went on for about a year to 18 months before the supplies dried up. He estimated that about £10,000 of damage was caused on board the ship.

In the January storm of 2005 some empty bottles were washed up and some of the £3m of Jamaican currency. Some believed that it was to support the Royal family if they had to evacuate to the Caribbean if the war went the wrong way.

There have been theories about why the ship ran aground. One is that there is a magnetic anomaly in the rocks at the south end of South Uist and that this could result in a magnetic pull which would put a ship off course.

Compton Mackenezie described the incident as 'like a folk tale. What the sea gives is a gift.'

In August 1942 Charles McColl, the Lochboisdale Customs Officer, reported to his superiors that the 'scrapping operations have now ceased. Any dutiable cargo was destroyed by gelignite.'

When my friend Iain Davidson, a Stornoway hotelier and keen diver, decided to have a dive on the wreck to mark the 25th anniversary, I accompanied him to cover the story. A few bottles were salvaged but the contents were not drinkable. However my bottle made a good conversation piece in my lounge for many years.

In 1990 when a house at Bruernish on Barra was being renovated a cache of four bottles was found underneath the floor but the whisky had evaporated because the cork seals had corroded. Here's an anonymous poem about the great event.

The Politician

Och times were hard in Barra, you'd hear the bodachs cry,
No food to feed a sparrow and every bottle dry!
Old men once fresh and frisky, so full of ploy and play,
dropped dead for want of whisky, the blessed uisge-beatha

Now the dusty dry Sahara is a thirsty barren land
but the drought that year in Barra was more than man could stand.
Aye, life was hard and cruel, and the days were dreich and sad,
When the strongest drink was gruel and the war was going bad.

A clever man old Hector, and wise the words he said,
'Without the barley's nectar, a man is better dead.'
But strange the ways of heaven, when men in darkness grope,
Each sorrow has its leaven, each tragedy its hope.
The great ship 'Politician,' its hold all stocked with grog,
Steamed proudly past the island - and foundered in the fog.

One case was rent asunder, twelve bottles came to grief,
when the Barra surf like thunder, came pounding on the reef.
And then the scent of nectar, came on the wild wind's breath,
'I smell it,' cried old Hector, 'It's whisky sure as death.'

He cried out: 'Kirsty, Kirsty, hand down my oilskin coat,
No more will I be thirsty, salvation's on that boat.'
Now 'Chon Macneil' was dying - the death that's far the worst,
No end so sad and trying as the awful pangs of thirst.

He cried 'We are delivered, from torture we are free'
And his nostrils flared and quivered in the glory of the sea.
Poor Sandy in a coma, was stretched upon his bed
when the lovely sweet aroma came wafting round his head.

For weeks he had been lying without a spark of life
And all the neighbours crying for his nearly-widowed wife
He shook just like an aspen, the man they thought was dead,
Then sighing, gulping, gasping, he vaulted out of bed.

Barefoot in his nightie, he slipped from out their reach,
With steps both long and mighty, he headed for the beach.
Old bodachs in their dotage and cailleachs by the score,
came streaming from each cottage and mustered on the shore.

Now Sarah Jane Mackinnon, a lady through and through,
was just a wee bit partial to a drop of 'mountain dew,'
She knelt there at the ingle, her form all crooked and bent,
When her nose began to tingle at a well-remembered scent.

One sniff and she was rising, two sniffs and straight outside,
where odours appetising were blowing from the tide.
She knelt in deep devotion with reverent pious face,
and blessed the stormy ocean and the Lord's abiding grace.

By jove she went full throttle across the Barra turf
when she heard a tinkling bottle in the pounding of the surf.
She ran - but so did others - aye, hundreds maybe more,
As uncles, cousins, brothers, descended on the shore.

And then the boats went dashing across the crested wave,
the long oars dipping, splashing, to their Aladdin's cave.
Each man took turns at rowing, a job no man would shirk,
and the spirit they were showing, was better than Dunkirk.

They climbed aboard the liner, the lame, the halt, the old,
no Vikings e'er were finer, no pirates half so bold.
And then with eager faces, they gazed into the hold,
and saw a thousand cases of liquid, shining gold.

'A shame, a shame,' cried Kirsty, 'it is an act of God,
just think of Barra thirsty, and all this going abroad.'
But joy was there abounding and every heart did leap,
for all were in communion with the spirits of the deep.

Oh the ceilidhs and the pleasure, and the drams in Castlebay,
As the gurgling golden treasure chased the cares of war away.
Man, the bottles that were hidden, buried deep beneath the croft
Aye, the cases in the midden, and the joy up in the loft.

Who would heed air raid sirens, who would hide himself in fright
with a 'muchkin' in the morning, and a bumper every night.
And Barra boys hard fighting on land and ocean wide,
deserved a wee bit parcel, with a glook, glook, glook inside.

Aye, Hector cried, 'We're winning, it's very plain to see,
Tonight is the beginning of the victory at sea.
He swigged another bumper, and happily he sighed,
'The Germans sure have it, now that Barra's fortified.

Slaithe now to Churchill, whose name we proudly recall,
But the Barra 'Politician' was the greatest of them all.

****

The guga hunters, the men from Ness in Lewis who annually go after the young solan geese on the remote Atlantic Isle of Sula Sgeir, 40 miles north of the Butt of Lewis, always interested the news desks. The men leave by fishing boat from the Port of Ness and spend two weeks catching the gugas with long poles. The birds are considered a delicacy by the people of Ness who queue up to buy them when the guga hunters return. The birds are cleaned and salted before landing. Responding to calls for the cull to stop, Donald Murray, a former fishing skipper and councillor said in Ness they had been in harmony with nature and God's providence was their inheritance.

Vaila survivors in Sailor's Home

Provost Sandy Matheson receives the ship's bell and the name plate of the Iolaire from Customs Officer 'Peter' Cunningham watched by some of the Iolaire survivors.

The SS Politician

Diver Iain Davidson with a bottle of Polly

Timber galore - a listing SS Stassa

John F Macleod, the seaman hero and boatbuilder

The rocks at the Beasts of Holm where Iolaire perished

Flannan Isles Lighthouse dining area

The Flannan Isles Lighthouse

Rockall

Winchman Chris Murray

Queuing up for the gugas at Port of Ness

TIMBER GALORE

There was timber galore when the 2000 tonne Panamanian cargo vessel 'Stassa' went aground on the southermost point of Harris on Thursday, July 28, 1966. In addition to the timber in the holds she had timber loaded on her deck. She was on her way from Archangel to Limerick when she grounded and was listing badly.

She was pulled off the rocks by the Stornoway lifeboat which had been called out along with the Life Saving Apparatus team from Tarbert in Haris. The LSA team went out in a small boat to the stricken vessel and took off 12 of the crew. The captain, his wife, the chief officer and the radio officer, remained on board. The other crew members were taken to the nearby Rodel Hotel and then to the Sailors' Home in Stornoway.

The captain left the ship on the Sunday night. A new rescue lifeboat, on its way from Scrabster to Mallaig, stood by the Stassa for two days to pump water from the engine room. A tug then took the vessel in tow to Stornoway.

The crew were claiming that they had not been paid and there was a confrontation between one of the crew and the Captain which I filmed while on board, as well as taking photographs. There was also a dispute at Stornoway as to whether they should be regarded as shipwrecked mariners and kitted out with clothing.

The sequel was heard at Stornoway Sheriff Court on November 29 when three men faced trial on a charge of theft of timber from the vessel and from the sea around the vessel after she had grounded on July 28. The accused were defended by Laurence Dowdall, doyen of Scottish criminal lawyers.

The Depute Procurator Fiscal, Colin Scott Mackenzie Jnr, claimed the men were in Rodel Bay with their lobster boat 'Tudor Rose,' when they took the wood which he said should have become the property of the Receiver of Wrecks.

Police witnesses gave evidence that 334 lengths of wood were found in a Mallaig boatyard.

Mr James R Cordiner (60) director of timber merchants James Cordiner and Son, Aberdeen, said in the witness box that that wood was similar to the timber from the Stassa. He said he had bought the deck cargo from the insurance company after the ship had gone aground. He could identify it by markings on the wood and some lengths were also marked with oil.

It was after the court adjourned for lunch that the trial took a new twist. On being cross-examined by Mr Dowdall as to how he knew that the timber was from the deck and not from the sea, he said he had run his finger along the lengths to see if there was any salt on them and he had also chewed some chippings.

Mr Dowdall enquired as to when this had taken place and he was told that it had happened during the lunchtime recess. Samples of the timber were in the well of the stairway in the court building and the Procurator Fiscal was present with him. He had chewed it to see if it tasted of salt. It did taste of salt.

'And why wasn't I invited to this pine tasting party? queried Mr Dowdall.

Mr Dowdall submitted that the wood was flotsam and had been found floating and was 'like pack ice.'

Sheriff Hamilton Lyons, in admonishing Mallaig skipper Duncan Henderson, said he did not think what they had done was greater damage than what might have been done by storm and sea. A crew member from Eriskay was acquitted and the charge against another crew member from Malllaig was dropped.

However there was a further unexpected sequel. I was building our present house at the time and my contractor had bought some of the timber from Cordiners. So my roof beams came from the Stassa!

****

THE IRISH STOWAWAYS

Two Irish colleens who stowed away on a ship which they thought was going to London -- but was actually bound for Russia -- were admonished when they appeared at Stornoway Sheriff Court in September 1977.

They were charged with an offence under the Merchant Shipping Act of 1970 and were liable to a maximum penalty of £100 or three months in prison.

The girls, both from County Cork, pleaded guilty to stowing away on board the 500 tonne London registered cargo vessel 'Torridge' when she was berthed at Foynes on the River Shannon in Eire, without the consent of the Master or other lawful authority. They had boarded the vessel on a Friday night.

The girls thought the vessel was going to London but it was on its way to Archangel in Russia to pick up a supply of timber.

The Procurator Fiscal said that a short time before the sailing the two accused went on board unseen or were taken on board, he did not know which, but it was without the Captain's permission.

On the Saturday afternoon the Captain discovered the presence of the two accused. He immediately contacted his company by radio and he was instructed to put the girls ashore at Stornoway.

They were landed at Stornoway on the Sunday morning and were then charged at the police station and released. The Fiscal said: 'They thought the ship was going to London. I presume they thought it was like a bus with the name on its stern.' Both were unemployed. The shipping company has agreed to pay the expenses regarding accommodation and for their return to Ireland.'

An agent, Ken Macdonald, said the offence was of a fairly minor nature. They had hidden in a storage cupboard but came out when they got hungry and went to the galley and the cook reported them to the Captain. They had been hoping to get to London but were horrified to discover that the vessel was on its way to Russia. They had no previous convictions and he understood they were both married.

Sheriff Scott Robinson said he was concerned as to how their departure might be supervised and he was informed that the Social Work Department were handling the matter.

He told the accused: 'I suppose by now you realise you have behaved very foolishly. You are perhaps fortunate that you were landed at Stornoway. I am going to admonish you both on the understanding that you will go back to your families..'

Both girls gave an undertaking that they would.

After the court the 22 year old accused told me: 'I'm very glad that's over. The people here have been wonderful and the Sheriff was wonderful too.'

Her 18 year old co-accused said: 'The Sheriff is a fine man. We could not have landed at a better place than Storrnoway. We are both separated from our husbands. I was sick 12 times on board because it was a very rough passage. On one occasion I was nearly swept overboard while being sick but one of the crew caught me.'

****

THE IOLAIRE TRAGEDY

Like the Politiician the loss of the Admiralty yacht HMS Iolaire on January 1, 1919, with the loss of 205 men at the Beasts of Holm at the mouth of Stornoway Harbour, has been one of the stories which keeps recurring on the anniversaries of the disaster.

What made the Iolaire so tragic was that these men had just survived the horrors of the First World War and then perished virtually on their doorsteps and only 20 yards from land.

A booklet published by the Stornoway Gazette stated that the men had survived 'not only the perils of the deep, but all the new infernal inventions of man for the destruction of human life - the floating mine, the cowardly submarine, the deadly torpedo.'

What should have been a happy homecoming turned out to be the bleakest New Year and lead to anguish, desolation and despair.

During the time she had been based at Stornoway the vessel had never entered the harbour at night.The returning servicemen had boarded at Kyle of Lochalsh.

Seaman John F Macleod of Port of Ness managed to swim ashore with a lifeline by means of which a hawser was pulled ashore and made fast between the beach and the ship. About 30 or 40 men got ashore by way of the rope. Altogether 75 men were saved from the wreck.

The jury at the public inquiry returned a unanimous verdict that the Iolaire went ashore and was wrecked on the rocks inside the Beasts of Holm about 1.55 on the morning of January 1, resulting in the deaths of 205 men: that the officers in charge did not exercise sufficient prudence in approaching the harbour; that the boat did now slow down, and that a look-out was not on duty at the time of the accident; that the number of lifebelts, boats, and rafts was insufficient for the number of people carried, and that no orders were given by the officers with a view to saving life; and further, that there was a loss of valuable time between the signals of distress and the arrival of the life-saving apparatus in the vicinity of the wreck.

In 1970 a party of divers recovered the ship's bell and name plate and these were presented to Stornoway Town Council. In addition to the 1958 memorial overlooking the scene of the tragedy at Holm Point, a plaque and pathway were provided in 2002.

I interviewed John F Macleod, known as the Ness boatbuilder, on several occasions for radio and newspaper articles, and I always felt privileged that it was he who made a pair of oars for my boat.

His grand-daughter Sandra Murray, who now lives in Inverness,, became an official dressmaker for HM the Queen and designed and made the outfit for HM when she opened the first Scottish Parliament for 300 years on July 1, 1999. She also made a Harris Tweed jacket for Princess Anne, and in 2007 designed a stunning yellow and black Macleod tartan outfit for Tartan Week in New York which was modelled by Ivanka Trump, daughter of billionire Donald Trump, whose mother came from Tong in Lewis.

****

The Flannan Isles lie to the west of Lewis and it was there that three lighthousekeepers vanished without trace in December 1900.

They were James Ducatt, the Principal Keeper, Assistant Keeper Thomas Marshall, and keeper Donald Macarthur, who came from Breasclete in Lewis, where there was a shore station for the families of the lighthouse keepers.

The last entry had been made on December 15 which showed that the lamp had been trimmed and the oil fountain and canteens were filled up and the lens and machinery cleaned.

The tragedy was discovered on Boxing Day. The lighthouse ship Hesperus called on a routine visit. The light was unlit, there was no sign of life, the landing stage had not been prepared for their visit, and there was no response when they fired a rocket.

On entering the lighthouse it was found that the clock had stopped and a meal had been left on the table. A chair had toppled over.

There have been many theories about what happened. There had been a storm the previous day and there has been talk that the men went to see what damage had been done when they were washed away by a massive tidal wave.

The Flannan Isles light became automatic in 1971 and I was taken out on the lighthouse ship to witness the evacuation of the last men to serve there, to see the logbook, and take photographs. Shortly after that as a result of a Royal Navy facility flight on a helicopter I was able to take some aerial shots of the lighthouse. These have been reproduced in many publications over the years, from books on great mysteries to children's educational books.

A helicopter is now used to take out personnel to service the light.

****

This brings to mind an attempt in 1983 to put a party of lighthouse personnel on to Rockall, the 60 ft pinnacle of rock out in the Atlantic, 240 miles west of the Hebrides.

The Royal Navy laid claim to the tiny finger of rock for Britain in 1955. After that both Ireland and Denmark made claims for the Rockall plateau which is believed to be immensely rich in oil.

Rockall comes under the administration of the Western Isles Council but there have been no site visits!

The Northern Lighthouse Board had chartered a British Airways Boeing Chinook helicopter to land personnel on the rock to replace the existing beacon there. The operation called for two mountaineering policemen to be landed on the rock first to provide handholds and safety ropes before the lighthouse personnel and the equipment was winched down to the rock.

Anyway I was commissioned by the Boeing public relations department in the States because they wanted film and photos of the personnel being winched down on to the rock from the chopper.

To achieve this I had to charter a fixed wing aircraft and the only one with fuel tanks capable of getting there and back was engaged in carrying out surveillance work for the Department of Agriculture and Fisheries who were keen to catch trawlers poaching within British territorial limits.

The charter cost £1000 and we set off in the morning after the helicopter took off. It was a two hour flight. However the visibility was down to about 200 yards and for safety reasons it was decided to abandon the attempt.

I brought the Boeing PR man up to date and he surprised me by just saying: 'These things happen.' I told him the charter plane had returned to other duties but as the Chinook was planning to have another go in the evening I would see if they would take me out and put me on the Pole Star, a lightouse ship which was standing by, where I would be able to film and get some photos.

I was taken out but the second attempt also had to be adandoned because the Chinook only had sufficient fuel to hover for 1 hour and 50 minutes which was not enough time to enable the party to complete the service of the beacon. I did get a photo of Rockall!

In 1985 adventurer Tom Maclean managed to spend four weeks in a cabin on the rock.

****

During my coverage of the isles there have been many stories concerning ships in distress -- too many to recount. However some stick in the mind.

One was the French trawler 'Cite Daleth' from St Malo. She was drifiting 20 miles south west of Barra Head in storm-tossed seas in January 1976. There were two rescue operations. The first was called off when she was taken in tow by another French trawler but there was another alert when the tow rope parted. The Barra lifeboat had also attempted to reach the trawler but was ordered to return to port because of the conditions. It was revealed that a British nuclear submarine, HMS Churchill, was standing by to rescue the crew if all else failed.

The trawler's ordeal began at dawn when the crew were having breakfast. There was a sudden flash and explosion from a leak in a gas pipe leading to a refrigerator near the crew's quarters. They rushed on deck because the ballast fuel tanks were underneath the cabins. The skipper reached the wheelhouse and managed to call up the St Briac which sent out a May Day message. Meanwhile the crew began fighting the flames.

Several attempts were made by the St Briac and the Mont Cenis to get tow lines on board but all were unsuccessful. Then the tug Lloydsman, on course for Iceland, said she would stand by to assist if the crew took to the liferafts. The Lloydsman had suggested that they abandon ship.

Then the Mont Cenis managed to get a line on board as the vessel drifted only six miles off the Sherryvore near Tiree. When the line was safe they ran before the storm.

The blackened and fatigued 10-man crew were eventually landed at Stornoway after battling their way for 130 miles through 40ft high waves and hurricane force winds.

When he came ashore Skipper Louis Riqual denied that he had rebuffed rescue attempts by the tug Lloydsman and RAF choppers.

He told me in the Sailors' Home (through interpreter Jacques Mesleard): 'I have the greatest admiration and respect for the RAF but I cannot say the same for the behaviour of the Lloydsman. I feel the tug wanted us to abandon ship so that they could claim salvage. But we had no choice in the matter. It would have been sure death to try and abandon ship in such conditions. These were the worst conditions I have seen in my 26 years at sea. I felt it was safer to stay on board. In fact I doubt if the crew would have obeyed an order to abandon ship.'

Some of the crew were taken to the Lewis Hospital for treatment for eye irritation caused by the smoke and fumes on board. Within a few days the trawler was towed back to France.

****

Another story gained the headline 'Deja vu, Spanish style.' It concerned the 132 ft Ormaza trawler which ran aground twice within 24 hours - once after leaving Lochinver on the mainland, and later near the Butt of Lewis in Ness.

On Monday, September 20, 1999, the Spanish trawler ran aground at Ness and was badly holed and leaking diesel.

The bad luck had started at 6am on the Sunday when Coastguards received a mayday signal that that Ormaza had gone aground on rocks in Lochinver harbour. The vessel, which had 14 tonnes of fish on board, had to be towed off by the lifeboat. A diver checked her condition before she went back to sea.

At 3am a garbled mayday call was picked up from the skipper of the 1973-built trawler. The crew also contacted the Spanish rescue controllers in Madrid who in turn called Stornoway Coastguard. The rescue helicopter was scrambled and the 14 men were winched off the vessel aground near the Butt. There were no injuries. The skipper and two other crewmen were questioned and later released by the police.

****

Mystery surrounded the tragic sinking of the 600 ton French trawler Sneckar Arctic' from Dieppe which went down 360 miles west of Lewis in February 1986 with the loss of 15 of the 27 crew members. A crew member of another trawler which took part in the search was also lost.

The nine survivors arrived at Stornoway on board the French trawler 'Dogger Bank' about midnight and shortly afterwards two other French trawlers arrived with two bodies.

After being kitted out with new clothes the survivors attended a memorial service in the town. Sandy Matheson, the Convener of the Western Isles Council, also attended the service and expressed the condolences of the community. The survivors were then taken to the airport where a chartered plane flew them to Octeville Airport near Le Havre.

None of the survivors were able to say what caused the sinking. The vessel had suddenly listed to starboard and then went on her beam. She then setttled down on her stern before going under. It all happened in a matter of minutes.

******

A modest local hero is Chris Murray, who has completed over 700 mercy missions as a Coastguard rescue helicpopter winchman.

Twice he was awarded Coastguard commendations for meritorious service, but he dismisses the idea of local hero. He says: 'I am a plain old Joe who gets on and does the job.'

On receiving one award he said: 'The only reason I am getting this award is because of the skill and determination of the rest of the helicopter crew - not forgettting the engineers back at base.' He became a winchman in 1988.

On one occasion Chris was washed overboard from the Spanish trawler Moraine on April 1995 when it was 90 miles south east of Rockall in the Atlantic.

There had been numerous attempts to land him on the deck of the trawler in difficult weather conditions. Due to the extreme range fuel was a critical factor and the helicopter Captain decided that he would need to refuel at Benbecula and then return to the Moraine.

On returning Chris was successfully landed on the trawler but shortly after detaching himself from the winch line he was washed overboard by a heavy sea. He sustained a dislocated finger and severe bruising to his legs and body, but signalled to his fellow helicopter crew members that he wanted to be put back on board to complete the rescue mission of helping a sick trawlerman. The mission was accomplished.

The Chief Coastguard at the time, Commander Derek Ancona, said at a commendation ceremony in Stornoway that he did not give them away lightly.

He added: 'This incident is a good example of the risks, professionalism and courage that helicopter crews have to face and undertake during the course of their duties. It must have been a terrifying experience for Chris but we have to remember that he was a clearance diver in the Royal Navy. The award reflects credit on the rest of the crew who must have watched in horrror as he was washed overboard.

'The courage, determination and dedication to duty demonstrated by Chris Murray was entirely within the keeping of the finest traditions of the servive.'

Chris also rescued nine men from a liferaft from the sunken German registered trawler Hansa in a massive international search operation 240 miles west of Tiree. Sadly six crew members lost their lives.

At the time of writing (2007) Chris has completed 760 missions and has received the Queen's Gallantry Medal as well as numerous other citations. Provided he keeps passing the medical examinations Chris hopes to continue in his work. Who knows he might notch up 1000 missions.

AIR AFFAIRS

Two Cessna Citation private jets were on their way to Stornoway on the evening of Thursday, December 8, 1983. The weather was North East 6/7, cloudy and clear. One landed safely and the other plunged into the sea off Arnish Point in Stornoway Bay with the tragic loss of 10 lives -- three couples, two young children and two pilots.

It sparked off a massive sea and air search but to this day mystery surrounds the crash.

The aircraft was on its way from Paris to Liverpool enroute to Stornoway when it disappeared off the radar screens and ditched into 360 ft of water. Those on board were going to spend a shooting week-end at the luxurious Garynahine Lodge on the 12,000 acre estate which belonged to 40 year old millionaire Mike Carlton, a property and finance tycoon. He had arrived in another Cessna Citation jet at Stornoway Airport just minutes before the other disappeared. He owned a number of planes including two Royal Navy Gannets.

On board the ditched aircraft were Inspector General Henri Gimbert (53) of the French Airforce, his wife Charlette (53): Air Commodore John Parker, RAF Director of Quartering and his wife Jill, of Cranwell in Lincolnshire: 37 year old Liverpool solicitor John Wallace, his wife Allison (27), their two young children Claire (3) and 7 month old baby Jonathan, all of Five Oaks, Hay Lane, Williston, South Wirral: and the two crew members, Captain Stewart Patterson and his co-pilot, Tim Ridgeway.

Stornoway Lifeboat was called out -- it was the first occasion that pagers had been used to summon the crew, prior to that rockets were fired to call out the lifeboat as well a telephone calls.

They had received a callout from Stornoway Coastguard that the Controller at Stornoway Airport had reported that a private jet had disappeared from the radar screen. The position given was off Arnish Point at the entrance to Stornoway Harbour.

By 1995 hours a Nimrod and a rescue helicopter from Lossiemouth were in the area. The Lochinver Lifeboat, the Fishery Protection Vessel Jura, MFV Radiant Way and MFV Shona, joined the search. The Caledonian MacBrayne car ferry Suilven - on her way to Stornoway -- also assisted.

Coastguard rescue teams from Gairloch, Loch Ewe, Ullapool, Dunvegan, Portree, and Duntulm were told to stand down after the Stornoway Coastal Rescue team was called out.

Radiant Way picked up a body at 22.55 hours and the Lochinver Lifeboat picked up a second body. The search was called off at 0204. The Lifeboat then refuelled and was again ready for service at 0520.

On December 9 the search was resumed at 0830 hours. At 10.46 the lifeboat recovered an aircraft seat and an article of child's clothing. At 10.45hours the lifeboat recoverd a body and a second at 11.12 hours. Two life jackets were then recovered. The search continued until darkness at 15.53.

On December 10 the lifeboat was launched again and the search resumed until it was discontinued.

The Cessna which plunged into the water was one of several planes belonging to Mr Carlton who lived at Albert Lodge, Victoria Grove, London.

I interviewed a shaken Mr Carlton about midnight at his luxury lodge 16 miles from Stornoway. He told me that the two aircraft had not started off together for Stornoway. The Cessna Citation had left three hours early to go to Le Bourget in Paris to pick up some friends and then also picked up some others at Liverpool.

He said he himself had left in a friend's aircraft from Biggin Hill about 4pm and had then flown the plane directly to Stornoway.

He said they were all personal friends of his who were coming up to the lodge as guests for a shooting week-end.

He told me: 'I have no idea what could have caused it. The weather was good and we landed some little while before the other aircraft. There was no obvious reason for the accident. We had heard the other plane talk to Stornoway Tower just a few minutes before we ourselves talked to the tower.'

The Citation had mysteriously disappeared from the radar screen about 5.45 pm.

Although the majority of the bodies were recovered over the first few days, it was months later before all were recovered.

On December 12 the Department of Transport anounced that an Air Accident Investigation inspector would be arriving on the island to organise a sea search for the wreckage of the plane. A Department spokesman said: 'A limited salvage attempt using a local trawler will carry out a dredge of the area for four days. We have a good radar fix of where the aircraft disappeared.'

On December 13 the Air Attache from the French Embassy in London and the Consul General for France in Edinburgh formally identified the fourth body found as that of Madame Charlette Gimbert, wife of the French Air Force General.

That same day the Stornoway fishing boat 'Sandy Bay' returned to port to land the body of a young child, believed to be that of 3 year old Claire Wallace. Like the other bodies it was sent to Inverness for a post mortem examination and for formal identification.

Two other fishing boats also found items from the plane. 'The Alpha' found a compass and the 'Fear Not' a parachute.

The following day the trawler 'Grampian Heather' -- which had been chartered to search for the plane wreckage -- found the body of one of the jet pilots off Kebbock Head, the same area where the bodies of the two children had been found. A major part of the wreckage had been found but the net broke when trying to bring it to the surface.

On December 15 the Department of Transport announced that the search for the wreckage had been officially abandoned. A spokesman said that the 'Grampian Heather' had left the scene as it had been decided to call off the search. He added: 'The vessel located what appeared to be a major part of the jet but their net broke and they lost it. Despite an intensive dredge of the area they were not able to pick it up again. Although they had a good fix on it the problem was one of cost. To bring in a proper salvage vessel and divers would cost a minimum of £25,000 a day.'

He said that although the search for the wreckage had been abandoned the investigation into the cause of the accident would continue. He added: 'At the moment there is nothing to indicate what caused the accident.'

However an English Tory MP, Mr Tim Smith of Beaconsfield, pressed for a full and independent inquiry into the way the investigations were carried out.

Years later when a local fishing boat, the Diana, picked up the wreckage they were told just to dump it. An inquiry decided that the cause of the accident was pilot error and that seemed to be the end of the story.

Then 10 years later, in June 1993, the Stornoway pocket trawler 'Providence II' picked up the wreckage in her nets while fishing about 14miles south of Stornoway. The wreckage -- the fuselage, wings and engine -- was towed into port by Skipper Colin Mackenzie.

He told me: 'It took us about seven hours to tow it into Goat Island (in Stornoway Harbour). I put a buoy on the wreckage and then with the aid of two divers I towed it into No 2 Pier.'

The wreckage - believed to be about 60 per cent of the aircraft and weighing five tonnes -- was being lifted out by a crane and was almost clear of the water when the support straps broke and it sank to the bottom of the harbour.

A second attempt using chains and new straps was successful and the wreckage was placed on a lorry and taken to the fabrication yard at Arnish for examination by Richard Parkinson, a senior inspector of the Air Accidents Investigation Branch of the Depaprtment of Transport. Prior to this he had carried out a preliminary investigation on the pier. After his examination of the wreckage at Arnish he gave permission for it to be taken to the rubbish dump and buried there.

Still caught up in the wreckage was the cod end of the fishing net full of prawns.

Following the recovery of the wreckage in 1993 the MP Tim Smith asked why the wreckage had not been returned to the Royal Aircraft Establishment at Farnborough He told me: 'I came up against a brick wall. I even went to see the Minister and got nowhere. The whole thing is extraordinary. I cannot understand why the wreckage was not returned to Farnborough Many people think there was a cover-up of some kind.'

When the question was put to the Department of Transport the spoksman replied: 'The investigation is concluded. There was nothing to keep.'

I was then contacted by Captain Gordon Mills of Sidcup in Kent, a personal friend of Captain Stewart Patterson, who had seen my newspaper reports of the wreckage being found. He said he had asked the Department what the normal procedure was when aircraft wreckage was found and had been told that it was returned to Farnborough.

He told me: 'The official inquiry put the cause of the accident down to pilot error, but Stewart was one of the best pilots in the business.

'The plane was in perfect condition, it also had a new engine. Stewart was also an instrument reading examiner. He would not make that kind of mistake. I myself had flown it just a few days before. I also knew Mike Carlton. This only deepens the mystery surrounding the whole tragedy.'

In addition no Fatal Accident Inquiry was ever held the reason given being that it was 'outwith the court's jurisdiction.' That, however, did not explain why an FAI was carried out when a private plane crashed off North Uist the previous year (1992) where I was engaged as the official court shorthand-writer.

According to the Lord Advocate's office an FAI should be held if it appears that the death resulted from an accident occurring in Scotland while the person who had died, being an employee, was in the course of his employment or, being an employer or self-employed person, was engaged in his occupation as such.'

So if Captain Stewart and his co-pilot were employed at the time it would appear that an FAI should have been held.

Of course there were many rumours going around at the time as to where Mike Carlton obtained his vast wealth and there were suggestions that he was engaged in the arms industry and who better to have as personal friends than two high ranking air force officers.

Another twist to the strange saga was that Mike Carlton and his wife were killed when he was piloting an aircraft in 1985.

Like the disappearance of the lighthouse keepers on the Flannan Isles it will remain a mystery.

****

SHACKLETON TRAGEDY

Ten RAF personnel - the entire air crew -- tragically lost their lives on April 30, 1990, when a Shackleton Aircraft from No 8 Squadron from RAF Lossiemouth -- which had just completed a maritime patrol exercise -- crashed into a 900 ft high cloud-covered hill near Northton in South Harris just before lunchtime

The burnt wreckage was strewn over the top of Maodal and one engine was lying near the bottom. The bodies were taken to a temporary mortuary in the nearby village of Leverburgh. Later they were taken by helicopter to Stornoway and then conveyed to the police mortuary.

The Procurator Fiscal, Colin Scott Mackenzie, who visited the scene of the crash by helicopter along with Chief Inspector William Fraser, said that police were carrying out inquiries on his behalf. He said he also expected to receive reports from the RAF investigators and he would be reporting the matter to the Lord Advocate who would decide whether there would be a Fatal Accident Inquiry.

Members of the RAF's Board of Inquiry - equivalent to the civilian Air Accident Investigations Branch -- were quickly on the scene as well as experts from RAF Abingdon near Oxford, a maintenance unit, who were flown there to assess how the wreckage could be removed for further examination.

The Shackleton was taking part in Exercise Brushfire, which involved a total of 12 aircraft. There were five different types - Shackleton, Buccaneer, Nimrod, Tornado F3 and the NATO 3A. The aim of the exercise was to assess the RAF capability to counter incoming Cruise missiles. The role of the Cruise missiles was being simulated by a Martel which was an anti-ship missile fired by a Buchaneer.

A spokesman for RAF Strike Command in Stornoway said that the reason they were so certain that the missile had no relevance to the loss of the Shackleton was because the Martel had been fired one and a half hours before the crash. It was the first day of the exercise.

The Shackleton had carried out its part of the exercise and was continuing flying training before returning to base at Lossiemouth. He added that the Shackeltons were to be phased out by the end of the next year (1991). He said it would be irresponsible to speculate on the cause of the disaster.

However one theory circulating immediately after the crash was that the aircraft, which was out over the Atlantic -- had planned to come through the Sound of Harris because of the low cloud and then fly up the Minch but had lost its bearing and hit the 900 ft high hill.

Thirty seven year old Angus John Maciver, who was one of the first on the scene, said that the hill was covered with low cloud when he and the local policeman arrived. They had found two or three bodies near the top. He said there was a smell of burning fuel and wreckage was scattered all over the place.

Stornoway Fire Station Oficer John Norman Macdonald told me: 'There was nothing we could do when we arrived. In fact it was all over before anyone could get to the scene.'

Some rescuers described seeing half-eaten sandwiches among the wreckage. Northon crofter Malcolm Mackinnon (65) heard the roar of a plane's engine and remarked to a companion that it sounded very low. He said half a minute later there was a loud bang. He said there was a blanket of fog covering the hill at the time. He climbed up and could see red in the heather. At first he thought it was a fire but when he got closer he could see it was a red survival suit.

As the Shackletons did not carry flight recorders the members of the Board of Inquiry were talking to witnesses, the crews of other Shackleton aircraft, and looking at the wreckage. They will then come to an estimate of what happened. The President of the Board of Trade would decide whether the aircraft would be re-assembled.

The week-long exercise was immediately suspended but an RAF spokesman categorically denied that the remaining Shackeltons had been grounded. He said that one of them was still flying.

The Shackleton which crashed was aircraft WR965. It was nicknamed Dylan, after the character in the children's TV programme 'Magic Roundabust.' It was the first Shackleton crash for 22 years. Air historians recalled that the piston-engined Shackletons were often referred to as a 'million rivets flying in close formation.' The loss of the WR965 meant that there were then only five in service with the RAF.

Stornoway Police released the names of those killed: They were: Wing Commander Stephen John Roncoroni (44) of Murray Hall, Milton Duff, Elgin: Flying Officer Colin Hudson Burns (23) of Devron, Prospect Terrace, Lossiemouth: Squadron Leader Jeremy Iain Lane (53) of Templestones, Rafford, Forres: Flight Lieutenant Alan Duncan Campbell (36) of 64 Macdonald Drive, Lossiemouth: Wing Commander Charles Francis Wrighton (42) of Drainie House, Lossiemouth: Flight Sergeant Kieran Paul Rickets (39) of Rosehall Dyke, Forres: Sergeant Graham Robert Miller (23) of 26 Prince Road, Bishopmill, Moray: Flying Officer Keith Stuart Forbes (26) of Rooftoops, 8a John Street, Lossiemouth: Corporal Stuart James Boulton (23) of 21 Hillview Place, Lossiemouth: and Master Air Electronics Operator Roger Anthony Scutt (45) of Albert Street, Nairn.

The remains left from the NATO base at Stornoway Airport on the Wednesday morning after a short service conducted by the local RAF chaplain, the Rev Stanley Bennie. The service was conducted in the hangar. The coffined remains were then carried indivdually on to a Hercules aircraft.

Afterwards locals erected a cairn on the hillside to the memory of those who died.

An announcement of the crash near Northon with the tragic loss of all 10 RAF personnel on board was made in the House of Commons.

****

THE POLO WITH THE HOLE IN IT

There could only be one headline when on August 13, 1979, a Dan Air Hawker Siddeley 748 aircraft -- similar to the one which crashed in Shetland with the loss of 17 lives -- rolled off the apron at Stornoway Airport and caused extensive damage to a VW Polo parked in front of the control tower.

No one was injured. Only two people were on board the aircraft when it began its 20 yard journey down a slight slope towards the control tower -- 31 year old stewardess Angela Wakaling and 13 year old Calum Macrae, the son of a British Airways passenger officer.

The 748 had just landed from Newcastle with about 40 workmen employed at Lewis Offshore's oil fabrication yard at Arnish Point on the outskirts of Stornoway. The men had already collected their baggage at the terminal building and were boarding a bus when the aircraft began moving.

I was standing chatting to the Convener and Chief Executive of the Western Isles Council -- it was the day before the offical opening of the new Council headquarters by the Queen -- and I was therefore an eyewitness and had to quote myself in the story.

I said at the time: 'It just began moving slowly down a slight incline on the apron and headed for the control tower and then smashed into a light blue Volkswagen.'

Young Calum Macrae, who had been talking to the stewardess after the oil workers disembarked, said: 'I realised the plane was moving and immediately ran down the aircraft steps on to the tarmac. I was out of the plane before it hit the car. It was quite frightening.'

Stewardess Wakaling said she had been sitting reading a newspaper when young Calum came on board for a chat. She added: 'He felt it moving before I did. It just rolled towards the control tower. I was pretty shaken.'

The owner of the Volkswagen Polo, Airport Controller James Bricknell (29) who is also the Deputy Aerodrome Manager, said he had bought the car about 18 months ago. He said: 'The plane pushed the car right into the control tower building and it was extensively damaged. The side, roof and bonnet are all badly damaged. I suppose my car is now the original Polo with the hole in it. If it had not been for the car the plane would have hit the control tower direct.'

The plane, which is still towering over the car, will not be removed until a team from the Air Accident Investigation Branch of the Department of Trade and Industry arrive.

A spokesman for the Civil Aviation Authority in London said that it appeared that the cause of the accident was brake failure. He said that as there was no loss of life or injury involved the incident would probably be the subject of a local investigation involving Danair and the CAA at Stornoway He added that the aircraft had received only minor damage to its nose wheel doors.

Dan Air was not available for comment.

However the story did not finish there. Naturally I had also sent photographs of the Danair aircraft towering over the wee helpless Polo. It was used by papers up and down the country and Volkwagon were quick on the phone looking to use the photograph in full page advertisements to show how sturdy Polos were. I was told to negotiate my fee with their top level advertising agents - Doyle Dane Bernbach Ltd.

The full page advertisements appeared in the Daily Telegraph, the Guardian, The Daily Express and the Daily Mail.

This was a bit out of my league so I phoned a well-known Glasgow lensman and he told me I should ask for a new Volkwagen as PR firms hated parting with money but would cheerfully hand over a vehicle as part of their advertising costs. Alas it was not to be and it was a long hard haggle. However a German magazine also wanted the use of the photograh and then the Swiss insurance magazine 'Reinsurance' also used two photographs on its front page. The resultant payments financied a holiday to the Far East.

I often wondered what the Airport Controller's insurance firm made of his claim.

****

On the subject of air services the Scottish Government introduced an air discount scheme which gave a 40 per cent reduction on the price of core air fares. In addition a Road Equivalent Tariff scheme for island ferries is to be introduced which could cut fares by half and a review of all ferry services is to be undertaken.

****

As far as air waves are concerned the new Gaelic Digital TV Channel was launched in September 2008.

****

There's a yarn about the young Jewish boy coming home from school and proudly telling his mother that he had got a part in the school play. She asks him: 'What kind of part?' He tells her: 'I play the husband.' The mother tells him: 'You go right back to your teacher and tell her you want a speaking part.'

A waiter serving five Jewish women in a posh restaurant asks them: 'Is there anything alright?'

****

The little fellow was sitting at his desk on his first day in school. The kindly primary teacher asked: 'Calum, would you like to take off your anorak?'

Came the reply: 'I don't think so, I won't be staying.'

NORTH UIST CRASH

In October 1981 a light aircraft ditched off North Uist which resulted in the death of 50 year old company director John H Milne of Dunvegan, 14 Green Lane, Great Staughton, Huntingdon, Cambridgeshire.

The pilot, the only other occupant of the plane, Captain Francis H B Start (48) of Millhouse, Binbrooke, Linconshire, who escaped, suffering from shock and exposure, was taken to the Royal Artillery Range medical centre in Benbecula, where he recovered.

The aircraft, a Rockwell Commander, was on its way from Tiree to Stornoway, and ditched between the islands of Ronay and Floddymore on the east coast of North Uist.

This resulted in a Fatal Accident Inquiry being held on March 1982 at Lochmaddy Sheriff Court in North Uist where I was the court shorthand writer. Because of an electricity failure the inquiry had to be postponed as part of the evidence was a film of the plane ditching and there was no power to work the generator. When it finally started it set up a new record for the court by sitting until 2.20am the following morning.

The inquiry heard that the light aircraft was owned by JHM (Painters) Ltd of which the deceased was managing director. When a pilot was required he used one from Eastern Air Executive, an air taxi company. Servicing the aircraft had been done by several companies but latterly by Yorkshire Light Aircraft.

Captain Start, with 5500 hours of flying experience, told the inquiry that on the day before the tragedy they had landed at Tiree because of a power failure experienced after passing through heavy rain. After a flight check the following morning they took off for Stornoway but 15 miles east of Benbecula when flying over the sea at a height of 3000 ft the engine had failed.

He said: 'At that time there was a loud bang. It certainly startled me and there was a loss of power and I could not maintain altitude. The engine was turning over with a heavy clanking sound. It was perfectly obvious to me that there had been a catastrophic loss of power.'

He contacted Benbecula control tower but then it became apparent he would not make the airfield. Mr Milne had asked him: 'Are we going to get there?' and he had replied: 'No,' Just before ditching Mr Milne had been strapped into a rear passenger seat with a dinghy on his knee.

Captain Stark said the sea was 'pretty white.' However they came to rest with the aircraft floating level and they both got out on to the wing He then noticed that Mr Milne did not have the dinghy with him and asked him to get it. Before he could go back for it, however, the plane began to sink. They were both wearing inflated lifejackets and they jumped into the sea.

They both got to a seaweed covered rock and held on. Captain Stark said he managed to scramble up on top but Mr Milne did not seem to get a hold properly and was washed away. He was picked up about an hour and a half later by an RAF Sea King helicopter which had already picked up Mr Milne. They were both taken to the Army Medical Reception Centre on Benbecla but Mr Milne was found to be dead on arrival.

The inquiry also heard from Loganair pilot Captain Edmund Bewley who was on a flight from Stornoway to Benbecula. He said he saw the other aircraft 15 miles out and that the engine was spluttering and it was losing height rapidly. He followed him and gave him directions for a fairly flat piece of ground on the Island of Flodday More. However it became obvious that he was not going to make it and he ditched the aircraft.

One of the Loganair pasengers, Frank Cavanagh, a British Airways clerk at Stornoway, actually filmed the Rockwell Commander as it ditched and this was shown to the inquiry.

Mr Steve Moss, a member of the Air Accident Investigation Branch, told the inquiry that the ditching had been done skilfully. He felt the cause of the loss of power was due to some external factor, either carburettor icing or contaminated fuel.

Procurator Fiscal Colin Scott Mackenzie drew the Sheriff's attention to the fact that it had taken an hour-and-a-half to rescue the two men. While he was not criticising the rescue services or other agencies, he felt the tragedy highlighted the need for 'some sort of rescue service to be based on this side of the Minch' in view of the amount of air traffic and shipping in the area.'*

In his determination Sheriff Morris Rose said the cause of the engine failure had not been proved and the post mortem had shown that the deceased suffered death by drowning.

*Later a Coastguard Search and Rescue helicopter service was established at Stornoway and also a Coastguard tug.

******

BARRA: THE AIRPORT WITH A BEACH RUNWAY

One of the attractions of Barra is that it it the only airport in the UK where the runway is washed twice a day by the tide! Many like it that way, others pine for a tarmac runway which would not be dependant on the tide.

Matters came to a head when there were numerous aborted flights on the Loganair service to the island after the Shorts 360 replaced the Twin Otter on the route at the end of March 1994.

There was a packed public meeting in Castlebay to confront the Loganair men.

Local priest, Father Donald Mackay of Castlebay, said: 'It seems strange that 25 years ago we were able to land on the moon - now we cannot get a plane to land on the beach at Barra.'

Referring to the Otter aircraft he declared: 'The old rule seemed to be that if the seagulls were walking on the beach you could land, if they were paddling the pilot had to be a wee bit more careful, and if they were swimming you did not land at all at all!'

Another priest, Canon Angus John Macsween, told the meeting: 'There must be a plane somewhere in the world that can land on Barra.'

HIA chairman Peter Grant said they would do everything they could to ensure improvements and added: 'We believe that service reliability can best be served by the construction of a tarmac runway adjacent to the beach.'

This idea, however, split the island's population. Local taxi operator Dan Cowie said he did not want to see the tradition and romance of a beach runway taken away and added: 'A beach landing is popular with the tourists. The problem isn't the beach, it's the Shorts 360. Loganair should be looking for an aircraft more suited to landing on Barra.'

Loganair proposed to station an Islander aircraft on Barra five days a week to act as a feeder service to Benbecula and Tiree on days when the Shorts aircraft could not land on the beach.

At the time of writing the island still does not have a tarmac landing strip.

I met Scott Grier of Loganair at a CalMac dinner a few years ago -- he is now a director of the ferry company -- and I was reminding him of the meeting in Castlebay that night. He made to open his shirt and told me: 'I've still got the scars.'

****

On air matters there is the story told of a chartered plane with the pilot, the Brain of Britain, a Church of Scotland minister, and a Boy Scout, on their way to the USA.

The Pilot says everything is fine, it's a good aircraft, and they should be on time. There was only one small problem and that was that there were only three parachutes, but they wouldn't need them anyway.

After a few hundred miles one engine cuts out. He still assures his passengers everything is fine. A few hundred miles more and the second engine cuts and he tells them he's sorry but the company had invested a lot of money in training him and he will have to take one of the parachutes and bail out.

The Brain of Britain says he must get to America for the sake of his country's reputation as he is taking part in the World Brain Contest. He too leaves.

The Minister tells the Boy Scout to take the remaning parachute and he will stay with the plane. The Boy Scout tells him: 'It's OK there are two parachutes left.'

'That cannot be' says the minister, the pilot took one, and the Brain of Britain took one, that leaves only one.' 'No,' said the Boy Scout,' the Brain of Britain took my rucksack. There are still two left.':

PAN AM EMERGENCY - October 26/90

A Pan Am Airbus 'Constitution Clipper' with 183 people on board had to make an emergency landing at Stornoway Airport in the Hebrides yesterday afternoon (Friday). The aircraft was on its way from Vienna to New York.

The airport fire tenders were augmented by units of Stornoway Fire Brigade. Ambulances also stood by and the Stornoway Coastguard Search and Rescue helicopter was scrambled in case the aircraft had to ditch.

However the plane landed safely although one of its tyres deflated. Captain Curtis Briggs said that the emergency was caused by a loss of oil on the No 2 starboard engine when they were 50 miles south of Stornoway. The tyre was a controlled deflation. He said that there were 183 people on board including the crew.

After telephoning Pan Am operations in London he said that a maintenance crew were being flown to the island and that arrangements were being made for the passengers to be flown to London on a 727 aircraft.

Passengers were served their dinner while the aircraft was grounded at Stornoway.

Because there were no suitable gangways the passengers had to be taken off in a basket rigged to a hydraulic hoist. They were then taken to the terminal building to await the arrival of the 727.

One passenger said he thought there was something wrong after they left Vienna but he gave full credit to the crew that after they identified the problem they did something about it.

A woman said that she was very relieved when they were on the ground. It had been rather frightening as they were coming in to land to see water on both sides of them.

Stornoway airport is also a reserve NATO base and the fact that the main runway was lengthened over two years ago as part of a £40 million extension to the base enabled the Airbus to use the airport.

Later, however, the passengers were told that the Boeing 727 would not be coming from London, and that accommodation would be provided for them in Stornoway hotels.

A British Airways spokesman said that because it was the end of the tourist season they were able to secure accommodation in local hotels.

The Pan Am maintenance crew were expected to be air ferried to Stornoway and were due to arrive at 10.30 pm.

The passengers stayed overnight in five different hotels in the town. They were flown to London on Saturday morning on board a Pan Am Tri-Star and those who had later connections in the States left on the British Airways Glasgow flight.

There was cheering when the replacement aircraft touched down. One group produced a bottle of champagne and toasted the arrival of the aircraft.

Luis Gaona, owner of Pacific Express Travel from Los Angeles, said: 'We enjoyed our stay in Stornoway. Perhaps they should make it a regular stop-over on the Vienna - New York flight!'

The passengers were extremely appreciative of the courtesy of the British Airways staff (who had to cope with such an influx of passengers) and of the locals -- from the coach drivers to the hotel staff -- who provided for the 'accidental tourists.'

A replacement engine was flown in from Frankfurt on Sunday and then installed. After tests on Monday afternoon the aircraft took off for London Heathrow at 4.15pm.

****

TWIN TOWERS TRAGEDY - *November 17, 2001*

While the Twin Towers terrorist disaster occurred 3000 miles away from the Hebrides, there was a connection: it resulted in the first UK funeral of a British victim of the World Trade Centre disaster taking place in Lewis.

One of the victims was 47 year old Gavin Cushny, whose family lived in Ness. He worked as a computer consultant on the 104th floor of the north tower of the World Trade Centre.

The remains arrived on the island from the States in a Customs sealed coffin, draped with the American flag, and were kept at the mortuary of the Western Isles Hospital in Stornoway until the funeral on November 17, 2001.

About 40 mourners - including his mother 78 year old Mrs Sybil Eales-White of South Dell in Lewis, his brother Rupert, his sister Myra, and his fiancee Susan Brady -- attended the funeral at the cemetery which overlooks the Atlantic.

The service at the cemetery was conducted by the Rev Stanley Bennie of St Peter's Episcopal Church in Stornoway, and a Gaelic prayer was said by the Rev Kenneth Ferguson of Cross Free Church in Ness. After the remains were interred the American flag was presented to his mother.

Gavin had changed his name to Cushny to preserve an old family name.

Following a request from the family no Press photographers were allowed to be present at the cemetery and two police officers checked vehicles at the entrance to the cemetery.

Gavin, who would have been 48 on Thursday, and his blond fiancee, 43 year old Susan from Montclair, New Jersey, had plannned to marry at St Molug's Episcopal Church in Ness on October 28. The church is across the bay from the cemetery at Habost.

His mother, who has lived on Lewis for the past 32 yeas, attended a special memorial service for Gavin in America. His father, Donald Eales-White, an Episcopalian minister who preached at St Molug's, died in March this year.

The family had made it clear that they did not wish to be interviewed by the Press but issued a statement through the Northern Constabulary.

It said: 'Our lives changed forever on September 11 and the loss of Gavin has been a terrible shock to us all.

'Gavin worked for the brokerage firm Cantor-Fitzgerald on the 104th floor of the North Tower of the World Trade Centre and the shock of what happened, as you can imagine, has not left us.

'Gavin had two brothers and two sisters who tragically lost their father earlier this year. The very public way that Gavin was tragically killed further emphasises the fact that we would like to keep his return to Scotland a private family occasion.

'We understand that the media have an interest in the events of today, however we ask that you respect our privacy at this extremely sad time and let us come to terms with our grief in the quiet of our family. We will not be making any further statements to the Press at this time.'

****

BOMB SCARE EN ROUTE TO STORNOWAY

While it must have been a terrifying ordeal for the pasengers on board the two hijacked planes which crashed into the World Trade Centre on 9/11, 2001, passengers on the flight to Stornoway on March 15, 2004, suffered fear and alarm as a result of a bomb scare on the aircraft. The man who caused it was none other than a part-time Sheriff. Here is the the story filed at the time.

A former part-time Sheriff, Advocate Dr Raj Jandoo, was fined a total of £2500 at Stornoway Sheriff Court yesterday (March 18/05) when he was found guilty of causing a bomb scare on a flight into Stornoway a year ago.

The offences occurred while he was a passenger on the Edinburgh to Stornoway flight on March 15 last year, just four days after 10 bombs exploded on four packed early morning commuter trains in Madrid, killing 191 people and leaving at least 1800 injured.

Since his first appearance at Stornoway Sheriff Court on March 16 last year Jandoo -- who made history when he became Scotland's first Asian Advocate -- voluntarily stood down from further service as a £500 a day part-time Sheriff until proceedings in his case had been concluded. He was on his way to sit on the bench at Lochmaddy Sheriff Court in North Uist when the incidents occurred. He was arrested at Stornoway Airport and spent the night in the police cells. (Local duty solicitor Angus Macdonald discovered his custodial client was a Sheriff).

Dr Jandoo could now still face disiplinary proceedings before the Faculty of Advocates which could impose penalites ranging from a verbal admonition, a formal written reprimand, a severe written censure, a substantial fine or suspension from practice.

Yesterday, defence witness Dr John Crichton, a forensic psychologist, said that at the time of the incidents Dr Jandoo was suffering from abnormal grief reaction and had a deep psychological wound following the death of his wife in a car crash.

Last month during the first three days of evidence the trial heard that during the flight people on board were alarmed when they heard the accused say in a loud voice on his mobile phone that 'they probably do not see many black persons up here. Maybe they think I am a terrorist going to bomb their plane.'

Sheriff Principal John Macinnes found 47 year old Jandoo, of 54 Blacket Place, Edinburgh, guilty of making referenes to a bomb on board the aircraft and repeatedly pressing buttons on his watch whilst looking around and placing the occupants of the aircraft into a state of fear and alarm, and committing a breach of the peace.

He was also found guilty of a charge that whilst on the flight between Inverness and Stornoway that he acted in a manner likely to endanger the aircraft or any person on it by failing to comply with a safety instruction given by the stewardess and did fail to sit in his allocated seat with his seat belt fastened and that he stood in the aisle, opened the overhead lockers, searched them and refused to desist, all during the approach to and landing of the aircraft at Stornoway Airport.

A charge of failing to comply with a safety instruction to switch off his laptop on board the aircraft was found not proven.

He was found not guilty of another charge that while the plane was stationary at Inverness airport he conducted himself in a disorderly manner and made a reference to a bomb, placed the occupants into a state of fear and alarm, and committed a breach of the peace: and that he failed to obey all lawful commands given by the commander to secure the safety of the aircraft by failing to swith off his mobile phone and his laptop computer, failing to remain in his seat and fasten his seat belt, and desist from opening and searching an overhead locker.

Last month the trial heard evidence that passengers on board the Loganair plane flying from Edinburgh to Stornoway became nervous, restless and alarmed as a result of a 'bomb' scare on board the aircraft. They said that Jandoo had been speaking on a mobile phone in a loud voice saying that people were looking at him as if he had a bomb on board. Another said that he had used the word terrorist.

A police officer told the trial that on the way to the police station Jandoo had said he was 'in deep trouble for being a fool.' He had also said: 'I am finished as a Sheriff.' When he was cautioned Jandoo had replied: 'I am a very silly man, I am sorry. I should have done what I was told.'

An aviation consultant told the court that such equipment as mobile phones and laptops could reduce the safety margins on an aircraft, not just navigational equipment There were about 80 items which could be the victims of interefrence from mobile phones and laptops. The most crucial times were when the aircraft was taking off or landing.

The trial also heard that Dr Jandoo was always nervous when flying and was always fidgetting: that he had consumed three glasses of wine at Edinburgh Airport and then a brandy on the flight: and that he was still suffering from unresolved bereavement reaction to the death of his wife who was killed in a car crash in 1997.

Dr Jandoo's partner, 40 year old Catriona Munro, a high profile solicitor with qualificatiions to practice in both England and Scotland, said in the witness box that he had told her on the mobile phone that some people were staring at him. She said: 'I think he was trying to make light of it. He had added: "They probably do not see many black people up here. Maybe they think I am a terrorist or something." She said that was said in a light-hearted tone.

Yesterday (Friday) Dr Crichton told the court that after examining Jandoo on two occasions he had concluded that he suffered from abnormal grief reaction characterised by anxiety and post traumatic stress. This followed the lingering death of his wife who had been injured in a car crash It was recognised as a mental illness when grief extended over an abnormally long period of time. There would be a preoccupation with grief going into floods of despair. Most people recovered from grief in six to 12 months except when there would be an anniversary or birthday. He said Jandoo would avoid subjects in connection with his wife's death, even the locus of the crash.

Dr Crichton said: 'During my interview with him he broke down in tears and showed distress. He has flash bulb recollections of his wife being in hospital as a result of the crash. He has obsessional and personality traits. He is a people watcher and has staring eyes. He will show anxiety in social gatherings. He has difficulty in coping with confrontation. His mannerisms therefore could be misinterpreted. If somebody was staring at him he would feel anxious and intimidated. He relieves his anxiety by fidgetting, staring at people, and searching for things.'

Asked how he could cope as a lawyer Dr Crichton said: 'When he puts on the uniform or the robes of court he can cope, and can be in control in that environment. Take him out of these circumstances and he cannot cope. The silver lining of the case is that he has been given the opportunity to address the deep psychological wound which has otherwise been covered up.'

Dr Crichton said that there was also a tremendous sense of guilt established after he became involved in a new supportive relationship. With the problems Dr Jandoo was carrying around with him it did not surprise him what had happened on the flight. There had been a number of unfortunate events which had interacted with each other.

In his summing up the Procurator Fiscal David Teale asked his Lordship to accept the evidence of the passengers on board the flight that the accused had been using his laptop. The accused was reported as saying on his mobile phone that they had never seen a blackman and a terrorist with a bomb.

Mr Teale said: 'This was during a background of heighted tension just a number of days after the Madrid train boming. It was said in an enclosed space with a view to challenge and to provoke some sort of response. It did provoke a response. People were upset and alarmed by his conduct, people were shouting and the air stewardess was summoned. There had also been a reference to a bomb when the accused spoke to the stewardess. He had said: "I hope we do not have problems with bombs on board."'

Donald Findlay QC for Jandoo, said that much of the evidence during the trial had been contradictory. It was appropriate to consider the background of the tragic events in America and in Spain. However there were two sides to a coin. He submitted that against that background people had reacted in a way that was disproportionate to the facts which confronted them.

He said his client had been 'footering about in a locker,' and that there was no danger to anyone. It may have been foolish but it was not reckless or negligent. He added: 'If it had not been for the Spanish bombings people would not have reacted in the way they did. I submit that the Crown have not proved their charges.'

In delivering his verdict Sheriff Principal John Macinnes said that there had been terrorist activity within the previous few days which would be more likely to make reasonable people very apprehensive than they would have been in other circumstances. He did not regard it as a trivial matter.

Mr Findlay QC said that at the time of the events Dr Ranjoo was not aware that he was suffering from a mental illness due to his personal tragic circumstances. He took the matter very seriously and he regretted any offence or harm or distress caused to anyone else. It was a desperately unfortunate incident. Dr Jandoo had a high respect for the law. He was a member of the Faculty of Advocates but he had not been in a position to pursue any practice since the time of the incident.

He added: 'I can assure the court that this is something that Dr Jandoo will regret for a very long time indeed. It has caused him considerable personal embarrassment and distress.'

The Sheriff Principal imposed fines of £2000 on the breach of the peace charge and £500 for failing to comply with the safety instructions on board the aircraft.

Mr Findlay asked for four weeks to pay the fine.

It was later learned that there was to be appeal against the sentence.

Dr Jandoo's principal areas of interest as an Advocate were Discrimination Law, Employment Law and Education Law - special educational needs.

****

Cessna wreckage

Shackleton victims being flown off from Stornoway Airport

The Polo with the hole in it and owner Jim

A hoist and a basket had to be used to allow these Pam Am passengers to disembark at Stornoway Airport

First Twin Towers funeral in Britain - remains leave mortuary at Western Isles Hospital in Stornoway for burial at Ness

Dr Raj Jandoo

THE INQUIRIES - Nato

On March 15, 1981, the tiny Western Isles Council took on the mighty Ministry of Defence in another David and Goliath contest concerning the £40 million proposals for the upgrading of the NATO base at Stornoway Airport.

The two week public planning inquiry -- ordered by the Secretary of State for Scotland following the Council's refusal to grant planning clearance to the MOD -- was heard before Mr A G (Sandy) Bell, the Chief Inquiry Reporter at the Scottish Office.

The Inquiry was expected to cost the Council £12,000 but they levied a charge of £70 per day on the Secretary of State for use of the Council's convening chamber for the inquiry. Presenting the Council case was the Dean of the Faculty of Advocates, Mr Charles Kemp Davidson QC., and representing the Ministry was Mr David A O Edwards QC.

Both sides had about a dozen witnesses appearing for them - several of them eminent experts in the field of noise pollution and defence studies.

The MOD already owned the land. They claimed that Stornoway was of strategic importance to NATO to help plug the defence gap between the UK and Iceland.

The islanders' underlying fears were that their concerns might never get an airing because it had been made clear that the issues of national defence policy for the UK role in NATO would not be heard.

The other fears were that it would become a full time base -- swallowing up their language and culture -- and that it would turn Lewis into a large aircraft carrier which would be a prime target in the event of war. It was also feared that nuclear weapons would be stored at the base.

From the time the proposals became known there was a vigorous protest campaign launched by the KNO (Keep NATO Out) Group.

This organisation was ably led by Angus McCormack, a Stornoway teacher. They issued leaflets, a booklet entitled 'Islands at Risk', and there were even song sheets by peace groups.

A total of 4300 people signed the KNO petition opposing the escalation of Stornoway Airport and a further 2000 people sent individual objections to the Secretary of State for Scotland, George Younger.

The MOD case was that Stornoway was already capable of being used as a full operational airfield. However they claimed that in its present state the airfield was not suitable for operation of the more advanced aircraft, particularly the Tornado, which was due to come into service in the next decade.

They were therefore proposing to upgrade Stornoway as a Forward Operating Base by the provision of better refuelling facilities, lengthening the runway and providing a better taxiway. They would also need to provide hardened aircraft shelters. The project would be funded by NATO. The base would be restricted to short exercise periods of up to 2 weeks duration up to three times each year.

They said that while they had just enough facilities in Scotland for peace time training, in wartime they must get their aircraft as close up to the operational area as possible, to maximise their quick reaction capability to block Soviet egress into the Atlantic and to protect their own sea forces.

Geographically Stornoway was closer that any other UK airfield to the operational area and there was no alternative but to update the NATO reinforement airfield at Stornoway to modern standards for use in war.

The night before the Public Inquiry KNO organised a ring of fires around Broad Bay, the area to be most affected by the MOD proposals. A KNO spokesman said: 'The fires will symbolise the call to arms of those who are in opposition to the NATO plans the same way that the Fiery Cross called clansmen to arms in the past.'

On the fifth day of the inquiry they also had another surprise up their sleeve. Just before it was due to start there was the deafening noise of a Tornado aircraft flying overhead. The noise was produced through a battery of amplifiers. Angus McCormack stood up and announced that the inquiry had been very 'low key' and that despite the main planning issue being noise, very little had been produced. They therefore intended to demonstrate what kind of noise the island people would be subjected to by a Tornado aircraft.

There then followed two minutes of deafening noise reaching 118 perceived noise decibles, which had officials and members of the public putting their hands over their ears. Noise contours shown earlier at the inquiry revealed noise levels of up to 130 PND round Stornoway Airport.

Professor Elfyn J Richards, an eminent noise expert, and a witness on behalf of the Western Isles Council, told the inquiry that the World Health Organisation recommended only 35 decibels as a total time noise dose. The communitees near the Stornoway Airfield would be subjected to 30 to 40 in excess of that figure.

He said that in terms of noise energy received this meant that the inhabitants close to the airport would be expected to tolerate 1000 to 10,000 times the noise energy they should do if they were to be guaranteed no sleep disturbance from noise. These areas included Melbost, Branahuie, Sandwick, Holm and other close in areas.

He said the degree of startle would also affect two schools near the airport, Tong and Sandwick. The startle could cause heart attacks and palpitations for up to a minute because of the sonic afterwards. Indoors it would be worse because the sonic boom sounded worse indoors if windows were open. He added: 'Indeed the startle effect is the same as an explosion, you jump a mile.'

The Reporter Sandy Bell concluded that on local planning grounds there was a presumption against the development which could only be overcome by convincing evidence of a national need which could not be met elsewhere. However as there was no evidence led on the latter point at the inquiry, he was unable to make any recommendations for or against the development.

On December 1, 1981, George Younger MP, the Secretary of State for Scotland, decided that the development should proceed.

This decision left island organisations seething - they had won on planning grounds but had lost out in the national interest.

The Rt Hon Donald J Stewart, SNP MP for the Western Isles, said the decision was a total disregard for the way of life and interests of the island people. He said: 'The people who planned and approved this development differ only in degree from the attitude of the Russians in Afghanistan. We in the isles will organise to frustrate the intentions of MOD and NATO. I know that at an earlier stage trade unionists threatened to black materials for the base. The Government has a real fight on its hands.'

Reacting to the decision, Angus McCormack of KNO -- who also organised a car cavalcade protest of 50 cars -- said: 'The Seretary of State for Scotland has declared war on the Western Isles. His decision flies in the face of democracy and his much vaunted wish to show humanity to the people of Scotland.

''He is in effect thrusting upon the people of Lewis and the Western Isles a living death from constant and pervasive noise. His action will reinforce the determination of KNO and the people of the Western Isles to resist the montrous imposition of a full time NATO base at Stornoway. Let there be no mistaking the great resolve of the people to oppose the intention of the MOD to escalate war preparations.'

The Rev Donald Macaulay, the Council Convener, said he felt the Council should demand compensation of £10 million - £5 million to preserve the Gaelic language and culture and £5 million to aid crofting and the fishing industries of the Western Isles.

The Vice Convener, Sandy Matheson, said that further political pressure should be put on the Secretary of State. He said it was perfectly clear from the terms of the report that the case was prejudged by the Secretary of State's decision that the National need was not to become an issue at the planniing inquiry. He added: 'That in effect lost us the case. We won the case on planning grounds.' His call for a further inquiry into the national defence issues was rejected by Mr Younger.

So the upgrading went ahead and we finished up with an extended runway and the airport is still used for NATO exercises each year. There was a £1 million noise compensation scheme by the MOD for 670 houses surrounding the NATO base. This provided triple glazing.

The need to 'plug the Icelandic gap' receded becaues of a thaw in relations with the Soviet Bloc. In 2000 Highlands and Islands Airports Ltd paid £1million to the MOD for the airport which was placed on the open market following the closure of the RAF station there and the NATO base. This deal included runways of 2280 metres and 1000 metres, a modern air traffic control building -- since upgraded -- and the air terminal building. In 2002 a new £2.8 million terminal building was opened which replaced and tripled in size the original 1940 buildng.

Since then HIAL have been seeking a commercial partner to develop a hotel at Stornoway Airport and have outline planning permission for it. They are also keen to lease ground for light commercial developments and for a mixture of private and social needs housing.

The RAF Station -- No 112 Signals Unit -- closed down in March 1998 after a presence of 50 years at the airport. It had opened in 1941 on the old Stornoway Golf Course. In 1944 there had been 150 officers and 1200 airmen stationed at the base and Lews Castle College had been the officers' mess. Flying boats also used Cuddy Point in front of the Castle.

On two occasions RAF Stornoway received the Wilkinson Sword of Peace for promoting community relationships and for charity work. In 1996 the base - with only 29 personnel -- had raised £37,000 for the BBC Children in Need appeal. They had also raised £3000 for local charities. The Peace Swords were presented to the Western Isles Council and are on display in the reception area.

Many of the servicemen posted to RAF Stornoway counted themselves the happiest in the Service. Many asked for their posting to be extended and several married local girls. Three former Commanding Officers settled on the island following their retirement.

****

Lingerbay

The time taken to get a decision on a 1991 planning application for the Lingerbay Coastal Superquarry in South Harris was stated by one Councillor 'to be longer than the Second World War'.

When the company took a decision in April 2004 to pull out of their plans for a £70 million superquarry it brought down the curtain on a scandalous 13 year old planning farce.

The development would have provided 200 direct or indirect jobs for a depopulated area of Harris. It would have meant the extraction of 600 million tonnes of anorthosite over a 60 year period and would have created one of the larget holes in Europe. When the quarry finished operations this was to be flooded to make it into a marina.

The delay in giving a decision on the 1991 planning application was described as 'scandalouos and unfair' by Scottish Judge Lord Hardie and former Energy Minister Brian Wilson MP described it as a fiasco.

It was ironic that on the day before Lafarge, the giant French minerals company, decided not to pursue any further appeals against planning refusal, that the Scottish Executive announced modernisation of the planning system which called for 'speeding up decisons' and 'allowing quicker investment decisions.'

Lafarge Aggregates UK -- who had taken over Redlands Aggregates who made the original planning application -- announced that it was withdrawing from the proposed coastal superquarry at Lingerbay following the decision in the Court of Session on Janaury 2, 2004, to reject its appeal over the extent of the existing planning permission granted in 1965. They were also withdrawing their outstanding appeal in pursuit of its 1991 planning application.

This let the Scottish Executive off the hook as the 1991 application had still to be redetermined by the Scottish Ministers.

There were mixed views following the Lafarge decision but those for and against the proposal both condemned the Scottish Executive and their predesors - the Scottish Office -- for the time taken.

John Macleod of Northton in Harris, chairman of the Coastal Quarry Local Supporters Network, summed up their feelings. He said: 'The decision to pull out is so disappointing, particulary for Harris. We are losing in excess of 200 jobs, a Royalty of 3p per tonne for a community fund, and losing wages in excess of £3m a year. The decision will also have a marked effect on the economy of the Western Isles. There is talk of a Sound of Harris causeway to link up with Uist and Lingerbay could have provided the rock. The project could also have helped engineering businesses.'

The local Councillor, Morag Munro, said: 'Those who supported the development must not feel that they did not lobby hard enough and those who opposed it must not feel triumphant. Harris has been portrayed as being divided, this is not the case. There are strong differences of opinion on this issue, but we all share the same over-riding motive -- we want the best for Harris, we just differ on how that can be achieved.'

The public inquiry into the 1991 planning application --which started in 1994 -- lasted 8 months, the longest public inquiry ever held in Scotland and cost about £2 miillion. Most of the 83 days of evidence (I covered them all) was heard in Stornoway with two sessions in Harris.

Of the 800 representations made to the Secretary of State for Scotland about the project, only 17 came from the Western Isles.

At times it seemed the only show in town with a cast of characters as colourful as the anorthosite rock which was to be extracted from the quarry - white, pink, deep purple, green and black. They came from all quarters and few with local voices were heard.

There was evidence from a Free Church Professor, a Quaker human economist, and a Red Indian Chief in full regalia. A letter opposed to the development was submitted by a Prince, a nephew of the Aga Khan. Another opponent was millionairess Tessa Tennant -- whose mother once owned an estate in South Harris -- and who confessed that it was there she had kissed a boy for the first time! A hotelier from Uig in the extreme west of Lewis claimed that if there was a quarry in South Harris (over 60 miles away) it would have a detrimental effect on his world-wide clients. There were even claims that the large hole would be seen by transatlantic aircraft passengers.

In June 1993 the Council decided by 24 votes to 3 to approve the project and had informed the Scottish Secretary that they were minded to grant the application. However on the day before the the inquiry closed in Harris the Council -- many of them new members following the local authority elections in 1994 -- decided by 21 votes to 8 to withdraw their support. This followed a recent referendum in Harris which resulted in a 2 - 1 vote against the project, although two years prior to that they had voted in favour of it.

This all left Dr Robert Reed QC-- now a Judge -- Counsel for the Western Isles Council, in a difficult situation. He told the Chief Inquiry Reporter, Miss Gillian M Pain, that he had received instructions to inform her that according to a resolution on the Monday night that they were no longer supporting the quarry project. However he had clear instructions from the Council that they did not wish to withdraw any of its evidence which had come before the inquiry. Neither did he wish to amend any submission nor to make new ones. Nothing was being departed from which had come before the inquiry.

Miss Pain warned the parties that it was open to the Secetary of State to order the inquiry to be re-opened if necessary.

Mrs Lynda Towers, for Scottish Natural Heritage, the principal objectors, said that the decision was a material consideration that the Council, at the end of their evidence, had reversed their view.

She said that it was inconsistent with Dr Reed's closing submission asking the Secretary of State to grant planning permission.

She said it affected the status of the evidence from the Council as local planning authority. She submitted that Dr Reed's instructions were going to cause some difficulty to the Secretary of State and to the Reporter in drawing up her recommendations.

Mr Lloyd Austin of the LINK group of environmental organisations who were also objectors, also submitted that the Council's resolution was inconsistent with the closing submission by Dr Reed.

However Mr Roy Martin QC for Redlands, said that the SNH submission was another attempt by the agency to try, at any cost, to prevent the application being approved.

He said the answer to the problem was quite simple. The decision taken by the Council on June 24, 1993, to approve the application was the decision of the planning authority. The planning authority's function -- so far as the application was concerned - ceased when the application was called in by the Secretary of State.

After allowing an adjournment to seek clarification on certain points the Chief Inquiry Reporter then ruled that she would close the inquiry.

It was 7pm . Miss Pain said she believed that it had been the longest planning inquiry to be held in Scotland. She expressed her thanks to everyone involved -- including the islanders - for the courtesy extended to her. As the sheep continued to bleat outside the village hall where the inquiry was being held, she remarked: 'It looks as if the sheep will have the last word.'

So time passed... and passed... and passed. Nothing seemed to be happening despite protests from the Council about the length of time it was taking Scottish Ministers to reach a decision.

Then on July 12, 2000, Sarah Boyack the Evironment Minister, delayed matters further by deciding to ask for more information before taking a final decision on the Lingerbay application.

She wanted Scottish Natural Heritage -- who were the principal objectors at the inquiry -- and the Joint Nature Conservation Committee to say whether the proposed site should be designated as a Special Area of Conservation under the EC Habitats Directive.

This resulted in Lafarge Redlands lodging an application with the Court of Session in Edinburgh for a judicial review and seeking a decision by Scottish Ministers on the planning application within 21 days of the review being granted.

It was only as a result of the judicial review that Lafarge Redlands learned that the Chief Inquiry Reporter's recommendation had been with the Scottish Ministers for 20 months and that she had given the development a resounding seal of approval.

In her conclusion Miss Pain said: 'I am satisfied that the proposed conditions and the matters already secured through the completed Section 75 Agreement and the proposed Ballast Water Management Plan would provide for adequate controls and that legitimate interests would not be prejudiced should the Secretary of State be minded to accept my recommendation that permission should be granted.'

She continued: 'Some adverse effects will inevitably result from the proposed development but I am satisfied that these have been considered properly in the course of the inquiry and that the design and preservative measures proposed by Redlands and the conditions proposed by the Western Isles Council would limit the area affected. The whole approach to the scheme has been based on precautionary principles.

'I conclude that the considerable additional evidence made available at the inquiry has provided sufficient environmental information on which to make an adequate assessment of the environmental effects of the proposed development. I am satisfied that the environmental effects would be acceptable in the context of the potential employment benefits for the Western Isles and the wider national interests in the development.'

In his judgement in October 2000 Lord Hardie described the delay by the Scottish Executive as 'scandalous and unfair.' He also found that the delay was a breach of the Convention for the Protection of Human Rights.

Lord Hardie also concluded that Scottish Natural Heritage could not be impartial in any recommendation they gave to the Environmental Minister as to whether part of Lingerbay should be proposed as a Special Area of Conservation.

This information resulted in John Leivers, Director of Lands and Planning with Redland Aggregates. to issue the following statement: 'We are naturally delighted to know at last that all of our efforts during the application and inquiry stage have been vindicated and we were pleased to learn in open court on Monday that Miss Pain has given our application such a resounding seal of approval.

'I am particualrly pleased for all our supporters on the island and would like to thank them publicly for all the encouragement they have given us over the years.'

Redland's delight at the Reporter's recommendation was short lived. On November 3, 2000 the new Environment Minister Sam Galbraith refused planning permission. The announcement came in response to a parliamentary question by Rhoda Grant MSP.

John Leivers of Redlands said they were 'extremely disappointed' with the decision and that 'the arguments put forwards at the public inquiry have not gained the support of the Scottish Executive in spite of the fact that they were totally in line with Government policy and the fact that the Chief Inquiry Reporter had recommended that permission be granted.' The company would now determine any future course of action.'

The Western Isles Council said that there was relief that a final decison had now been made but called for an inquiry as to why it had taken so long for a decision.

John Macleod of Leverburgh, Chairman of the Quarry Supporters Network, said the decision was very disappointing to Harris and the Western Isles 'where jobs are scarce and people are leaving.' He said that recently four families had left Harris within a month.

He added: 'It seems that the Scottish Executive would rather curry favour with the environmentalists than support the survival of Harris. This decision will reflect badly on the Scottish Executive and will put investors off because they will feel that green issues are more important than people.'

The development could have netted a community trust fund £140,000 per annum based on the tonnage of rock removed. This would also have been topped up by money from the landowner and the man who held the quarry rights, Iain Wilson of Dunblane.

Councillor Angus Graham accused Sam Galbraith of trying to appear macho to resurrect his own political career.

Redlands appealed and also appealed against the Western Isles Council's refusal to accept a 1965 planning permission for the Lingerbay quarry as valid. This resulted in a five day public inquiry held in the Anchorage Restaurant in Leverburgh. The 1965 planning application was for a much larger area than the 1991 application and there were fewer conditions attached.

Mr Colin Campbell QC for SNH told the Inquiry Reporters James M McCulloch and Mr Donald W Jackson that the planning procedure adopted in 1965 by Inverness County Council mirrored what was now known as 'outline and detailed planning consent.' He submitted that the appeal be refused.

Andrew Devline for objectors Scottish Environment Link stated that the 1965 planning application was unlawful. He claimed that once a site had been adandoned a new planning permission had to be sought.

However Mr Roy Martin QC for the appellants, Lafarge Redlands, submitted that there was a valid planning permission for the quarry at Lingerbay in 1965: the Inverness County Council stamp on the plan stated "consent"; the quarry was on the Council's valuation roll for five years: and rock from the quarry was exported by sea and the Council had used it for their own use.

Lafarge Redlands lost and appealed.

Then came the shock news in April 2004 that Lafarge had decided to abandon its plans for the £70 million coastal superquarry at Lingerbay, and that they would be withdrawing its outstanding appeal in pursuit of its 1991 planing application. This followed the decision of the Court of Session on January 2, 2004, to reject its appeal over the extent of the existing planning permission granted in 1965.

Ronald Mackinnon, a 17 year old from Stockinish in Harris, did get a bursary from the company to support his studies for a structural and civil engineering degree at Aberdeen Univeristy.

The company also presented a cheque for 50,000 Euros (£33,860) to launch the fundraising campaign for the refurbishment of the Leverburgh Playing Field in South Harris.

In May 2004, John Leivers, the man who had masterminded the proposal for the £70 million coastal superquarry since 1987 and who clocked up many air miles travelling to and from the island, made a final trip to Harris to host a buffet at the Rodel Hotel for members of the Coastal Quarry Supporters Network to express his thanks to them.

The company had announced that they were abandoning their plans for the superquarry when he was out of the country.

John, who was by then a consultant for the company, told the network supporters that he was sorry he had failed them. He said: 'I have a very healthy respect for you all. You have supported, challenged and asked the right questions and put me on the straight and narrow when I was wrong. You have done it all without payment.'

He then added: 'When the decision came I was flabbergasted. It was not a scenario which I had expected. Do not ask me for an explanation, I was not a party to it. I do not know the issues they had to consider in making the statement two or three weeks ago. Personally I felt it was a flawed decison, but then I am purely a planner and developer.'

He said he was amazed that the Chief Reporter's decision to grant the 1991 application had been repelled by the Scottish Ministers. However he reminded the supporters that there was still a planning application for a small area of Lingerbay. Someone would have the right to work it!

****

Thomas Freeman from Alabama, a singer with a Paul Robeson voice, was one of the guest artists at the launch in 2005 of 'Salm and Soul' a bilingual CD in aid of funds for Bethesda Hospice and Care Home in Stornoway. He was one of the members of the Black Presbyterian Choir which visited Lewis earlier in the year and also performed at the Celtic Connections concert in Glasgow where the CD tracks were recorded. Yale professor Will Ruff believes there is a link between Black Gospel music and Gaelic Psalm singing which he has described as the DNA of all Afro-American music. He said the lining-out style was not something brought over by slaves from Africa but learned from the Gaelic Psalm singing of the Highland overseers on the plantations. Thomas was a grave digger by profession. His business card reads: 'I will sing you a song and be the last one to let you down.'

The Rocket Range

While there was no planning inquiry into the land and sea grab by the MOD for the extensions to the Rocket Range in the Uists there were several public meetings and the MOD found they had a fight on their hands with very angry crofters and fishermen.

Much of the land was owned by the Department of Agriculture so it was a case of it remaining under Government control.

RAF Benbecula was established as an operational airfield in 1942. The Rocket Range -- correct name Royal Artillery Range Hebrides -- opened in 1959. According to the official blurb the range provided 'unparalleled facilities for the testing and evaluation of all conventional land, sea and air launched weapons.'

In 1968 there was a £6 million extension to the range and in 1972 a further £20million was spent.

One crofter, Donald Macdonald of 13 Aird, Benbecula, faced a sixth application for resumption of his land which was described by Donald J Stewart, the SNP MP for the Western Isles as 'callous bureaucracy.' He said Mr Macdonald was being robbed of his land piece by piece.

The crofter told me at the time that he had lost a few acres at the start of the war. Then in 1950 Inverness County Council resumed two acres for a housing scheme: in 1967 there were another two acres for a similar purpose: in 1969 he lost six acres to the MOD for houses for service personnel at the rocket range: then the same year the Department of Agriculture (his landlords) resumed six acres for a new primary school to meet the needs of the service children. Then came another demand for six acres for more houses for service personnel and for county council houses.

He added: 'They have already taken the best of my land. I have only 38 acres left but only 14 arable and I have 32 head of cattle and 100 sheep. They offered me £1650 in compenstion but I refused. I'm too old now to get any other type of employment and if I have to give up crofting I feel they should pay me at least £10,000. That would be a fair and reasonble settlement. In the South Uist Estate land there goes for about £2000 an acre. I wrote to the Department in July refusing their offer and asking then to reconsider their figure but got no reply. I took the matter up with my MP.'

However that was only an individual case. There were also confrontations between the crofters in Bornish in South Uist and the Army regarding compensation terms for a landing strip for a Skeet, a model aircraft, at Ardvule Point on the range head.

At a public meeting in Stoneybridge School there was an Army presentation with a film and slides. Brigadier Paddy Ryan, Commandant of the Range, said that two types of weapons systems were used at the range -- Rapier missiles and the Blowpipe, which was a short range shoulder held missile defence system.

The Blowpipe required a moving aerial target. At present they used a target towed by a Buccaneer aircraft but this was not very satisfactory. Short Brothers had now developed for them a model aircraft with an 11 ft wing span which would be much cheaper and more relistic as it would "waggle like an aircraft." The model aircraft, called a Skeet, was remotely controllled.

The Brigadier said the Skeet would be landing up to 24 times per day, Monday to Friday, for about 10 months of the year. ('The compensation will have to be very high' cried one crofter.) However because it could only land into the wind the landing area, within a circle with a 400 yard diameter (about 26 acres) would have to be moveable. The areas the Army had in mind were to the north and the south of at road at Loch Bornish.

It was at this point in the meeting that the Skeet flew into a lot of flak from the crofters. The Brigadier was told that next year the area to the south would be ploughed, which meant that all the cattle would have to be moved into the north area. Hoping for a quick compromise the Brigadier assured his audience that they had no wish to upset the ploughing programme and hoped the crofters could assist in the mornings by moving the cattle out of the landing circle in the north.

'We'll be at work,' said one man, 'so you'll have to ask the cows themselves to move.' It was then seriously suggested that the Army should provide a cowherd if the crofters agreed to make the land available.

Another shouted that before there could be any agreement in principle they would have to know what compensation was going to be offered, but this was not acceptable to the Lands Defence Officer.

If the Army had trouble with the crofters it was nothing to the broadside they encountered from the local fishermen which lead to a number of boisterous public meetings.

The fishermen were furious at the plans to extend the danger area over which the missiles were fired. The extension planned, added to the area already in existence, would amount to about half the available lobster fishing grounds for the Uists. There were about 50 boats in the area. Lobster fishing was the main industry and single source of income on the island. The Highlands and Islands Development Board had invested £20,000 in a new lobster factory at Grimsay which exported to London and the Continent.

Previously the boats had been asked to leave the danger area when firing took place. Now, because of frequency of the firing, -- 40 weeks of the year for five days a week -- the area would no longer be available unless a compromise was reached.

Concessions of a day here or there were of no use to the fishermen who felt it would be a serious threat to their livelihoods. It was also feared that the long term future prosperity of the islands could be jeopardised for short term military objectives.

In order to allay the fears of the fishermen, Brigadier R C Winfield, the Projects Diretcor of the Range, attended a public meeting at Paible School. He had already claimed that the fishermen's concern was based on a misunderstanding of what the extensions would involve.

The Rev James Morrison, the Free Church minister at Bayhead and also an Inverness County Councillor, said that there was a great deal of disquiet.

About 200 people, many of them fishermen from the other islands and the mainland, attended the three-and-a-half hour meeting in April 1969.

It was chaired by the Reverend Morrison who told the meeting: 'I am persuaded beyond a shadow of doubt that if the basic industry of fishing is interfered with in this island the government may as well initiate a mass evacuation scheme to remove us from this island. This industry has been in operation for many years. It is of very serious concern that any interference should be allowed.'

Brigadier Winfield, who had been sent by the MOD to pour oil on troubled waters, said: 'Time is on our side, and by that I mean both the Army and fishermen. There will be a gradual build up of procedure. We had to negotiate these extensions of the range which has been in operation for the past 11 years. We made applications for extensions to the north and the south. We were told that firing could not be allowed in the north and that in the south there would have to be co-operation with the fishermen.

'I know what is worrying you is not the extension so much as the existing area. This is where we will have to come to some arrangement. However unless the danger area is activiated, there is no restriction whatever to fishing.

He explained: 'We will have to post notices when they are going to be used and use black balloons. There will have to be a means of informing you. One suggestion which has been made -- and it is a good one -- is that we should appoint a Liaison Officer between the range and the fishermen. He would provide a direct link between you and the army. There will be a radio telephone on the Monach Islands where the lobster fishermen spend the night in bothies after setting thir creels. We will also have a fast boat so that we can talk to fishermen at sea. It is proposed to start firing at 10.30 am although a later start might be made in the summer months. They would finish by 5pm. He said they had gone to great pains and trouble to get consultation at all levels.

Questions from the fishermen came so fast they made have been launched from the rocket range itself. They were adamant that firing should not commence until 1pm . The pointed out that because of the tides some of them could not leave their anchorages when they wanted. Lobster boats were not equipped with radios, and a launch, no matter how fast, would not be able to cover all the area from Barra to the Monach Isles.

At one point when a Lieutenant Colonel was giving an assurance that at certain times he would guarantee them safe passage through the danger zone from north to south, one wag asked: 'What happens if we want to go from south to north?'

County Councillor Ian Hilleary said that although the Army claimed that they had taken appropriate consultations there had been no consultations at all at a local level with the fishermn.

Father John Maclean of Eochar said: 'If they do not get this time extension they may as well draw their boats ahsore and give up their livelihoods.' He also asked what the consequences would be if they entered the danger zone but the Colonel said that was something that would have to be examined very closely.

The Rev Roddy Mackinnon of Daliburgh pointed out that the

fishermen could not be expected to invest in new boats if their fishing was to be restricted.

Duncan Erskine, manager of the lobster factory, wanted to know if there would be any compensation to the fishermen for the loss of earnings, but was told by the Brigadier that he was not in a position to answer that question.

The MP for the Western Isles, M K Macmillan, said he would be pressing the Brigadier's political chiefs to give answers to the questions which had been raised and to look at a compromise on the firing times.

In August, Donald J Stewart, the prospective SNP candidate for the Western Isles, attended a meeting in North Uist and said that it was clear to him that the MOD, with the support of the Scottish Development Department, were determined to bulldoze the fishermen into submitting to their arrangements. He added: 'The whole discussion was conducted on the basis of the fishermen being obliged to meet the requirements of the Rocket Range instead of the military fitting in with the needs of the fishermen. It is intolerable that a region which suffered so much loss of life in the wars and is trying to maintain itself in difficult conditions, should be treated in this way.'

However there was some compromise and the MOD provided a 20 knot fibre glass patrol boat, the Fulmar, to cover the rich Atlantic lobster grounds and to warn fishing boats when there was going to be any missile firing.

But the troubles were not over. As one crofter succintly put it: 'The Army arrived with kid gloves, but since they became entrenched, the gloves are off and they are down to the bare knuckles.'

A fine example of their insensitivity was the choice of street names for the new married quarters for the officers and men. Despite their talk of wanting to integrate with the local community they named the streets at their housing sites after officers who had been most involved in the Rocket Range project. So instead of the usual island steet names the locals had to get used to Tuzo Close, Tindall Road, Close and Place, Windfield Close and Windfield Way.

However when the first of the 139 houses was to be officially opened in 1971 it proved rather embarrassing. As the key was handed over by Col A W R Currie, the smiles of the assembled brass hats and civilians turned to puzzled frowns, as the front door of the three-apartment refused to open.

An official, however, saved the situation by entering the house by the back door and then opening the front door from the inside with the key.

While everyone on the island loves a ceilidh and dance that did not seem to apply to the service families who were living less than 20ft from the village hall and there were complaints not about the rockets but the racket. While the Army owned the land all about the hall the feu it stood on belonged to the islanders. The Army then offered a choice of buildings which they no longer required.

There was further embarrassment when the Duchess of Gloucester, Colonel in Chief of the Royal Army Educational Corps, was invited for a two day visit in 1978 for the 21st anniversary of the range and to officially open the new building complex at the Balivanich domestic site of the Rocket Range.

The 'blacking' of the Royal Visit by members of the Transport and General Workers Union was called off at the last minute after assurances by their union that they would discuss their grievances. Their dispute was over variations in the District Island Allowance among their members. There were four groups involved - some got nothing and others received up to £288 a year.

The TGWU secretary for the Uists said that he did not think the

Royal visit could have taken place if they had continued their 'blacking.' Most of his 130 members on the MOD establishment were drivers, cleaners and waitresses. He did not think the Army would have dared to bring in service personnel to do their work because of the 'blacking' of goods for the MOD by Caledonian Macbrayne.

As a result there were no pickets at the main gate to the Headquarters and a few rude graffiti signs were quickly covered over prior the the arrival of the Duchess.

There was a piper's welcome for her when she arrived and a military band, which had been flown in for the Royal occasion, played background music in the splendid new physical and recreation training centre during the official reception and luncheon

Well known milestones such as empty beer cans and half bottles disappeared from the surrounding ditches and roadside and almost everything in sight had been painted or polished.

Another classical touch was the rubber soled boots worn by those who would be within earshot of the Duchess or on hand to open doors or carry umbrellas in case of rain.

However the highlight of the visit was to have been a demonstration of two Rapier surface-to-air missiles being fired at the Rocket Range. At that time the range was believed to be the most sophisticated and best instrumented missile range in Western Europe.

You could say this plan backfired and caused many red faces among Army and RAF personnel. The missiles were to be fired by an RAF Detachment from the No. 3 launch area at the rangehead.

We all assembled in the bunker with great expectation.

The first one misfired and the destroy button had to be pressed at command control. Everyone waited while the target towing aircraft circled again and fresh tracking began. Alas the second missile suffered the same fate as the first.

No more could be fired because of budget restraints! However the Duchess emerged smiling from the bunker and then went to have lunch in the Sergeant's Mess before leaving the island in an aircraft of the Queen's Flight.

Captain Jimmy Shovlin told me: 'The RAF detachment have been here for the past two weeks and have had 25 successful firings. They were so unfortuante today it just wasn't true. The Duchess however thought everything was superb.'

(However Royal security was still tight in those days and despite my persuasion they declined to take my cine film for TV back to Glasgow on the Royal flight.)

The following year (May 1979) the Army made it a happy birthday for 86 year old South Uist crofter Donald Mackay of 24 Ardivachar, when they handed back to him a 300 year old cannon which had adorned the entrance to the Rocket Range headquarters in Balivanich for 10 years.

The 3 inch cannon, made of high grade cast iron and weighing nearly half a ton, was found by the Mackay family way back in 1902. They took it back to their croft after discovering it on a wrecked 17th century Swedish vessel lying offshore from their croft.

They left it near an outhouse near the beach and about 10 years ago a party of divers from the Rocket Range sub-aqua club came across it and took it back to their camp. It was then mounted and took up residence outside the guardroom.

However the newsletter published by the Uist Council of Social Service revealed that the cannon actually belonged to the Mackay family and suggested that it be returned.

The Army took the hint and at a ceremony at the Mackay croft house an Army delegation headed by Brigadier Paddy Ryan, Commandant of the RA Range, arrived with the polished cannon, a birthday cake and two bottles of whisky for Mr Mackay.

In 1970 when seeking election to Parliament Donald Stewart warned that like other military etablishments the Rocket Range could be closed down overnight at the whim of the MOD without regard to the civilian population who had come to depend on it for their livelihood.

Well it almost happened in 1993 as the result of a wide-ranging review by the MOD of military facilities in the UK. At that time the Rocket Range was pumping £10 million a year into the local economy and providing 800 jobs, which represented 40 per cent of the total number of Full Time Equivalent jobs in Uist. They also provided apprenticeships. Its closure would have been devastating. There were representations made by the MP, the Council and Western Isles Enterprise.

However it survived. Altough still owned by the MOD the range has been operated by private contractors such as SERCO. DTEA and now QinetiQ.

****

The MP Donald Stewart always told the story about the Russian spy sent in when the Rocket Range started up. He took the name of Maclean and settled into the community.

The KGB heard nothing from him for five years so they sent in another spy to seek him out. He asked the first person he met if he knew Maclean.

'You mean the postman?' 'No.' 'Would that be the teacher then?' 'No I don't think so.' 'Oh, I know who you're looking for, it'll be Maclean the Russian spy, he lives down there.'

****

A Deacon on his rounds was told by an elderly man living alone: 'You never know how lonely you are until you have a visitor.'

THE BCCI FIASCO

Like the Robert Kennedy assasination or the 9/11 terror attack you always remember where you were when momentous events occur. Such was the case with the BCCI disaster in which the Western Isles Council - one of the smallest local authorities - lost £24 million in July 1991 when the Luxembourg-based Bank of Credit and Commerce International collapsed leaving debts of £10 billion throughout the world.

I had been covering Lochmaddy Sheriff Court in North Uist -- one of the cases involved a Western isles Councillor and his trial had finished on the Tuesday evening (July 9). I was ready to board the flight at Balivanich the next moring for Stornoway when I was tipped off that when I got there I should go directly to the Council headquarters as something big was breaking.

When I arrived the first information was that the Council had lost £2 million but no one would confirm anything. No one wanted to be seen talking to the Press. It was finally announced that the Council losses were 'substantial,' but as the day progressed it was like an auction with the loss figure going to £5m, then £11m then £15m. By the following day it was £22 million and then £24m. A special meeting of the Council was called.

Calum Macdonald the MP issued a statement calling for urgent talks between the Council and the Scottish Office.

The money lost was equivalent to the cost of the new Western Isles Hospital which was about to be built. Islanders did not think the Council even had that kind of money to invest.

Likewise few had ever heard of BCCI. It was later learned that it had been founded in 1972 by a Pakistani banker Agha Hasan Abedi, with the support of Sheik Zayed bin Sultan al Nahyan, ruler of Abu Dhabi, and head of the United Arab Emirates, who owned 77 per cent of the Bank which was represented in 130 countries.

Time magazine described BCCI as 'a notorious cash conduit for drug smugglers, arms dealers and rapacious tyrants.' Investigators had called it the most corrupt enterprise in modern history.

There was even a link between Saddam Hussein and Osama bin Laden - they used the same bank: BCCI.

BCCI was closed down by the Bank of England amid fraud allegations on July 5. It was one of the most recent list of investment banks approved by the Bank of England and circulated by the Department of the Environment just two weeks previously. Nearly £90 million was lost by UK councils with the greatest loss being suffered by the Western Isles Council. Ross and Cromarty lost £1.8 million.

A number of years before the Council had been reprimanded for borrowing for the purpose of on-lending to local authorities outside Scotland. The Commission for Local Authority Accounts in Scotland said such transactions were unlawful but did not recommend that a surcharge be made in the case of the Western Isles or Lochaber District Council.

Despite being informed of the loss the Council Convener, the Rev Donald Macaulay, left for a conference in Newcastle where the other delegates wondered why he was there when there was such a crisis back in the Stornoway HQ.

The Director of Finance, Donald George Macleod, was informed of the loss late on Saturday, July 6. He informed the Convener but could not get the Chief Executive, Dr George Macleod. He was reluctant to phone him on a Sunday because of the Chief's strong Christian convictions and disapproval of Sunday working.

However the Chief Executive left on the early ferry on Monday morning for a holiday in France. He was finally contacted by phone on the Tuesday in London and agreed to return to the island.

On Monday, July 8, the Director of Finance and the Depute Director of Legal Services (Wendy Geddes) left the island for Edinburgh to meet COSLA., the Convention of Scottish Local Authorities, to discuss the crisis. No other senior officials in the Western Isles Council were told of the loss and staff in the Finance Department who knew were told to tell no one.

The Chief Executive, Dr George Macleod, returned home on the lunchtime ferry on Thursday (July 11) where he was met by a posse of Pressmen and cameras.

Asked for his immediate reaction to the crisis facing the Council he said: 'It is one of shock and dismay. But I cannot comment further until I have the facts from the Director of Finance.'

He then drove home returning to the office just before an informal meeting

The Director of Finance, Donald G Macleod, was suspended from his £35,000 a year post on full pay pending a full investigation into the loss of the £23m (with interest the figure was rounded up to £24 million.).

Mr Macleod , aged 49, who had been the Director since 1974, slipped out the back door before the announcement was made to avoid a Press corps of 20 and three TV camera crews.

The announcement was made at 10.30 pm after a heated six and a half hour private informal meeting of the Policy and Resources Committee where Members were briefed about the crisis situation facing the Council. The meeting adjourned for a few minutes after 6pm and then continued without officials.

 At 8pm the Council had sympathy with the large number of media representatives who were waiting for a statement and provided them with coffee and sandwiches.

In a prepared statement at the conclusion of the meeting, the Vice Convener Murdo Afrin -- who was also chairman of the Policy and Resources Committee -- roundly condemned the system which allowed banks, subsequently found to be in a weak financial state, to be operating in the money market.

He added that the Council obviously recognised its own responsibilities and it was therefore actively pursuing means of mitigating the loss. He hoped that Central Government would understand the council's situation and give 'sympathetic and urgent treatment' to them.

The Western Isles branch of NALGO issued a statement fully supporting the Council's stance in blaming the Government and the Bank of England for the losses incurred.

There was a feeling in the community that a Council with a Sabbath observance policy and strong Christian views should not have been investing in a bank with such a questionable reputation.

On Friday, July 12, the Convener, the Rev Donald Macaulay, stated that there was no question of impropriety regarding the suspension of the Director of Finance, Donald G Macleod. He was responding to a question regarding the relationship between the Director and a senior member of the staff of the Edinburgh brokerage firm R P Martin. It was one of a number of brokerage firms used by the Council. Mr Donald Macleod and Mr Iain Macleod of Edinburgh were second cousins.

He said they should now be looking forward and try to assure the people of the Western Isles that they would provide the services as best they could in the future. He also said he was unaware of the bank's reputation which had only been revealed in the previous few days.

Mr Macaulay added: 'When the Bank of England did not know, how could our financial officers? It makes people wonder whether you can trust the Bank of England. We look to them as a guiding light on financial matters. If they are unable to judge how can we judge? They want to wash their hands of it but all the perfume of Arabia will not sweeten their hands in this matter.'

The Chief Executive, Dr George Macleod - who had taken the decison the previous night to suspend the Finance Director pending an investigation -- said it might be necessary to recall him to clarify certain matters. If he was called in he would be entitled to be represented by a union official or his lawyer.

He explained that the money invested represented revenue support grants from central government usually made available at the beginning of the financial year. They were invested on a short term basis.

During Saturday July 13 Dr George Macleod and a number of senior staff were preparing a report (never published) on the situation. The report filled out the background of the Council's invovlement with BCCI and the sums and investments made. It concluded that the Director of Finance should be dismissed immediately.

On the Sunday morning the Rev Angus Macrae -- who had been licensed to preach by the Presbytery just a few weeks previously -- took the service in Stornoway Free Church.

He based his sermon on James 4: 13 - 14 and James 5: 1 - 2.

'Go to now, ye that say, today or tomorrow we will go into such a city and continue there a year, and buy and sell and get gain: whereas ye know not what shall be on the morrow.

'Go to now, ye rich men, weep and howl for your miseries that shall come upon you.

'Your riches are corrupted and your garments moth eaten.'

This was all happening against a background of a unemployment rate of 10.2 per cent in the Western Isles. The Council had £2 million in poll tax arrears over the previous two years. The poll tax at the time was £77 - one of the lowest in the UK - which included a £26 water rate. At that time £1 on the poll tax brought in only £22,000.

Disillusioned islanders were reckoning that it would therefore take a poll tax of £1100 to cover the £23 million loss sustained in the BCCI collapse.

There was another problem on their doorstep. If Mr Macleod's suspension turned into a dismissal, the Council would find themselves in great difficulty as the Depute Director of Finance, Brian Lawrie, had accepted an appointment a month previously to become Director of Finance with North East Fife District Council and would be leaving in a few weeks time.

Also moving was Lorna Eller, the Department's Chief Accountant, who was due to take up a university lecturing post in New Zealand which had been arranged in November. Meanwhile, another member of the Finance Department, Kenneth Flagg, had confirmed that he was considering early retirement for some time.

Like the Watergate scandal more information was being leaked each day. It was revealed that at the briefing meeting that the Director of Finance had deliberately distanced himself from the day to day transactions concerning the BCCI investments because he was related to one of the brokers in the Edinburgh firm of R P Martin. The work had been delegated to Mairi Macmillan, a senior accountant.

Calum Macdonald the MP for the Western Isles, who had met the Convener and senior officials on the Friday evening, said that the briefing paper presented to Members had revealed that following concern voiced about BCCI by officers that two representatives of the brokerage firm R P Martin -- including the Director's second cousin Mr Iain Macleod -- had visited the Council headquarters in

September to allay their fears and to assure them they could keep on investing with BCCI. Mr Macdonald said it appeared to him to be an appalling piece of advice and it had to be questioned.

Mr Macdonald said: 'This crisis ought to be seen as an opportunity to expose some weaknesses in procedures and decision making. It will need to be tackled if we are to restore the Council's credibility which has taken a huge body blow. Tough decisions will have to be made at the emergency meeting on Tuesday.'

He said it appeared that at various times in the previous year a total of £90 million had been invested with BCCI, and on that sum the Council had made £100,000 in interest.

By the Monday (July 15), following a Press conference, confusion reigned as to whether the Chief Executive, Dr George Macleod - the man who had suspended the Finance Director - was about to resign himself.

Rob Barnett, the Director of Administration, read a statement at the Press conference which did not reveal anything new. He said that 'whilst the investigation continues it would be premature and prejudicial for there to be announcements allocating blame.'

It was then time to start blaming the Press. He added: 'Until the facts are known and reported to the Council, there can be no basis for the critical statements which have appeared in the media.'

Sensing blood, the Press corps were in no mood to accept such a bland statement.

Had the Chief Executive resigned or walked out that morning? Why was he not at the meeting?

We were told that Dr George Macleod was in his office attending to his work. He was not at the Press briefing because he had not been asked to attend.

In response to another question the Convener said that he had not asked the Chief Excutive to resign. He added that he was 'reflecting on his position' and had been discussing it with friends and advisers because he was worried about press satements and statements on radio and television.

Dr George had gone home on Monday, July 15, following a statement on radio by Councillor Mary Bremner that 'When a ship hits the rocks I hold the Captain responsible, not the First Mate.' The Chief Executive was demanding a retraction of the statement and an apology, otherwise he would not return. He was eventually persuaded to return on Tuesday (July 16).

Asked about the responsibility of the elected Members the Convener admitted that they had a responsibility and part of that was to delegate matters to responsible officers who had the expertise, skill and experience.

When asked: 'Will Dr Macleod have effectively resigned his position by not attending tomorrow's meeting?' the Convener replied: 'You may put that question to him.'

The corridor to the Chief Executive's office was immediately invaded by the Press representatives but this only resulted in a statement being read by an Assistant Director that 'Dr Macleod was considering his position.'

A special meeting of the Council was held on Tuesday, July 16. NALGO had urged the Council not to take any panic decisions. They said that any panic measures -- incuding cuts in services and job losses -- would have a serious effect on the local economy.

It was a case of standing room only at the special meeting. Even the public seats were full 40 minutes before it was due to start. Traditionally all Council meetings start with prayer and Councillor Donald I Nicolson asked for 'guidance and wisdom for the councillors from the Lord who knew the end from the beginning.'

Brian Lawrie, the Depute Director of Finance, who presented a report on the financial implications following the collapse of BCCI, told the meeting that the Council had received offers of help from other local authorities and financial institutions. He put a number of options before the Council.

He told them that the full impact of any aditional borrowing would commence in 1992-93. The estimated cost of additional borrowing of £24 million over 30 years at 11 per ent -- using the equal instalment principle -- would be £3.4 million or £3.8 million over 20 years. Funding £3.4 million was equivalent to adding £157 to the community charge. With water rates that would be a total of £273. It was agreed to borrow £23 million over the next 30 years.

Former Convener Sandy Matheson said that the crisis had not done their credibility any good because of the way it had been handled.

Councillor Angus Graham observed: 'Yesterday can be described as a Hebridean farce and the only person absent was Compton Mackenzie to write about it. We can claw back our credibility by being seen to take decisive action.'

It was agreed to establish - without delay - an independent external inquiry and to invite Professor Alan Alexander to undertake the inquiry with powers to retain such expert financial and legal services as he saw fit. They wanted the findings to be submitted not later than August 31.

The Council then went into private and at a Press briefing after the 2 1/2 hour meeting it was announced that they had decided by 22 votes to 8 not to suspend their 49 year old Chief Executive, Dr George Macleod, pending the outcome of the Alexander Inquiry.

Dr George thought he had been vindicated. He was unaware of the voting at the meeting. The decision had been a compromise between an original motion to suspend him immediately and an amendment to exonerate him.

The following day (July 17) the Finance Director Donald G Macleod, who had been suspended, was re-instated to assist with the inquiry.

Professor Alexander arrived on July 18. He said he would outline the terms of his remit at a Press confence on the Monday and added: 'Thereafter I'll being going into purdah until my investigation is concluded.'

The national Press representatives departed leaving only the local Press corps. The Press room in the Executive corridor at the Council HQ -- a hive of activitiy over the previous week -- was closed down and given over for a Financial Management Services pilot scheme.

The Convener -- whose own handling of the media had been criticised -- then sent a letter to all Members advising them not to make statements to the media.

Concerning an 'unhelpful' statement by the Scottish Office that £17 million had been borrowed to invest, the Council issued a terse statement which said: 'The Council has been made aware that the Scottish Office has issued a statement suggesting that it borrowed £17m for the purpose of on-lending and that this was part of the £23 million deposited with BCCI.

'In view of the inqiury which is being undertaken by Professor Alan Alexander and which is now pending, it would be premature for the Council to comment on these most unhelpful statements which are being issued by the Scottish Office.'

The result of the Convener's 'media embargo' was that at the week-end public meetings were held by two councillors - one in Stornoway and one in Barra.

At the Stornoway meeting there were calls for resignations not only of chief officials but Members as well. Another speaker called for the resignation of the Convener because of the way he had handled the crisis in front of the largest media coverage of any event in the Western Isles.

In Barra there was further criticism of the Chief Executive for permitting the Director of Finance to go on holiday two days after being re-instated to his post following his suspension. His holiday in France had been booked some time previously.

Meanwhile feelings amongst the staff were tense. It was felt that while recruitment to the Council's top posts might now prove difficult, that might also be the case for staff who wished to leave and seek employment elsewhere.

By this time there was a new acronym for the Western Isles Island Council (WIIC) - Worst Investors in the Country.

There was a stormy and confused special meeting of the Policy and Resources Committee on August 13 when they recommended savings of almost £2 million in the current financial year.

There were recriminations and accusations that Members were not being told the truth, and that information that Barclays Bank had issued a writ on the Council the previous Friday suing the Council for almot £300,000 had been withheld from the councillors.

Councillor Donald Mackay, a former Vice Convener, declared: 'I feel we are going to make a bigger laughing stock of ourselves. We learn more at our cornflakes in the morning by listening to the radio than we learn here as elected Members of this Council.'

The meeting was an excellent example of the Council tearing itself apart with little or no guidance coming from senior councillors or senior offcials.

The Convener, the Rev Donald Macaulay, left the chamber at the height of the crisis debate, and there was then a demand that he return to the chamber to explain the meaning of a letter which he had sent to members.

The Director of Administration, Rob Barnett, explained that Mr

Macaulay had left because he had an appointment with Professor Alexander. He returned to the chamber 20 minutes later.

Most of the confusion centred around the Convener's letter to members which stated that the Secretary of State was not able to give any indication of how he might react to the Council's position.

However the Vice Convener Murdo Afrin said that the Scottish Secretary had given a clear indication that there would be no assistance to the Council in that financial year.

When challenged about the meaning of the letter the Convener said it had been written by the Director of Administration, but it was pointed out that he had signed it.

Vice Convener Murdo Afrin said that he had proposed to inform them of the Barclay's writ at the private session of the PR meeting on the Thursday, but the information had leaked out.

Despite calls for leadership and unity at a meeting of the Council on August 16 it resulted in the very opposite at a marathon session. Again the public gallery was packed - many of them Council employees -- and it seemed as if some one had pressed the self-destruct button as the accusations and recriminations were made.

The Council were given an update of their existing capital debt which was just under £146 million . By August 1 a total of over £16 million had been received in Revenue Support Grant.

The Finance Director Donald G Macleod also informed the meeting that external auditors had visited the Council 9 times since January 1, 1990, for a total of 90 days and normally they brought four staff members with them. Asked if they had made any observations on the transactions he said that no critical comment had been made by the auditors.

Former Convener Sandy Matheson criticised the lack of leadership in such a traumatic time for the Council. He said his fear was that they would be in a horrendous financial situation one year on. A loss of £23 million was catastrophic.

Barra Councillor Captain Roddy Mackinnon made a plea for unity. 'Let us put an end to this downward spiral. It will be hara kiri if we continue like this. We have to uproot the seeds of destruction which have been sown. Let us show the people of Scotland that we are in control of our own destiny.'

Concerning the press release by the Convener which seemed to have indicated that there was hope of assistance from the Secretary of State - when in fact the opposite was the case - Councillor Angus Graham commented: 'Denis Healey said that when he got into a hole he stopped digging. We have not stopped digging yet.'

While agreeing that two committees be set up to deal with disciplinary matters that might arise from Professor Alan Alexander's independent inquiry -- one for investigative purposes and the other for appeals -- it was also agreed that they should seek expert legal advice as to whether their present procedures were really flawed.

After hearing a statement by Chief Executive Dr George Macleod on the meeting with Ian Lang, the Secretary of State, on August 2, several members voiced the opinion that if the information had been made available at the PR meeting on the Tuesday, that it would have saved a lot of time and trouble.

Dr Macleod said that Mr Lang had made it clear that the Council must decide how it got through the next eight months. He had indicated that if the Council had to increase its community charge by £150 that it would still keep it below the national average, and that there was a rebate scheme in operation. While summing up the Secretary of State had reiterated that there was absolutely no question of the Council receiving full recompense for the loss.

Mr John Broadfoot, the Controller of Audit for Scotland, arrived on August 21 for a two day visit to look into the how the money was lost. He interviewed members and officials. He declined to comment on the previous vists of the external auditors.

Councillor Kathleen Macaskill was appointed as chair of the 15 member comittee to deal with any disciplinary action against senior officials recommended by the independent Alexander Report. John Wallace, a former Chief Executive with Tayside Regional Council, was appointed to be clerk of the committee.

On Friday, August 30, the Alexander Report was handed over to the Council and was immediately deposited in the local branch of the Royal Bank of Scotland. It would be taken out on the Monday when the adjourned investigative committee would reconvene to study the report and its recommendations. After the meeting all copies of the report would be returned to the bank.

It was estimated that it would be well into October before the 15 member committee would complete their task. The report was not to be made available to the other council members until all the disciplinary implications -- if any -- had been exhausted.

On September 2 the Convener, the Rev Donald Macaulay, resigned from his post. He had previously served two four year terms as Convener when the Council was established in 1975.

He said his resignation was a matter of principle and it was a decision he had taken after much heart searching to indicate to the people of the Western Isles his distress over the collapse of he BCCI.

The following day it was leaked that the 42 page Alexander Report had been highly critical of the Chief Executive and the Director of Finance. The chair of the investigating committee, Councillor Kathleen Macaskill, was furious that the information had been leaked and declared: 'The person who leaked it is not worthy to be a councillor.'

A source revealed that Chief Executive Dr George Macleod, had been slammed for his lack of leadership immediately after the news broke and especially for going home on the morning of the special meeting.

The Director of Finance, Donald G Macleod, was understood to have been criticised for the overall running of his department and for not revealing his relationship with a partner in the brokerage firm of R P Martin, although there was no suggestion of impropriety. He was also criticised for not acting on the early warning signal regarding corruption within BCCI, given by a member of his staff, Mrs Mairi Macmillan.

Councillors were criticised for not asking enough questions. The role of Brian Lawrie, the Chief Financial Officer, the Depute Director of Finance, was described as 'blurred.'

The Press were finally given a portable cabin with phones outside the Council building.

In a letter to the Scottish Secretary, Calum Macdonald MP, told him that the people of the Western isles were 'innocent bystanders in the sorry saga of BCCI, and must not be allowed to become its chief victims.'

He also reminded him that the Council was the single largest employer in the Western Isles.

Finance Director Donald G Macleod, who said he had been advised to speak out in view of the leaked allegations made against him, said he had no intention of resigning.

He said he would like to defend himself and his department against allegations which had been made against them in a report which he had not yet seen despite wide publicity of part of its contents. He added: 'One point I would like to clear up is that it is my responsibility and mine alone and has nothing to do with the dealer. There is no question of me pushing the blame from myself on to anybody else.'

'I have been living a nightmare existence for the past two months. The harassment from the national media - not the local Press corps - has put me and my family under a great deal of pressure. I feel my position has been prejudiced because of the leaked information.'

NALGO asked for a copy of the Alexander Report because they could not defend their members without a copy.

The Investigating Committee announced on September 11 that they were suspending the Chief Executive and the Finance Director with immediate effect on full pay. Hearings would be held in October.

Then on September 17, to everyone's surprise, Councillor Donald Macleod of Shawbost , education chair, was elected as the new Convener. It was described by one wag (John Clark) as 'an immaculate election,' because he defeated Councillor Kathleen Macaskill, chair of the Investigating Committee, by 16 votes to 14. She had expected to win easily and had even bought a new outfit. She refused to shake hands with the new civic head.

The following day there was a call for the resignation of Mr Macleod as Convener. This was made by the chairmen of six council committees. They called for his 'resignation forthwith because of the 'widespread sense of outrage in the community' and because they shared the public's lack of confidence in him.

This was no doubt a reference that 'Domhnall Easy,' as he was known, had been jailed for a driving offence while working in Glasgow.

His view was that he had been democratically elected to the office and had no intention of resigning. Anyway his election did nothing to unify the Council.

Facing the media and camera crews he was not put off by questions relating to indiscretions in his youthful past. Although he did not say it the message was clear - people should judge him on his Council performance and not on his past.

The questions began to get nearer the bone. 'Why do you think the resignation call stated that people were outraged?'

'I have no idea.'

'There have been various attempts to bring your past personal life into this, what's your response?'

'Maybe my past will be my strength. We all learn as we go through life. Sometimes it can be a really tough path. The rougher it is the more one respects life.'

He called on the Council to unite.

Two members of the 'gang of six' who called on the Convener to resign, quit their posts as chairmen.

The Investigating Committee announced on September 26 that they were to hold disciplinary hearings against the officers named in the Alexander Report, but refused to divulge how many were named. However a source revealed that there were six -- all in the Finance Department..

In an interview with myself on October 2 the Convener came away with a classic quote: 'Every saint has a past and every sinner a future.'

It followed the latest revelation in a Sunday newspaper that he had also served six months in jail in 1967 for assaulting an island policeman.

He had been reluctant to give me an interview . Remembering he had been in the Lifeguards during National Service, I left a note with his secretary Sybil to give to him. It just said: 'Donald, remember the Guards motto - 'Evil be to him who evil thinks.'

I got a phone call to come and see him.

In the Convener's panelled office - and accompanied by the Director of Administration Rob Barnett - he responded to accusations made in the Sunday newspaper.

He told me: 'The people of the island knew about the six months in jail in 1967 after being found guilty of a police assault. It was a skirmish in a lay-by at Brue on the west side. I went initially to Porterfield Prison and served the rest of the sentence at Perth Prison.

'The 20 previous convictions referred to in the report of the court case in the local paper were to do with driving offences in Glagow 25 years ago. I have already admitted that I had been fined and banned for a drunk driving offence while working as an engineer in the city. However during that ban I was caught driving without insurance, driving while disqualified, and speeding, and served a prison sentence in Barlinnie.'

Mr Macleod continued: 'That is all in the past and I paid the penalty prescribed by law. Reasonable people would see that I have paid my debt to society. Am I being tried for my past all over again when I have been nine years a member of the Western Isles Council, two years as vice chairman of the Education Commitee, and five years as chairman of that committee? Now I have been democratically elected as Convener.

'I cannot understand why all this is being resurrected and why my persecutors are taking this course of action. We all make mistakes. These were the sins and faults of youth. Every saint has a past and every sinner a future.

"For the sake of the Council and the community I would humbly beg the media to let me now get on with the heavy task of leading the Council into better days.'

The Investigating Committee -- which became the Disciplinary Commmitee -- agreed to delay the disciplinary hearings for 21 days following a NALGO request to give them time to prepare a case for their members.

On October 29 the Secretary of State Ian Lang granted the Council borrowing consent for £24 miliion.

The following day the Council received the report of the Comptroller of Audit into the £24million losses sustained in the BCCI collapse.

The same day John A Wallace, who had been called in to advise the Investigating Committee, resigned. He said he had anticipapted the hearings to have been completed by the end of October. He was replaced by Steven Hamilton, retired Chief Executive of Glasgow District Council.

At the beginning of November Rae Mackenzie, one of the six chairman who resigned in protest at the election of the Convener, was re-elected as chairman of the Environmental Services Committee.

A redundancy policy paper was drawn up by officials. A Revenue Estimates Working Party considered cuts of 8, 10 and 12 per cent. NALGO was getting agitated.

About this time church presbyteries in the Western Isles agreed to observe a Day of Humiliation and Prayer 'because of the BCCI crisis.' It was to be held on December 14

The BCCI disciplinary hearings finally commenced on December 4. Chair Kathleen Macaskill explained that 28 days would be allowed for appeals and then 14 days would be required to convene a meeting. Naturally the hearings began to run behind schedule.

The Convener sent a letter to the Prime Minister John Major inviting him to the Western Isles to see for himself the problems facing the island communities.

The Disciplinary Committee decided to sack both the Chief Executive, Dr George Macleod and the Director of Finance, Donald G Macleod. The hearings had lasted 8 days, and had cost £60,000.

There were six officers targeted in the independent Alexander Report. One - the former Depute Director of Finance - had already left to take up another appointment on the mainland. Of the remaining five, one was cleared and complaints against the four others were upheld.

Sources revealed that members of the committee were 'surprised and angry' that warning letters concerning the Council's financial and managing practices had never been brought to their attention. The letters were from the Scottish Office and the Audit Commission.

At a midnight Press conference the Depute Director of Administration Donald Martin read a statement. It said the Alexander Report Investigating Committee had now discharged its remit.

They had made the following decisons. In respect of Mrs Mairi Macmillan, a senior accountant, they found the grounds of the complaint had not been substantiated and that there should be no further action.

Lorna Eller - Chief Accountant, three out of the four complaints had been substantiated and agreed that she be given a written warning.

David Rattray, an Assistant Director of Finance, three out of five grounds of complaint had been substantiated, and that he be given an oral warning.

The Committee found that a number of serious complaints against Donald G Macleod, the Director of Finance, had been substantiated, and that the responsibility for losses incurred by the Council following the collapse of BCCI lay primarily with the Director of Finance.

The statement added: 'In view of the very serious nature of these complaints and bearing in mind the Director's failure to comply with a previous Council decision in November 1988 -- to cease the practice of borrowing to on-loan -- the committee agreed to dismiss him from the Council's service with immediate effect.'

While agreeing that the responsibility for the losses lay primarily with the Finance Director, the committee nevertheless found that serious complaints aginst Dr George Macleod -- on the basis of his failure to carry out adequately his general managerial responsibilities as Chief Executive - had been substantiated.

Accordingly, the committee agreed that Dr Macleod should be 'dismissed from the Council's service with immediate effect.'

Unfortunately before Councillor Mackaskill got a chance to go from the convening room along the corridor to inform the Chief Executive of his dismissal, Dr George already knew his fate. He had been looking out his window and saw and heard a Grampian TV reporter announcing the news on camera. He had started clearing his desk by the time the committee chairwoman reached him.

The day following the Council began the task of implementing severe cuts to pay off the £3 mllion a year loan charges as a result of the BCCI affair.

Financial controls on revenue expenditure were so bad (no accounts had been done for three years) that none of the cuts were actually implemented.

Then came the Broadfoot Inquiry conducted by Mr John Broadfoot, the Controller of Audit. He found that three senior officals of the Council had acted 'contrary to law' in borrowing to invest in BCCI. He concluded that the disastrous exposure to BCCI was due to negligence by the Finance Director Donald G Macleod, his Depute Director Brian Lawrie, and the Council's Assistant Director of Finance, David Rattary.

The other finance officials linked with the Council investment - Lorna Eller and Mairi Macmillan -- were exonerated by Mr Broadfoot. He stated that they had sought guidance and instruction from senior staff and satisfied the Controller that they did not act negligently or commit misconduct in terms of the law.

He found no evidence of impropriety in the family relationship between Donald G Macleod and his second cousin Iain Macleod of R P Martin, the brokers.

He said concerns about BBCI were brought frequently and persistently to the notice of senior finance staff by Mairi Macmillan and Lorna Eller. In response the Director took advice from other parties. The Controller pointed out that in taking advice from one of BCCI's representatives in Scotland, the Director of Finance could hardly be expected to receive information which would discourage continuing to deal with those who stood to gain most from the continuing relationship.

He concluded that of the deposits with BCCI at July 5, 1991, £16.5 million or thereby 'represents monies which the authority borrowed and on-lent outwith its statutory powers.'

At that point in the saga, Councillor Luis Maciver, chairman of the Education Committee who had proposed Councillor Donald Macleod as Convener -- jetted off to the Azores to give a talk at the Conference of Peripheral Maritime Regions on -- believe it or not -- 'The Management of Islands Councils.'

In March 1992 the Chief Executive Dr George Macleod was refused early retirement. At that time he was not yet 50.

In May he was given a 15 per cent pay rise, bringing his salary to £54,000 a year. This followed pay rises for all chief officers of Councils and followed a recommendation by COSLA consultants.

In June his second application for early retirement was successful. (He left his employment in September when he reached 50).

The following month the well known Glasgow disclaimer 'It wisnae me' summed up the Audit Commission's three day inquiry at

Stornoway into the loss. As each Council official was called upon to make his submission in response to the findings contained in the Broadfoot Report it became evident that no one seemed to have been in charge of the Council's loan fund, that there had been no written guidelines regarding its administration -- only verbal instructions - and that money had been borrowed illegally in advance of need.

The inquiry heard that £19 million of the £23 million need not have been lost. It had been placed with BCCI solely as a result of excess borrowing. The Council's need at the time was only £4 million. The Council had continued to borrow to on-lend at a profit after they had been warned about such practices in 1988.

Even the sacked Director of Finance told the inquiry he was unaware of the £5 million which had been borrowed in 1985 from Scottish Widows and invested with BCCI, and of £4 million from the City of Edinbrugh District Council, which had also been invested with the bank.

The Depute Director of Finance, who admitted responsibility for it, said that when he heard about the £5 million he had given instructions to close the account immediately. However he had not realised that there were other accounts with BCCI.

The solicitor for the external auditors also categorically denied any responsibilty for the losses sustained by the Council.

The Council also distanced themselves. Their view was that they had relied on their professional officers.

Chief Accountant Lorna Eller (by that time lecturing in New Zealand) and Senior Accountant Mrs Mairi Macmillan - who were both exonerated by the Controller -- said they had expressed concern about dealing with BCCI on two occasions. The first because of the laundering of drug money in the States and when the bank was restructured. However after seeking advice from brokers and financial advisers the Director had decided to continue using BCCI.

The Audit Commission was told that a large part of the Director's time had been taken up by his work as the Council's European Officer in attending meetings on the mainland and abroad, as well as preparing submissions and reports when he was back at his council desk. His subordinates too spoke of their heavy workload. It was even suggested that one of the reasons for borrowing larger sums than required was because it involved less administrative work.

Mr Broadfoot submitted said that it was 'not a comfortable experience for the Commission to spend such a substantial part of this hearing listening to senior staff disclaiming responsibilty for the management of such a key function in this authority.'

The Council welcomed the Bingham Report which was an Inquiry into the Supervison of the Bank of Credit and Commerce International and chaired by The Rt Hon. Lord Justice Bingham. It had been ordered by the House of Commons and it criticised the Bank of England on its supervison of the fraud-hit bank.

In his 218 page report he stated it did not pursue the truth about BCCI with the rigour which the scandalised Bank's reputation justified. The Bank came to rely too heavily on the auditors of the international bank.

He added: 'The Auditors have a crucial role to play, but the duty to supervise is placed on the bank and it is a duty which cannot be delegated. It is the bank, not the auditor, which is the supervisor. In these respects the Bank's supervisory approach to BCCI was, in my opinion, deficient. How different the course of events would have been had these deficiences not existed, one can only speculate'

Western Isles MP Calum Macdonald demanded the resignation of the Governor of the Bank of England, Sir Robin Leigh-Pemberton, and compensation for local authorities who lost millions in the forced closure of BCCI.

In a Press release the Western Isles Council stated that the report demonstrated quite clearly that the Bank of England was at fault in its licensing of BCCI. The Council, however, deplored the inordinate delay in the release of the report and the fact that it had not been released in its entirety.

However they said that the report, as released, 'confirmed a lack of adequate supervision by the Bank of England and a reckless disregard for the depositors whose interests and assets it was supposed to protect.'

The Council added: 'The report provides an overwhelming vindication of the position consistently held by this Council and other depositors that the Bank of England, as the body responsible for the supervision of BCCI, failed in that duty and should now compensate the depositors in full.'

By April 1993 the second part of Professor Alexander's report was published on 'Procdures, Policies and Structures of the Western Isles Council', but it was decided to defer consideration until the new Chief Executive, Brian Stewart, took up his post. The report had 56 recommendations and cost £50,000.

The upshot was that in December 1993 there were radical proposals for the restructuring the Council which meant the disappearance of some departments and the axing of some top posts. They wisely decided to appoint a Communications Officer -- Nigel Scott.

While the Scottish Office had made it quite clear that they would not help out financially they had granted borrowing consent for £24 million. But strange the ways of central government: there was a fortuitous review of the SINA (Scottish Islands Needs Allowance) a support mechanism, in 1992/93. As a result the Council share went up from £5.5 million a year to almost £10 million in 1993/94, and reached just over £10m in the following years, which helped with their loan repayments. Orkney and Shetland did not mind the Western Isles getting a bigger share but they wanted more money put into the pot, and Argyll was screaming because they wanted a share for their islands.

The Scottish Office maintained that there was absolutely no link with the BCCI losses and the SINA money as the independent review had been carried out by Touche Ross.

In November 2005, Deloitte, the BCCI liquidators, dropped their near £1.3 billion lawsuit plus interest against the Bank of England after a 12 year litigation batte This followed a reserve judgement from the Chancellor of the High Court who said it was no longer in the best interests of creditors for the litigation to continue and directed it to end.

The lawyers for Deloitte had alleged that the Bank of England had failed to protect depositors when the world's biggest bank fraud resulted in BCCI collapsing owing more than $16 billion or £9 billion.

The previous month the Bank of England rebuffed an approach to settle the lawsuit, and said it would not make any deal or negotiate a settlement. The liquidators alleged senior Bank of England officals were guilty of misfeasance.

The case began in January 2004 and made English legal history for the two longest opening speeches, followed by seven weeks of testimony from the central bank's first witness. At that time Deloitte said its current legal costs were £38 million. The Bank had spent over £40 million defending the case in the previous two years and said it expected to spend another £23.5 million in that year (2005).

Repayments to the Council began to filter through from the BCCI liquidators. They received £18.8 million from the liquidators, £2.7 million as a result of favourable currency transactions (all BCCI deals were in US dollars), and they had also repaid £2.2 million.

By March 31, 2005, they had cleared their debt. On December 21 -- a nice Christmas present -- they also received another dividend of £1.6 million, which went straight into their own coffers. Then in February 2008 they received a further £679,000 which meant they had recouped 90 per cent of the money they lost.

Tom Carter, the former Grampian Finance Director, who spent 9 months as Acting Director of Finance for the Western Isles Council picking up the pieces, said in an article in Treasury Management, a CIPFA (Chartered Institute of Public Finance and Accountancy) publication: 'One thing is very clear: that it is essential in matters as weighty as the Treasury functions to have written instructions for staff so that there can be no doubt as to their responsibilities and authority.'

He said that in the early days after the disaster a great many potential lenders refused to lend to the Council but added: 'Fortunately, more recently a wider range of local authorities now appear willing to lend to the council. After all, a loan to the Western Isles Council is sounder than one to a bank!'

Quotes from the time: Prime Minister John Major, who was criticised at a meeting of the Treasury and Civil Service Select Committee for failing to take action against the Bank when he was Chancellor, said: 'It is not a matter for us. It is a matter for individual councils.' He urged the Western Isles Council to increase their community charge closer to the Scottish average.

The Governor of the Bank of England -- Robin Leigh-Pemberton - said: 'If we close down a bank every time we find an individual act or two of fraud we would have rather fewer banks than we do at present.'

Reports also showed that a seat on the BCCI board was offered to Julian Amery but he was 'sheered off' from taking it by the B of E governor at the time.

****

In the early days of the Council the Environmental Services Committee was working its way though the agenda when Councillor Angie Allan asked: 'What about the septic tanks at Marybank?' Chairman Donald Mackinnon said: 'Mr Macleod, we're on Item 4, Noise Pollution.' About 10 seconds went by then Angie said: 'Well you know they make a bit of noise as well!'

The KNO car cavalcade protest

Police meet with the KNO demonstrators and those who did a sit down protest at road to airport

John Leivers

Chief Stone Eagle at Lingerbay Inquiry

Corporal Missile at Rocket Range

Entrance to Range Headquarters in Balivanich

The 'White House' the Council HQ

BCCI Council in session. Top table:-Dr George C/Ex: Murdo Afrin, Rev D Macalay, Rob Barnet: Gordon Frith. Front row: On left is Brian Lawrie, Dep Dir of Finance and various committee chairmen.

Dr George Macleod

Donald G Macleod

Rev Donald Macaulay

Donald Macleod

Professor A Alexander

Auditor John Broadfoot

RENEWABLE ENERGY

Plans for windfarms meant the possibility of more public inquiries lurking down the road. Council reports told us that we were to be the 'alternative energy capital of Europe', they designated the Western Isles an 'Energy Innovation Zone' with the possibility of 1000 jobs in future years. We had the wind and the tides to make it all possible as well as a fabrication yard at Arnish to manufacture the turbines and other structures.

One seminar was told the large scale wind farm proposed by Lewis Wind Power - one of the biggest in the world - was our 'Get Out of Jail ' free card in economic terms which, if seized, could turn the tide of our depopulation and economic leakage and bring a rich harvest of community benefit. It was all great stuff and made good copy and headlines.

The proposals, of course, were linked in with the fabrication yard at Arnish. In 1974 the Stornoway Trustees concluded a deal with Fred Olsen Ltd for the 60 year lease of 93 acres of land at Arnish Point for an £8 million oil development for fabrication and engineering facilities incorporating a supply base. It was thought we would cash in on the oil fields to the west of the Hebrides. The Trust were to receive a rent of £32,620 per annum and there would be a review every 10 years. The project was to give work for 1000 by 1982. There was to be no Sunday work.

Mike Thompson, managing director of Fred Olsen (UK) Ltd told a packed public meeting in Stornoway Town Hall that they were there to stay.

There were a number of disputes and strikes and workers were on unofficial strike in 1979, originally over safety measures ashore and afloat plus a row by incoming workers regarding lodging allowances.

One of the biggest contracts they pulled in was for the conversion of the drilling rig 'Drillmaster' into a floating production platform, the 'Buchan Alpha' for BP Petroleum. Work commenced in October 1978 and at its peak 1720 people were working on the project, many of them locals, and during that period it was estimated that more than £10 million was injected into the island's economy.

The estimated cost of the conversion was £75 million. Because of the number on incoming workers Lewis Offshore, as the company was known, had to use ferry vessels to provide floating accomodation. The first was the Borea and then the Nalja.

Initially workers were ferried from the harbour out to the rig. A poem circulatingat the time of the big strike caused much merriment.

>
> The playboys are on strike again
> But it isn't for more pay
> They havn't got their sea legs
> And they are falling in the bay.
>
> Now Glumaig Bay is mighty cold
> And the lads sure took fright
> So they want to tell us landlubbers
> the nature of their plight.
>
> We had to give them lifebelts
> and make their ferry bright
> for they told us of the hardships
> that they face up to every night.
>
> We had to give them thermal gear
> As they couldn't stand the cold
> now the rubber ducks in Woolworths
> Have nearly all been sold.
>
> They look so brave on Cromwell Street
> How could you we ever tell
> That these big men in cowboy boots
> were all as soft as hell.

The yard went through a number of ownerships -- including a management buy out -- after Fred Olsen left the island. It closed down in November 1999.

When it became vacant the Stornoway Trust took it back into their own possession. With the possibiity of windfarm developments other companies showed interest in the facility and Highlands and Islands Enterpise took over the lease and pumped in £12 million into it to make it a multi-purpose yard and Camcal began operations there.

Lewis Windpower - a subsidiary of AMEC and British Energy -- announced proposals in 2001 for a £600m 250 turbine windfarm on the publicly-owned 70,000 acre Stornoway Trust Estate. It was to be the biggest windfarm in Europe and provide jobs for 1000. The electricity generated would be sent by a sub-sea cable to the mainland costing about £400 million.

However their proposals ran into oppposition from Scottish Natural Heritage and the Royal Society for the Protection of Birds as well as murmurings from the Civil Aviation Authority. The result was that they had to spread the windfarm to two other estates - Barvas and Galson -- and then start pruning.

Energy Minister Brian Wilson declared: 'There are three reasons why this development is so important and must - I repeat must -- be brought to fruition. First, it is on a scale which will make a serious contribution to the energy needs of the UK: secondly, it will transform the economy of Lewis: and thirdly, it will regenerate the Arnish fabrication yard where the turbines will be manufactured.

The LWP project was cut back several times and the last planning application for 181 turbines was approved by the Council. The turbines would be 454 feet in height.

Moorlands Without Turbines ran a campaign which resulted in over 4000 objections to LWP's first application, and over 4000 to the second reduced application.

The company planned to issue three contracts - one for turbines, one for civil and electrical contracts, and the third for grid connections. There would be over 100 miles of roads, and 160 bridges and culverts.

The Stornoway Trust would get about £2 million per annum as landlowers, and £2 million for the crofters on the estate. Local communities would get £750,000 per annum and the Western Isles Development Trust £700,000 per annum.

The Council also originally approved an application by Beinn Mhor Power for 130 turbines on the 40,000 acre Eishken Estate, in South Lewis, owned by Nick Oppenheim, an investment manager. The community would be given 33 turbines which would bring in £16 million a year - a terrific boost for one of the most economically deprived areas of Lewis.

However this too was downscaled to 53 turbines to satisfy landscape, visual and ornithological concerns. The community would be given 6 turbines, which would net them about £1m a year. The result of a public inquiry is still awaited.

Then in October 2007 he submitted another planning application for just 16 turbines, part of the original 53. This was reduced to 13 and has been given the go-ahead. Under this proposal the community would get 1per cent of revenue from the windfarm, and the opportunity to own two of the turbines. The Western Isles Development Trust would get a 1/2 per cent of revenue.

A third big application was submmitted by Scottish and Southern Energy for a 57-turbine widfarm in the Pairc area of South Lochs in Lewis. The tip height of the turbines would be 145 metres making them the highest in the Western Isles. It was approved subject to a condition they remove or relocate 31 of the turbines.

All these windfarms would need a new inter-connector to get the electricity to the national grid otherwise the region's natural resources would remain untapped.

A Highlands and Islands Enterprise study also revealed that the cost of connecting in north mainland areas was many times greater than other EU countries, and 30 times higher than Denmark, one of Europe's leaders in renewable energy production. Island costs were even higher, "certainly higher than in any other European country,' said the report.

The issue was taken up by First Minsiter Alex Salmond with the electricity regulator Ofgen.

However in 2007 the 3-turbine windfarm on the Arnish Moor came into operation, and another 6-turbine farm on the Pentland Road on the outskirts of Stornoway is about to come on stream.

There are also hopes of wave and tidal projects off Shader in Lewis.

In 2003 Energy Minister Brian Wilson told a conference in Stornoway: 'These islands are surrounded by some of the best renewable sources in Europe, with strong prevailing winds and the power of the ocean. Today we are contemplating the real possibility that these islands could become a power house on the periphery, making a serious and environmentally sustainable contribution to the energy needs of the whole nation. That prize is worth pursuing.'

Many said Amen to that, but it was not to be.

In April 2008 the Scottish Government gave the thumbs down to the planning application by Lewis Wind Power for their £500 million development. Consent was refused on the grounds of incompatibility with European law. The applicants had spent over £5 million on preparing their planning application which included a number of bird surveys.

Energy Minister Jim Mather said: 'The Lewis Wind Farm would have significant adverse impacts on the Lewis Peatlands Special Protection Area, which is designated due to its high value for rare and endangered birds. This decision does not mean that there cannot be onshore wind farms in the Western Isles. An action plan for sustainable development on the islands will be ready in the autumn.'

(A few months later Scottish Renewables, the green energy trade body, said that new government research 'blew away' the myth that wind farms could not be constructed in peatland areas without causing massive release of carbon and condemned calls for a moratorium on wind farms on peatland areas as 'misguided and blocking effective action on climate change.'

It said that the research had shown that the carbon payback for constructing wind farms on peatlands could be under three years.

The Government decision was a bitter economic pill for the community to swallow as the project would have meant £10 million a year coming into the isles. The scheme had been backed by the Western Isles Council, the Stornoway Trust, Highlands and Islands Enterpise,and support from such organisations as the STUC, CBI and SCDI.

A conference in March 2008 was told that the Western Isles was the most designated area in Europe.

The Scottish Government decision cast doubt on the future of the Arnish fabrication yard outside Stornoway -- which manufactures turbines -- and the prospects of a new sub-sea High Voltage Direct Current cable linking the isles to the mainland so that the power from the island could be connected to the national grid.

However in July 2008 Scottish Hydro Electric Transmission Ltd (SHETL) a subsidiary of Scottish and Southern Electric, revealed that planning consent would be sought for a sub-sea cable linking the Western Isles with the manland.

Because of pressure from environmental groups they also announced that the pylons from Dundonnell on Little Loch Broom in Western Ross to Beauly in Inverness would be buried underground.

The LWP scheme would have meant the community owned Stornoway Trust having 55 turbines: the Galson Trust 61, and the Barvas Estate 60. There would have been £6 million per annum in community benefit, and £4 million in rental payments. The community benefits could be exchanged for 15 per cent ownership of the whole wind farm.

The project on the Specially Protected Area would have meant 400 construction jobs, 70 jobs at the Arnish fabrication yard, and 70 jobs associated directly with the wind farm. Each turbine would have had a 3 MW generation capacity, and the height would be 140 metres (454 ft) and 100 metre blades. It would have involved 104 miles of 5 metre-wide access roads, 9 wind monitoring masts, and overhead lines and underground cables. There would have been 134 pylons, each 27 metres high.

The Council and the StornowayTrust expressed bitter disappointment at the government's decision and Councillor Archie Campbell, chairman of the Council's Sustainable Development Committee, declared: 'Stay out of the Western Isles is the message being given to developers by the Scottish Ministers.'

LWP said the windfarm would have contributed 650 MW of renewable energy and added: 'Over the 6 years of this project we conducted extensive environmental and economic studies and designed the development around these findings. As a result, we believe we had put forward a detailed case showing the benefits of our proposal and the benefits it would bring to Lewis, the Highlands & Islands region and to Scotland. We also believe that during our discussions with the Government, we demonstrated that this proposal could have been approved without violating European law.'

'Sadly all of this has been lost because of the Government decision which, we believe, represents a huge missed opportunity.'

Arnish yard, Drillmaster rig, and accommodation ship

The 3 turbine windfarm on Arnish Moor near Grimshader

North Uist bulb scheme which came to nought in the 70s

Thoughts on wind, wave and tidal power reminds me of the story of the Scots tourist watching the 600,000 million US gallons of water per second pouring over the Niagara Falls in Canada.

The Scotsman was not saying anything and a big Cannuck said to him: 'Hey Jock, you ain't got anything like that in Scatland.'

Jock paused before replying: 'Aye, right enough, but I've a pal in Govan who's a plumber, he could fix it for ye.'

****

The guide on the small cruise boat on the Riddeau Canal in Ottawa was quite a comedian. He told us: 'There's a $50 fine for swimming in the canal, so if you fall overboard just float.'

The canal freezes solid in winter and becomes the longest skating rink in the world, so many commuters -- many of them working in Government offices -- skate to work as it is much quicker.

The guide told us that it had been so cold the previous winter that the Prime Minister had to put his hands into his own pockets!

****

It was a poor tourist season in Canada and it got so bad in one area that the hotel boss said he would have to start paying off unless things improved. He suggested one way to attract the tourists would be if there were more sightings of moose. He provided one female staff member with a moose costume and told her to cavort in the forest. To her horror on the first day she came face to face with a bear. She turned and ran but the bear was gaining on her. At last she gave up and stood there petrified. The bear said: 'If you don't start running again the two of us will be out of a job.'

THE ISLAND INDUSTRIES

I don't like to think of the number of times I have written that the Harris Tweed industy has been at a cross-roads. There were amalgamations over the years until Derek Murray finished up with the KM Group which controlled about 95 per cent of Harris Tweed production. That comprised Kenneth Mackenzie Ltd of Stornoway and Keneth Macleod (Shawbost) Ltd.

The Mackenzie family firm -- under the guidance of Harris Mackenzie -- won the Queen's Award for industry on three occasions in a 10 year period : 1977, 1981 and 1986.

That KM group was sold to Yorkshire man Brian Haggas who at the end of December 2006 formed Harris Tweed Scotland Ltd: not to sell Harris Tweed but to manufacture and sell gents jackets to the top end of the market from his company, Brook Taverner in Keighley. He reduced the number of patterns available to just five.
In 2008 he paid off 34 mill employees - half the workforce and put the main office block, a former yarn store, and a 1 acre gap site on the market.

That left an opening in the market for those customers who still wanted the normal range of colourful Harris Tweed. In stepped top Scottish international oil trader Ian Taylor who started up a new mill in Shawbost. Derek Murray had only sold the business name of Kenneth Macleod but retained the mill and some plant.

Ian Taylor is president and chief executive of the Vitol Group, the largest physical oil and gas trading comany in the world with 2006 revenues of approximately US $100 billion. He made the shrewd move to engage Iain Angus Mackenzie, who had been the Chief Executive of the Harris Tweed Authority, as his new C.E.O. and Rae Mackenzie as his sales director. Rae had just retired from the family firm as sales manager after 41 years' service.

The only other mill, HTT Manufacturing Ltd of Carloway, which had been producing mainly knitting yarn, is now once again producing Harris Tweed.

Meanwhile the firm getting all the publicity was the Luskentyre Harris Tweed Company run by my good friend Donald John Mackay and his wife Maureen.

They were successful in securing large orders for Harris Tweed from the sportwear firm Nike for their famous Dunk fashion shoe for ladies, and after that supplied tweed for the US Healthy Back Bag Company.

A new Association of Harris Tweed Weavers has been formed with Aneas Maclean as chairman. There are also plans for a Harris Tweed Visitor Centre in Tarbert, Harris.

The fishing industry has also contributed to the economic well-being of the islands over the years and it too has seen many changes.

The value of the farmed salmon eventually overtook the value of the fish landings. When first introduced to the island fish farming looked as if every crofter would have a fish farm at the bottom of the croft. But like crofts -- small agricultural holdings surrounded by rules and regulations -- it soon became apparent that no small farms could survive under new regulations and they were swallowed up by the larger international outfits.

The Stornoway Fishermen's Co-operative has experienced good times and bad, but overall has been a success.

Sadly plans for a large scale bulb growing development in North Uist came to nothing after trials at Paible had proved successul.

The other leg of the economy has been the tourist industry which has expanded over the years. There has been a lot of investment in improving hotels, guest houses and bed-and-breakfast establishments. The July Hebridean Celtic Festival, held in the Big Blue tent in front of Lews Castle, has been an international success. The islands can also boast of some of the best beaches, restaurants and hospitality in Scotland.

In May 2008 in Stornoway radical and controversial proposals for the future of crofting were unveiled by Professor Mark Shucksmith, chair of the inquiry into crofting. His committee had interviewed over 2000 people. He presented his report to Mike Russell, Minister for the Environment.

The far reaching proposals call for (1) the abolition of the Crofters Commission and the creation of 7 - 10 new Federation of Local Crofting Boards which would be elected: (2) all croft houses would be tied to residency: (3) all sub-lets and tenancies would have to be approved by the local crofting boards: (4) Registers of Scotland should be responsible for maintaining the register of crofts: and (5) there should be a review of agricultural subsidies.

To ensure that there would be no speculation on croft land, the Committee recommended that legislation should be backdated to May 12 to forestall any attempts to decroft.

Professor Shucksmith said: 'We firmly believe that these changes are necessary if crofting is to remain an important and viable part of our society. The recommendations come as a package, no single action on its own will achieve the vision.'

However the proposals ran into some opposition from crofters and it will be interesting to see how the Scottish Government deal with the proposals.

The Stornoway Trust is the oldest community-owned estate in the Western Isles. However new legislation gave communities the right to buy-out estates. Now almost 70 per cent of the population of the Western Isles live on community-owned estates.

One of the largest was Storas Uibhist. They bought out the 93,000 acre South Uist Estate -- the biggest community land purchase in Scottish history. The deal included almost the whole of the Islands of Benbecula, Eriskay, and South Uist, as well as a number of other small islands.

D J Mackay of Luskentyre with the Harris Tweed Nike shoes and some of his Harris Tweed below.

Ivenka Trump models a saucy Harris Tweed outfit by Sandra Murray at Tartan Week in New York and on right Alyth McCormack in a HT thistle pink gown from Thistle & Broom for her singing tour in Canada

Hebridean Celtic Festival's Big Blue tent in front of Lews Castle

The beaches are one of the attractions for tourists - looking towards Luskentyre

THE MISCELLANEOUS FILE

This file contains many of the headline stories I have covered over the years, as well as the offbeat and humorous.

These ranged from stories which received world wide circulation like the famous cherry brandy incident involving Prince Charles in June 1963. He was a 14 year old and visited Stornoway on the Gordonstoun school training yacht Pinta along with other pupils.

Before going to the local cinema to see a Jayne Mansfield film, the Prince and some of his friends were taken to the Crown Hotel in Stornoway for a quick meal. While there he left the company - including his private detective - and went into the cocktail bar and ordered himself a 2s 6d cherry brandy.

Alas I myself was not there to witness this having left to file my story, but a reporter on the local paper, Frances Thornton, was there with her parents and saw him being served. She broke that part of the story which was immediately denied by Buckingham Palace and also by the hotel proprietor who said the 'whole story is a complete fabrication and entirely unfounded.' However the Palace later retracted their statement. The licensee was charged with serving a person under age with alcohol but these charges were later dropped.

In a radio interview years later Prince Charles recalled that while they were waiting for the meal a lot of people were looking in the windows and he felt he had to get away somewhere. The only other place was the bar. He said the first drink that came into his head was cherry brandy because he had drank it before when it was cold out shooting. He added 'Hardly had I taken a sip when the whole world exploded round my ears.'

When Prince Charles -- who is Lord of the Isles - became engaged to Lady Diana, the new Crown Hotel management and staff sent them a telegram stating: 'Meal -a-Naigheachd - 'Congratulations on your engagement. We're toasting you in cherry brandy.'

The reply from the private secretary stated: 'Prince Charles and Lady Diana send you their warmest thanks for your extrememly kind and thoughtful message.'

Charles first visit to the Western Isles was in 1956 when he accompanied his parents and other members of the Royal family on the Royal Yacht Britannia during which time he inaugurated the foghorn at Tiumpan Head lighthouse. However there were other visits over the years. Princess Di was no stranger to the isles either because before her marriage she spent some holidays in South Uist.

He and Princess Diana carried out a three day tour of the Western Isles in July 1985 during which time they visited 10 islands. In addtion to the Scottish media there were also the 'Royal photographers' who follow them around wherever they go. Because the Royal couple were flying to various islands by helicopter there was no way to cover it but to 'leap frog' the venues when travelling by car and ferry.

I was to look after the representative from Synidcate International and I learned from him that these photographers operated in two packs. The ones he worked with joined up with me. These lads carry aluminium ladders around with them. One of them could not get his into my boot because it was longer than the others. He took out his Swiss knife and sawed about four inches off the legs. I always wish I had taken a photograph of that because I am sure I could have sold it to the Victorinox company.

During their visit the Royal couple stayed with Lord Granville, the Queen's cousin, in his circular house at Sollas.

On Barra they visited Kismuil Castle, the ancient stronghold of the Macneils of Barra. We have already mentioned the post-prandial customs associated with the castle when a trumpteter sounded a fanfare from the ramparts and proclaimed: 'Hear O Ye People, and Listen, O Ye Nations, The Great Macneil of Barra having finished his meal the Princes of the Earth May Dine.' In deferene to the fact that Prince Charles is also Lord of the Isles the proclamation was amended and heard by the many hundreds lining the pier: 'The Lord of the Isles and the Great Macneil of Barra, having finished their meal, the Princes of the Earth May Dine.'

I had arranged a boat to pick my party up to take us to Eriskay as it would be a good photo opportunity. The last Prince to stand on the strand at Eriskay had been Bonnie Prince Charlie in 1745.

My photo squad had picked out the spot where they wanted to take the picture but we were not getting much co-operation from the Scottish Office PR man. One of the photograhers, who knew a thing or two about covering Royal visits, told us: 'Nobody raise a camera when they come back towards the helicopter.'

This caused Charles to raise an quizzical eyebrow and he asked if there was something we wanted. He was asked if he would stand in a certain spot overlooking the strand and he and Di complied.

When our pack got back to the Dark Island Hotel fairly late for dinner we were being taunted by the other 'Royal' lensmen. However their faces fell when we told them about the photograph we had obtained on Eriskay strand.

When we got back to Harris the following day one of the photographers who worked for a German magazine said he wanted to get his pictures off the island. I told him there was no way as all the planes for the mainland had already left. 'Can you hire me one?' he asked.

I contacted a firm in Glasgow and he chartered the plane to come and pick up himself and a colleague. The arrangement was that they would take all the film back for processing while the two remaining photographers would cover the remainder of the Royal visit. They got the plane then a hired car and drove to London through the night and had the film processed at a 24 lab. The German magazine then sent their plane to London to pick up the film. It was an insight into how some of my colleagues operate.

In addition to covering my own clients I was also asked for a story of the visit by Majesty magazine.

In 1980 Charles also spent two days fishing in the Atlantic on the Hull trawler 'Junella' as a crew member and landed at Stornoway. (A year later Stornoway Lifeboat, under the command of Cox Malcolm Macdonald, rescued 29 crew members when the vessel went aground off Skye in a Force 8 to 9).

Then in 1987 Charles spent three days on croft on the Island of Berneray in North Uist where his hosts were Donald Alick Mackillop (known as Splash) and his wife Gloria. Charles helped in cutting peats and planting spuds -- which later became known as Prince Charles potatoes. He got involved in fencing, bringing in the sheep, and also went out creel fishing. He also enjoyed a ceilidh in the Mackillop home. It was not not until he attended a local funeral that the islanders knew he was there. However no one revealed his presence and he was off the island before the Press got to know of his visit.

He kept up his interest in crofting by opening the Crofters Union Conference in Stornoway in 1993. He greeted the crofters in Gaelic but cheerfully admitted that his Gaelic was helped by 'several short sharp drams.'

He also officially opened the £2 million TV studio complex in Stornoway on that visit, and the £25 million new Western Isles Hospital in the town and met up with 'Splash' Mackillop again.

In 2002 I was invited -- along with other journalists - to attend the media reception at Windsor Castle prior to the Queen's Royal Jubilee tour throughout the UK. There were 700 senior journalists present in St George's Hall. It was all part of a stategy to win their hearts and minds prior to her Golden Jubilee celebrations in June.
Donnie Macinnes from the Stornoway Gazette was also invited and although we flew down on different planes we were staying at the same hotel in Windsor. We had both agreed that kilts would be

the dress for the occasion. Donnie failed to turn up at the expected time and finally I got a phone call from the airport to tell me they had lost his luggage, which included his kilt.

They promised it would be sent the following morning by taxi to the hotel but it was an anxious time. It finally arrived about lunchtime after he had made several phone calls to the airline.
He was resplendent in kilt and waiting for me in the hotel lounge and began to relate the drama of the lost luggage to an Irish journalist who cut in with the riposte: 'So that's what's leaving you dressed like that!'

For some reason or other the Queen broke away from a group and headed to Donnie and I -- naturally the two best-dressed men present -- and chatted to us for about five minutes, and we told her about the great £1 billion wind farm proposal for the island. She asked: 'Don't those things make a terrible lot of noise?'

Later we caught up with Princess Anne whom I had met when she opened the Bethesda Hospice in Stornoway. I had been honorary secretary at the time. She was surprised when I told her that it was 10 years old. I also asked her if she remembered John Angus Patterson who had been the pilot when they used to stop off at Berneray in North Uist for a picnic when they were on the Royal Yacht Britannia. She said she remembered him well and I told her the story about the first time he was called upon to be their pilot.

He had arrived on board the Britannia and was pacing up and down the deck when the Queen came out and said to him: 'Ah, you must be my ferryman,' to which John Angus replied: 'Yes, and you must be my Queen.'

Princess Anne laughed and said: 'And he was quite right.'

When Prince Philip was asked by one journalist at the reception which part of the June-July Jubilee celebrations he would like most, he replied:'The beginning of August!'

During the Golden Jubilee tour the Queen and the Duke of Edinburgh visited Stornoway on May 27, 2002, and did a walkabout and also met several people in the Town Hall and also at Lews Castle College.

To mark her 80th birthday the Queen chartered the pocket luxury cruise liner 'Hebridean Princess' and had a nine day cruise throughout the Western Isles in July 2006.

The vessel was a former Caledonian MacBrayne ferry which had been converted into the five star 'Hebridean Princess'. It could accomodate 49 guests in staterooms and cabins all named after islands, castles and lochs. The Queen was accompanied by the Duke and other members of the Royal family, including Prince Charles and his new wife Camilla, his brother Prince Edward who carried his baby ashore followed by his wife, and Princess Anne and Prince Andrew.

The Queen and the other members of the family came ashore at Stornoway to head for the airport and Charles sailed on to Scrabster.

****

My Canadian friend Keith told me about a minister who was partial to cherry brandy. He asked one of his office bearers to get him a bottle and he said he would povided he would get a mention of thanks from the pulpit. On the Sunday the minister thanked the man for his gift of fruit and the spirit in which it had been given!

****

On December 1, 1962, Jack Coupar, News Editor of the Scottish Daily Express, had notched up 30 years in journalism and his devoted staff threw a party for him - they probably put it on expenses! I attended the celebrations. There was naturally a spoof paper to mark the occasion with a quote from Jo Magin the Night News Editor: 'Jack Coupar, who's he? Do you mean we've got people working during the day as well?' In the Facts Behind the News Desk it also noted that Jack, in three decades of devotion, had passed expenses totalling £1,676,000, and cut out expenses totalling £2,676,000 8s 5d.

A dramatic story which made the headlines around the world in 1968 concerned Europe's first lung transplant involving 15 year old Alex Smith from Breasclete in Lewis. He had drunk a weedkiller called paraquat from a bottle thinking it was Coca-Cola.

At the same time another Lewis boy, 11 year old Calum Macmillan from Lower Garrabost in Point, was in the Lewis Hospital after he had drunk the weedkiller. Fortunately he had taken it on a full stomach and his father had made him vomit by giving him salt and water. He was later released.

After being admitted to the local hospital young Alex Smith was flown by air ambulance to the Edinburgh Royal Infirmary. Less than 48 hours after the lung transplant operation - believed to be the first emergency one in the world -- Alex was eating fruit and ice cream.

ICI, Imperial Chemical Industries, manufacturers of the weed killer, confirmed that there was no known antidote to prevent destruction of the boy's lungs.

The weedkiller had been bought from Lewis Crofters Ltd. Although they sold it in their own tins carrying a warning label, it was a common practice to sell small quantities to customers who brought in their own bottles as it was very expensive.

An ICI spokesman said that a letter had been sent to all their agents in May 1967 insisting on strict compliance with the precautions on their labels. One condition was that products were only sold in the company's unbroken original packages.

Unfortunately young Alex Dan died three weeks later. The funeral took place to Dalmore Cemetery overlooking the beautiful beach. The mourners walking behind the coffin stretched for half a mile.

What impressed the many hard hacks who covered the story was the gracious way Mr and Mrs Smith dealt with their inquiries.

****

As recorded in the book entitled 'Alison - A Father's Search For His Missing Daughter' by Quentin Macfarlane, I broke the story in 1981 of the disappearance of 19 year old Alison Macdonald, a second year History student at Aberdeen University. She had been on a back-packing holiday in India in the Kashmir region with a fellow student, Liz Merry, who later became a GP. Both girls had arranged to work in a leper colony at the end of their trip.

Her father Kenny was a former Customs Officer in Stornoway and the family had lived in Coll in Lewis. A former amateur international footballer, Ken also became a Western Isles Councillor before leaving the island to study for the ministry at the Free Church College in Edinburgh. He was at the end of his first year when the tragedy occurred.

Alison and her friend had reached the village of Sonamarg, 9000 ft up in the Himalayas. Liz went off on a two day trip to see the Kalahoi glacier, and Alison stayed behind. On August 17 she went for a walk. She was last seen buying apples from a trader. Her clothes and rucksack were found in her room. It was six days later before her family were informed of her disappearance.

Her brother-in-law Donald Forsyth and her sister Mairi were living in Stornoway and the news leaked out. Donald was responsible for opening an account in the Stornoway branch of the Royal Bank of Scotland to help with travel expenses for Ken and his wife Reta to travel to India and people gave generously.

Ken has made 17 trips to India and Pakistan and also to Germany and Italy in his search. A reward Rs300,000 was also offered. He says: 'Alison belongs to Christ - she is His responsibility. We rely solely on His promises. We wait for Him.'

Ken became a Free Church minister and served at Rosskeen before retiring because of multiple sclerosis and he is also registered as blind. However he still serves as a supply minister. A man of great faith he is one of the most popular preachers in the Free Church.

****

The Molly custody case in 2006 certainly made the headlines in the UK and Pakistan.

It had started out as a possible abduction but it transpired that 12 year old Molly Campbell from Tong, a first year pupil at the Nicolson Institute in Stornoway, had absconded with her 18 year old sister Tahmina to fly to Pakistan.

As one former headmaster said: 'The Nicolson has not only a history but a geography.' There are four separate buildings one of them with four exits which would have made an abduction unlikely.

It transpired at a Police Press conference in the Caberfeidh Hotel - with Molly's mother Louise Campbell (38) and her partner, Kenny Campbell both present -- that the ploy had been well arranged.

Molly (aka Misbah Iram Ahmed Rana) was last seen within the school grounds at 10.50 am on Friday, August 25. She was met by her sister and they took a taxi to Stornoway Airport and flew to Glasgow where they were met by their father Sajad Ahmed Rana. They then boarded a flight for Lahore in Pakistan, where her father lived in a large villa.

However her mother Louise was the legal custodian. The three other family members were adults. She and Rana had married in Glasgow in 1984.

Louise made a tearful appeal at the Press conference for Molly to return. It naturally finished up in the courts and it began an international tug-of-war for the custody of the child. The father and Molly (who now insisted that she be called Misbah) played the media well.

A Pakistani court ruled that she be sent back to Lewis after her mother had lodged a legal petition claiming her daughter had been taken there illegally. Molly denied that she had been kidnapped and said she wanted to stay in Pakistan. There was a fine piece of emotional blackmail when she said in a messge to her mother on television: 'If you really love me you will let me stay here with my father.' She was also claiming that she had experienced racial abuse in the Western Isles, that her mother refused to allow her to perform Muslim prayers, and made her eat food forbidden by Islam.

Her father had filed papers seeking custody of his daughter claiming that no Muslim girl should be placed with a faithless mother in a 'sexually permissive society.'

Certainly the villa in a wealthy part of Lahore with a dozen rooms an expansive lawn and a 6ft high perimeter wall, was a far cry from the semi-detached Council home in Tong.

However in January there was surprise when Molly's mother decided to drop her claim at the Supreme Court in Islamabad for full custody of the child. While Louise was saying nothing in Tong, her lawyer in Pakistan told the Press that it was as a result of ill health that she wanted an out of court settlement for full custody as long as she had full access to Molly by telephone and internet, and have her home for holidays.

Later Louise and her partner Ken Campbell -- they had both come to Lewis several months previously to avoid Rana finding them -- split up.

****

Brian Souter of Stagecoach was the guest speaker at a Christian men's business lunch in Stornoway. Over coffee he was telling my table about attending a Garden Party at Holyrood. He espied one of his friends dressed up in his finery and shouted to him: 'Hey, Charlie, you didn't tell me it was fancy dress.'

Came the reply: 'I never do, that way I always win first prize.'

****

Another story which caught the attention of the News Desks was that of Lewisman Calum Murray of Gress who was kidnapped in Sierra Leone and held as a hostage for six months.

The Voluntary Service Overseas worker was among the first to be held by the Revolutionary United Front rebels, who were in conflict with the Government of the West African state.

Calum, a civil engineer, and his fellow hostages trekked for 16 days over rough terrain before being released into the care of the International Red Cross.

****

On three occasions the authorities recorded the death of a 70 year old island seaman Murdo Macleod, who even had a death certificate to show that he was buried in Holland.

During the Second World War Murdo was serving on the destroyer HMS Valentine when it was attacked by German bombers off the Dutch coast on May 15, 1940. He sustained two broken legs and other injuries. According to records he was 'seriously wounded and died there and was buried the following day in the Ternevzen Cemetery.'

When the remains of the victims were taken to a war cemetery after hostilities there was no trace of a grave for Murdo. A Dutch maritime documentalist wrote to the Stornoway Gazette to try and trace Murdo and they were put in touch with him at his home in Hill Street, North Tolsta.

At the end of the war he became a merchant seaman serving with the New Zealand Shipping Company and then the PO Line.

However Murdo was getting used to being written off. When his Merchant Navy pension stopped arriving at the bank each month he made enquiries. They told him they understood he had died but it turnout out to be another Murdo Macleod from Lewis. The same thing happened with his pension from the PO Line.

At the time of the interview Murdo told me he hoped to be around for a few more years!

****

In 1979 a South Uist crofter who had to send his children to school by pony because there were no roads, was granted an increase in his fodder allowance by the Education Comittee of the Western Isles Council.

The crofter, Eoghlainn MacLahlainn of 482 South Lochboisdale -- who had served as an officer with 'Mad Mitch' in Aden -- applied for an increase because inflation had gone up by 32 per cent since the last increase in 1977. Although he had three ponies -- Mairead, Sguab and Luchad - only two were used to carry his daughters Anna (11) and Seonag (6). They had to travel two miles over moor, a bog and a sea estuary to get to school.

The Council agreed to the fodder allowance of £1.50 per day with effect from the commencement of the winter term. However a road to his house was included in the Council's township road programme for 1980-81, when the allowance would be discontinued after the road was completed.

******

In the same year (1979) an application to allocate a beach for naturism got a chilly reception when it came before a meeting of the Council's Policy and Resources Committee which had four ministers, a priest, and three elders in its membership.

The letter, from the Central Council for British Naturism, stated they wished to help the island tourist trade and also to make 'thousands of British naturists happy.' The letter was noted with one councillor quipping: 'I don't think this is an area of desirable growth.'

Stornoway -- the Capital of the Hebrides -- was in the news when Stornoway Town Council decided to opt out of British Standard Time. A public meeting was to be called to set the date for turning the clocks back one hour.

The decision to defy the Goverment over BST was taken by four votes to two.

BST was introduced on October 27, 1968, and caused many problems in the island - probably the darkest place in winter in Britain. Not only is it far north but west of the Greenwich Meridian and darkness stayed till 10am. Provost Donald Stewart - who later became an MP - said: 'There is a great deal of danger to children and psychologiclly it is not good for people.'

For the sake of uniformity they were seeking support from Lewis District Council but this was not forthcoming. However the opt out proposal did get support from the Provosts of Wick and Thurso and by several MPs including Alick Buchanan-Smith, who described the Town Council's 'most praiseworthy unilateral decision.' MP Hector Munro said three-quarters of the people of Scotand wished to get rid of BST.

Captain Kenny Macleod, head of navigation at Lews Castle College, said Standard Time went against the law of the sun, but in winter months northern areas were affected far more than places further south. London had one hour 28 minutes longer daylight than Stornoway.

By 1970 Lewis District Council had changed their minds on BST and decided to oppose it.

After three years the BST trial finally ended on October 1971.

****

An Irish philosopher said that the only thing he was sure about was that a man entering a public toilet had the right of way.

Complaints by a Lewis Council house tenant about his 'magic floating carpet' resulted in a Residents' Association being formed at Vatisker Park in Back.

For over a year the Matheson family had been complaining about their floating carpet which took off every time there was a strong wind from a certain direction.

The tenant, Iain Matheson, threatened to report the Council to the Local Authority Ombudsman because he said the draughty conditions were now threatening the health of his two children. Following the publicity given to his problem Mr Matheson said he had received many sympathetic phone calls from neighbours, some of them with other complaints. As a result it was decided to form a residents' association.

He said he hoped his carpet problem would be near the top of the priority list they were drawing up because it had been reported to the Council 13 months previously. They had made an unsuccessful attempt to rectify the problem. His solicitor had a letter from the Council asking for more time.

****

An island cook who kept losing her voice when she went to church and only got it back again when she crossed the Minch on the ferry, baffled doctors and specialists with her problem.

She worked as a cook in the Crown Hotel in Stornoway. Her problem started about 1962 without any warning and without any prior illness. All the specialists could find no cure. She even tried hypnotism and although she got her voice back it did not cure her. However whenever she crossed the Minch her voice came back. Sometimes she was left completely mute and had to use sign language or communicate by writing notes.

She told me: 'My husband Alex and son-in-law think it's great.'

A fine example of Spin: The following e-mail was passed on to me from Rod the Gazette lensman. It alleged:

'Judy, a professional genealogical researcher, discovered that Hillary Clinton's great uncle Remus Rodham, a fellow lacking in moral character, was hanged for horse stealing and train robbery in Montana in 1889.

The only known photograph of Remus shows him standing on the gallows. On the back of the picture is the inscription: "Remus Rodham; horse thief, sent to Montana Territorial Prison 1885, escaped 1887, and robbed the Montana Flyer six times. Caught by Pinkerton detectives, convicted and hanged in 1889."

Judy e-mailed Hillary Clinton for comments. Hillary's staff of professional image adjusters cropped Remus' picture, scanned it, enlarged the image, and edited it with image processing softwear so that all that's seen is a head shot.

The accompanying biographical sketch says: "Remus Rodham was a famous cowboy in the Montana territory. His business empire grew to include the acquisition of valuable equestrian assets and intimate dealings with the Montana railroad.

'Beginning in 1883, he devoted several years of his life to a service at a govenment facility, finally taking leave to resume his dealings with the railroad.

"In 1887 he was a key player in a vital investigation run by the renowned Pinkerton Detective Agency. In 1889 Remus passed away during an important civic function held in his honour when the platform upon which he was standing collapsed."'

****

In the early 60s some people of Ness resorted to using the village well for water as their tap water was brown and dirty looking. They used a large circular hoop to prevent the two pails of water from colliding with their legs when walking back from the well.

A visitor in the early 60s was the Hollywood producer Alfred Hitchcock who arrived in Stornoway with his wife. He stayed at the Crown Hotel where I interviewed him.

He told me he was over to look at Amhuinnsuidhe Castle in North Harris as a possible location for a movie. He kindly posed for a few photographs.

As he had a reputation for making horror pictures, he was asked if there was anything in particular which gave him the horrors. 'Fried eggs,' he replied.

******

Also in the early 60s Stornoway-born Captain Donald Maclean, the former Commodore of the Cunard Line, was made an Freeman of the Burgh of Stornoway, along with two ex-Provosts, Roderick Smith and Alexander J Mackenzie.

Commodore Maclean was a former pupil of the Nicolson Institute and joined Cunard as a cadet. It was a Lewis family which helped establish Cunard and whose Gaelic name means 'high seas.'

While at the RN College at Greenwich he wrote the 'Maclean Pilotage Teacher.' During the war he served as a Lt. Cdr. on HMS Transylvania which was attacked and sunk. He was landed as a survivor at Gourock after spending a night in the water off Rockall. He was awarded the DSC in 1943 for sinking a U Boat.

After the war he returned to Cunard. In 1958 -- after commanding 8 passenger ships -- he was appointed to command the 34,000 liner Caronia on her Round-the-World luxury cruise. He also commanded the Mauretania and the Queen Mary. In 1960 he was appointed Commodore of the Cunard Fleet and appointed to Commodore and permanent command of the flagship Queen Elizabeth.

****

One seagoing man who endeared himself to the islanders was Captain John Smith, who during 35 years' service with MacBrayne's notched up over a million miles across the Minch.

He died while attending Communion services in Shawbost on the west side of Lewis. He was offering a prayer in a house gathering when he collaped and died. He was aged 77.

Captain Smith was one of the most accomplished and respected skippers in the MacBrayne fleet and retired about 10 years before his death. He inspired confidence in crew and passengers alike and when he berthed a vessel it was like a taxi pulling into the kerb. He had served on various ships in the fleet before being appointed as Master of the Loch Seaforth.

When he was presented with a silver salver by Stornoway Town Council in recognition of his 30 years' loyal service to the community -- why he was never given a gong we will never know -- he recalled that the Loch Seaforth had never missed a sailing due to bad weather during the 25 years she was under his command.

He told me: 'Some nights she found every hole in the Minch, but other nights she just danced across.'

****

Kilted Kiwi Sean Lineen -- who played centre 29 times for the Scottish rugby team and was a member of the notable Grand Slam team in 1990 -- visited Lewis in 1989 to visit his great uncle Murdo Macdonald at his croft in High Borve in Lewis. Sean's grandfatheher John Macdonald emigrated to New Zealand after the First World War. Sean's father was capped 12 times for the All Blacks. Sean is head coach of Glasgow Warriors.

On his visit to the island he was presented with a Stornoway Rugby Club tie by the vice-captan Iain Macleod.

****

In 1988 Lionel Morrison, president of the 32,000 strong National Union of Journalists, paid a visit to the island to meet the 12 union members and I had the pleasure of helping him to trace his roots as his grandfather had left the island at the turn of the century to emigrate to Africa. There he married an African woman who was the daughter of a Zulu chief. Lionel was named after the village where his father was born. He met up with several cousins and also visited the croft where his grandfather was born.

****

Over the years I have covered billionaire Donald Trump's connection to the island for various newspapers. His mother Mary Anne Macleod came from the village of Tong on the outskirts of Stornoway. She left the island as an 18 year old and met his father Fred, a carpenter and builder in New York. They built up an extensive property business and became millionaires. She returned to Lewis on several occasions to visit her relatives and was usually accompanied by one of her daughters, either Mary Anne, a lawyer, who later became a New York judge, or Elizabeth who was working in a bank.

In June 2008 -- on his way to a public inquiry in Aberdeen regarding his proposal for a £1 billion luxury golf resort and 1000 holiday homes on the Menie Estate -- he touched down in his private 727 jet. Along with his sister Mary Anne he visited the family croft house in Tong and met up with relatives.

At a Press conference he said he would be interested to hear more about plans to convert Lews Castle - which overlooks Stornoway Bay -- into a 5 star luxury hotel with 60 bedrooms.

****

Some islanders fondly imagine that the stretch of water known as the Minch adequately safeguards them from the various forms of legislation which are introduced from time to time.

Those dreading the new fixed penalties for parking offences -- which came into effect on December 1, 1986 -- must have thought that for once the Government had been defeated.

Stornoway motorists were convinced that the good old days of a smile and a warning - and sometimes a wee ceilidh -- by Stornoway's two Traffic Wardens were going to continue.

After two weeks no fines had been imposed by the two wardens - affectionately known as Pinky and Perky -- and the coffers of central government had received no contribution from the island.

However we established the cause from Chief Inspector William John Fraser who ruefully revealed that due to a hiccup in the system that the on-the-spot parking tickets never arrived on the island.

They were expected any day but as Christmas was approaching there would be a further amnesty period between the motorists and the traffic wardens. But he warned motorists: 'Beware, the new system will definitely come into effect on January 1.'

****

Because of the serious litter problem in Stornoway town centre on a Sunday morning a taxi was provided to convey a street cleaner to work on Saturday nights.

This followed a complaint to the Council by the Stornoway Chamber of Trade who felt that the 'unsightly mess on Sunday mornings could only be detrimental to the good name of Stornoway.'

Cleansing staff had indicated their 'total refusal' to consider Sunday working,' but the street sweeper was willing to do it late on Saturday nights. However he lived four miles away and had no car, so it was agreed to provide a taxi for him.

****

Well-known South Uist poet and novelist Angus Peter Campbell, was one of the nominees for best actor at the Lloyds TSB BAFTA Scotland Awards in 2007 for his part in the Gaelic film 'Seachd: The Inaccessible Pinnacle'. Like the rest of the cast he was not a professional actor and described his first acting experience as 'sort of winching with the camera.'

A story which amused the newspapers - and even Woman's Own -- was about the chastity belt worn by young sheep.

To safeguard gimmers -- a sheep only a year old -- from the ram crofters used to sew on a breid -- a patch or apron -- during the breeding season to prevent them becoming pregnant, especially if the crofter was planning to send it to market.

Although it has now died out a retired vet told me that it was 'a practice accepted but frowned upon.'

****

As the memory begins to fade the older we get it reminds me of two stories. The first was told me by friend over the years, fellow journalist Ron Lyon of Inverness. We were recalling old times but sometimes we could not remember the name of the colleague or which paper he had worked on. It reminded Ron of of the two old fellows living next door to each other and who helped each other out.

One day one of them asked his pal if he needed anything and was told yes he could get him some ice cream, then added: 'And get some of that 1001 dressing on it,' and 'Oh, aye, get one of these choco sticks too.' His pal came back an hour later with a hot pie and was told: 'You forgot the chips!'

That's like the elderly couple who came back from holiday with a great tan and at Glasgow airport were asked by the taxi driver where they had been to get such a good tan.

The husband said: 'It'll come back in a minute.' The taxi driver says: 'But you must remember where you got a tan like that.' He was pressed again by the taxi driver. The man asked him: 'What do you call that green stuff that climbs up the wall?'

'Ivy' said the taxi driver.' The man turns to his wife and says: 'Ivy, where were we on holiday?'

Ken Macdonald outside the hostel from which Alison disappeared

Harris crofter using an old oil drum for threshing

Bill & Donnie at Windsor

Prince Charles and Diana *Molly or Misbah*

Cdr Donald Maclean *Captain John Smith*

School transport - pony style - in South Uist

Ness water carrier coming from the well   *Sheep with chastity belt*

Alfred Hitchcock   *Rt Hon Donald Stewart*

Stornoway Town Council pose for Scotsman photograher
Clockwise from left of top table: M Macleod (Town Clerk) Provost
D Stewart: A Matheson, J Macrae, M McCallum (Burgh Surveyor)
K Nicolson (Burgh Treasurer): B Lucas, A Nicoll, Mrs Urquhart,
S Matheson and J Macleod

John Macleod of 5 Einacleit in Uig on the remote west side of Lewis lived in a traditional tigh dubh (a black house) with his sister Annie. Known as 'Brace' he decided to build a new house of natural stone and it took him 22 years!

He worked the stone from a nearby quarry, dressed it to size, and then transported it by wheelbarrow one at a time to the site of the new home which overlooks Little Loch Roag. He had started the work shortly after the Second World War. I wrote several stories about him, and then about 1969 he came up against officialdom. The walls were up and the roof rafters and he planned to cover it with corrugated asbestos which was commonly used at that time.

Not so, said the Ross-shire Planning Department, he must use tiles which would fit in better with the landscape. This placed the Brace in a difficult situation because tiles were far more expensive. However the Highland Fund stepped in a made up the cost difference and tiles were used.

John Macleod died in 1980 aged 78. The house is now occupied by a second cousin of the Brace named Neil Macritchie. Because some of the pointing between the natural stone work was beginning to wear and causing leaks, Neil decided to have it roughcast. The ruins of the old black house are nearby.

Billionaire Donald Trump at the entrance to the crofthouse at Tong in Lewis where his mother Mary Anne was brougth up

Donald with his sister Mary Anne, a New York judge (on left) along with relatives at the old family home in Tong

CIVIC DUTIES

When I left The Scotsman to set up my freelance agency my colleagues told me I would starve to death.

But I explained to them that all the statutory bodies on the island would provide the bread and butter for my news agency. There was the Stornoway Town Council, the Lewis District Council, the Stornoway Pier and Harbour Commission, the Stornoway Trust and the Health Board. Then I added: 'And of course there are the churches.'

This puzzled them but over the years, sad to say, there have been many church stories and not just from presbytery meetings.

It reminds me of the man who was marooned on a desert island and after a number of years he was finally sighted by a passing ship.

A launch headed for the island and the officer saw three buildings. He asked the castaway: 'What's that building in the centre,' 'That's where I live' was the reply. 'What about the one to the right?' 'That's the church I go to.' 'And what's the one to the left?' 'That's the church I used to go to.'

The Council, the Trust and the Harbour Commission meetings were held in the evenings and some of these could go on until midnight, depending on the mood of certain councillors.

Some of the Council meetings were rather boisterous. There was the occasion when an ex-Baillie had to be restraind after having a difference of opinion with a fellow councillor. The incident occurred when the Councillors were discussing a circular from the Scottish Development Department on the allocation of council houses.

Ex Baillie John Macleod declared that the council's method of allocation was 'as fair as you can get.' This caused Councillor Abraham Langley to laugh.

The Ex-Baillie snapped: 'Let Mr Langley laugh again and I''ll see him outside.'

'If you're able to see' came the retort.

At this Ex Baillie Macleod rose and made for the councillor saying: 'I''ll certainly see you now.' He was restrained by Dean of Guild James Maclennan who told him: 'Don't be so daft and sit down.'

By this time Provost Donald J Stewart was on his feet trying to keep order. The word 'nonsense' was muttered by Councillor Langley at this stage and ex-Baillie Macleod accused him of having 'given us nonsense for years.'

Earlier there had been a clash between the two members when the Council was discussing special inducements to attract industry, and Councillor Langley had said: 'At least I am sober.'

'And so am I sir, and if you'd like to have it out I'll see you outside,' said ex-Baillie Macleod.

Ex-Provost Mrs Anne Urquhart reminded those present of the Standing Orders,' and 'marching orders' were referred to by Councillor Langley.

'Ex-Bailie Macleod said: 'Marching orders, you never marched in your life.'

That was on the Monday night and it was not a good week for Ex-Baillie Macleod, affectionately known as John the Barber throughout the island.

On the Tuesday night at the Harbour Commission meeting he so riled the Harbourmaster that he threated to resign.

Friday night was the Stornoway Trust meeting. John was still on form but fortunately he nodded off at the start of the meeting and Slim Jim Macrae, the chairman, asked the other Trustees to keep their voices down in case they awakened the tonsorial artist.

John retired as a barber in 1973 after over 20 years of public service. He served as a 'bunting tosser,' a signalman in the Royal Navy during the Second World War. He recalled that when he started with the barber shop in Point Street he was a soap boy and sweeper. When he started his apprenticeshp he had to practice shaving on a blown up balloon with an open razor. 'If you could shave the soap off without bursting the baloon, then you were allowed to shave customers,' he told me.

For many years he gave free haircuts to many old and disabled people in their own homes.

At one point the Council served an eviction notice on Dean of Guild Donald Maclean (known as Basher) because of his rent arrears of £11.11s for his three-apartment council house. However the eviction notice was withdrawn when he paid up.

The Burgh of Stornoway was reckoned to be one of the top in the UK league for rent and rate collections for town council houses. Under the able guidance of Burgh Treasurer Kenny Nicolson it was 99.9 per cent. Even the shortfall was because a tenant was on holiday.

I myself eventually finished up serving as an elected member of the Town Council and also represented them on Ross and Cromarty County Council which meant travelling to Dingwall for the meetings.

One of the things I managed to achieve on the Town Council was a points system for the allocation of Council houses which was much fairer than what had occurred before when people were continually canvassing and it depended on who you knew.

The other thing which I have no regrets over is that I proposed Sandy Matheson as Provost. He became the youngest ever civic head of the burgh. He had second thoughts on the day of the meeting and came up to my house at lunchtime. We knew there was another candidate. But I persuaded him to let his name go forward. There was a tied vote and it was Sandy's name which came out of the hat.

When his photograph appeared in the local paper along with the two robed Baillies -- who were both over six feet -- one person remarked: 'I never realised Sandy was so small' to which Buck Forsyth said: 'What do you expect, he came out of a hat!'

Anyway Sandy went on to have an illustrious career. He was also chairman of the Harbour Commission and the Stornoway Trust, and became Convener of the new Western Isles Council and an Honorary Sheriff. He also served as chairman of the Islands Commission of the EU's CPMR (the Committee of Peripheral Maritime Regions). One of his virtues was that he has always been able to tell a story against himself.

On retiring from the local authority he became the successful chairman of the Highlands and Islands Airports Authority and was an excellent ambassador for the island wherever he went. He is the present Lord Lieutenant of the Western Isles.

While on the Council I was also involved in the Attraction of Industry Committee and produced a booklet and served on and later became secretary of the Lewis Development Fund which provided loans for island people setting up a new business.

While I served on Ross and Cromarty County Council I had the pleasure of moving the motion that we divorce ourselves from the mainland body and become our own Western Isles Council. At that time Lewis came under the administration of Ross-shire and Harris, the Uists and Barra came under Inverness-shire.

My motion came about following the Wheatley Report into the

Re-organisation of Local Government. All the local island bodies were in favour of the Western Isles becoming a multi-purpose authority under the new scheme.

So it eventually came to pass and the islanders themselves now make their own decisions. They were under-funded from day one, but they have survived. They took the bold decision early on to look after the needs of the Southern Isles which had been neglected by Inverness-shire. The new divisional administrative headquarters in Balivanich was erected before the Council had a proper place themselves and made do with the Town Hall for its meetings.The first new school was built at Lionacleit in Benbecula which became the Council's flagship.

They have also seen the islands linked up by ferries and causeways, which was only a dream at one time.

When I was absent from the meetings through illness on one occcason and then returned to my usual Press seat in the Chamber I was welcomed back by the PR chairman as the '31st member of the Council.'

The Authority has had its problems and at Press lunches I used to say that we did not make jokes about the Western Isles Council we only reported the facts!

One man who took them on following the loss of a five year street lighting contract was Lewis electrical contractor, Iain Crichton. After an 11 year battle he was awarded £139, 790, although he had sued them for £500,000.

The good news came just a week before Christmas, 2007, although Iain would have liked Santa's sack to be filled with something nearer to the sum he was seeking in the civil action.

At the time of writing a hearing on expenses has still to be heard. His solicitor, Mr Angus Macdonald of Stornoway, said that the expenses would be in the region of £100,000.

Iain told me after the Sheriff's judgement:'The position I adopted 11 years ago has been vindicated by the Sheriff's decision in my favour.'

From day one there was an avid interest in the case throughout the community and further afield.

After a number of callings the case began in July 2006 before Sheriff Desmond J Leslie and the final submissions were heard in June 2007. The Pursuer, Iain Crichton of Knock - who was represented by Stuart Buchanan, Advocate -- claimed that the award of the 5 year street lighting contract to the Council's Direct Services Organisation in 1996 was unfair and that the Council had acted in bad faith. The Council (the Defenders) was represented by Steven L Stuart, Advocate.

In evidence Mr Crichton said that the DSO had failed to include the price or hire of plant for the street lighting maintenance contract: they had failed to take into account a sum of £57,000 for stock: and the cost of £79,000 for the TUPE staff transference regulations Therefore the tender submitted by the DSO had been artificially low and Mr Crichton had been unable to compete fairly.

He told the court that he had submitted a very tight tender in 1996 because he had £50,000 of stock in hand and all the requisite personnel to carry out the work. He could not believe that he had lost the contract to the Council's DSO. His contract was £4500 more than the lowest tender of £171,776 submitted by the DSO. He also said that the contract accounted for 85 per cent of his work. He was suing the Council for £455,000 with interest at 8 per cent per annum from April 1, 2001 until any award is paid.

The Sheriff also heard of a confidential Council report which noted that the DSO were 'under pressure to win contracts at any cost.'

At one stage an Advocate was appointed as a Commissioner to ensure that all the relevant documents in relations to the contract were made available by the Council. The Sheriff was told that the Council had chosen to be selective in the documents produced.

The Sheriff found that the Defenders (the Council) had acted in a way which 'demonstrated inequality of treatment between the Defenders' DSO and the Pursuers by failing to evaluate labour, stock and plant costs to be incurred by the Defenders.'

In his judgement Sheriff Leslie stated: 'I am not satisfied that Western Isles Council, despite their forceful and occasionally bombastic efforts to do so, satisfied me that they acted in a way demonstrable of fair, transparent and equal treatment towards all tenders received'.

Sheriff Leslie said no secret had been made by the Council's officers (Donald MacRitchie, in charge of street lighting contracts, and Technical Director Murdo Murray) that the preferred Council policy was to have their public works undertaken by their own DSO. He could not discount the possibility that such a policy may have contributed to a diminution of objectivity when the assessment procedures were conducted.

The Council 'noted with disappointment' the Sheriff's judgement and said it would be examined in detail in the first instance.

******

I also served on the old Western Isles Tourist Association and edited their brochure which got up the nose of Sir Hereward the Wake who owned the North Harris estate. I had used a photograph of his home, Amhuinnsuidhe Castle, which he wanted dropped from the brochure as it would only encourage tourists.

The main road passed the front of the castle and was only a stone's thrown from the splendid salmon river. He was unsuccessful in his attempt to get the photogrpah dropped and also unsuccessful in trying to persuade Inverness-shire County Council to divert the road round the back of the castle.

Over the years I produced newsletters for the Council and the Health Board.

****

The Health Board has also had the knack of getting news coverage over the years.

In 1988 a four year dispute with the South Uist part-time consultant surgeon Mr Debarata Chatterje finally came to and end and cost the board £235,000. The result was that instead of being able as the GP to refer patients to himself as the Consultant, two new contracts were drawn up which covered his surgeon work and his non- surgeon work at Daliburgh Hospital. During the dispute the Board had been suplying consultant surgeons on a locum basis at the hospital - a very expensive business.

Then the Board took the controversial decision to suspend acute emergency operations at Daliburg Hospital. This was a result of a recommendation by a team from the Scottish Advisory Commitee on Medical Establishments that the single-handed surgical unit be closed on the grounds of 'inadequacy of workload and the safety of patients.' Cases would be transferred either to Glasgow or to Stornoway. Needless to say the locals were hostile to the proposals because for years they had been expressing the fear that the hospital would be closed.

The Board drew up a list of options and decided, after consultation, to implement Option 8 which meant that three GPs with an interest in anaesthetics, surgery and obstetrics should provide the cover required -- along with visiting specialists -- from the GP practice at Benbecula.

Don Cruickshank, the Chief Executive of the National Health Service in Scoltland, thought this was an 'imaginative proposal,' and that it was 'sensible and worklike.'

The Board then came up with a long-term option to provide a new multi-million purpose-built hospital on a greenfield site which would replace the two existing hospitals at Lochmaddy in North Uist and Daliburgh in South Uist.

But the Daliburgh Hospital Action Group, led by Canon John Angus

Galbraith, were opposed to this. They wanted to retain and enhance the surgical services at Daliburgh.

The Action Group's campaign increased in intensity and to show that they meant business they chartered the CalMac ferry and sailed for Stornoway with 500 protesters on board. They then marched to the Board headquarters. While the Board agreed to meet delegates the protesters declined the invitation because the Board would not come to their rally in Stornoway Town Hall.

Canon Galbaith told the rally that he was very sorry indeed that the Health Board had refused to come to speak to those who had travelled so far to 'demonstrate their profound dissatisfaction with the way the Health Board had been conducting itself.' About 560 people had attended a public meeting in Iochar School in South Uist - including representatives of many local organisations -- and they had made it clear that Daliburgh was the most central, nearest and most accessible place in case of emergencies. They would continue to bring the issue to the attention of the Scottish Office.

The Health Board chairwoman, Mrs Mairi Macmillan, isued a statement saying they were disappointed that representatives from the Action Group had not taken advantage of the opportunity to speak with Board members. She said it was wrong to claim that the Board was running the hospital down: the Board's plans were for improvement and development of services.

Eventually a new £8.5 million state-of-the-art hospital was built at Balivanich in Benbecula.

In Janaury 1995 the Board unanimously agreed not to re-instate Geoff Stobbs, their Director of Finance, who was sacked for 'gross misconduct' after he had accepted a free golfing holiday at The Belfry Club from the Board's travel firm when the contract was due for renewal.

However all these skirmishes were merely a training ground for what was looming ahead.

When Dick Manson became Chief Executive in April 2004 several of the old guard disappeared and from then on the Health Board was more like a TV hospital drama with a crisis every week.

For an 18 month period controversy surrounded the Board with allegations of bullying, a threat of industrial action, calls for senior officials to be sacked, and at that time there was an accumulated deficit of £2.4 million. There was stated to be a 'climate of distrust' between the Board and Council.

After the resignation of chairman David Currie in August 2006, Health Minister Andy Kerr and his team arrived to deliver a 'tough message to the Board and to give them one last chance.' However things got off to a bad start -- he and his team were locked out of the board headquarters and there was a frantic phoning by mobiles to get someone to open the door.

The chairman's resignation was followed by the departure of Dick Manson (he was seconded to a post in NHS Scotland), Dr John Smith, the Medical Director, and Kay Young, Director of Organisation and Learning.

John Angus Mackay, former chair of Gaelic Media Services, was appointed chairman, and in January 2007 Laurence Irvine from Norfolk took up the post of Chief Executive. However after queries about his CV he was suspended and the annual review by the Health Minister Nicola Sturgeon had to be postponed. John Turner was appointed as Acting Chief Executive.

In the latest audit report for the year 2006 - 2007 the Auditor General reported that the Board had an accumulated deficit of £3.364 million. It was the third year that he had issued a Section 22 report on its accounts. He highlighted 'serious weaknesses' in the board's governance arrangements: a failure to meet financial targets: saving targets which looked unlikely to be met: a 'lapse of budgetary control.': and a lack of corporate objectives. He would be holding an inquiry into their financial and managerial troubles.

On May 6, 2008, the Scottish Parliament's Audit Committee, highlihgted serious failures in the running of NHS Western Isles and a failure year after year to have in place adequate financial controls

The Committee also described the situation whereby the Health Board had three chief executives - one suspended, one on secondment and one acting - as unacceptable and called on the Scottish Government to work with the board to resolve the situation urgently.

Over all the report found that a number of factors contributed to the financial failings at the board, which had a cumulative deficit of £3.36 million at the end of the financial year 2006/07. These factors included external cost pressures from changes in the wider NHS and issues stemming from the design of health services in the Western Isles.

However, the report found that the situation was exacerbated by inadequate internal control systems and weak financial management at the board.

The committee went on to express concern over appointment processes used in the NHS, and considered there to be a lack of transparency in the way people were appointed to temporary posts and secondments. As such, the committee recommended that the Government reviewed its appointment processes and procedures for dealing with incompetence, inefficiency and failures in performance.

Committee Convener Hugh Henry MSP said: 'It is clear that there is considerable anger and dismay, especially in the local community, regarding the failures in systems and management that have taken place within Western Isles Health Board over a number of years. It is not acceptable for the same failures to keep occurring year after year, as happened within NHS Western Isles.

'This committee is deeply concerned by the fact that the board has three chief executives. This must be resolved urgently. We also believe that the Government must review its arrangements for appointing staff to temporary posts and secondments to ensure proper transparency.

'Where failure occurs, it is simply not good enough to keep moving staff on, often to senior positions. There is a worry that this occurrence might reflect a wider culture in the health service of failing to address performance issues and we would be concerned if this also happens in the wider civil service.

'The Permanent Secretary at the Scottish Government should review the procedures for dealing with incompetence and report back to our committee.

'The Committee believes that the Health Directorates must bear part of the responsibility for failures at the board, as they should have ensured that the clinical strategy being pursued by the board was sustainable. The Health Directorates should also have identified the management failures at the board much earlier and taken more decisive action.'

The Committee were also scathing of Mr Manson and Mr Currie's personal evidence to the inquiry during which they claimed not to recall the existence of the crucial 'Cook Report' into the board's finances. The Committee say that Mr Manson and Mr Currie's explanations were 'unsatisfactory and extremely unhelpful to the inquiry' and caused the commitee to find their evidence "unconvincing."

But there's always a silver lining. Health Minister Nicola Sturgeon announced that they had agreed to assist NHS Western Isles with their £3.097 million accumulated debt by giving them a loan over three years so that they can have a fresh start. She stressed that the island boards would remain independent and that the Government had concluded that no further investigation or inquiry was needed concerning the Western Isles Health Board

(Dick Manson left the Board's employment on September 5, 2008).

*******.

In April 2004 the new Stornoway Port Authority came into being in place of the Stornoway Pier and Harbour Commission which had lasted for 139 years.

In giving his valedictory address at the last meeting of the Harbour Commission -- which I had also served on for a number of years -- Chairman Iain Macleod said that it was more than just a name and boundary change. The title 'Commissioner' had reflected the original remit of the members of the port organisation who were charged with the establishment and commissioning of harbour facilities. That era, he said, had now passed.

He said they were now charged with running the port accountably, openly, efficiently, and effectively. The new method of appointment to the Board sent out a clear signal -- members had to be fit for the purpose and would be appointed on merit. (Previously members were appointed from the Town Council, the Stornoway Trust, the dues payers and one by the Sheriff Principal).

He stated that as well as managing port assets to the best effect, they would be expected to actively explore new business opportunities and to consider partnerships with other bodies. Less time would be spent on detail, much of which would be delegated to officers of the Authority.

What I was never able to understand was that if they were going to run the port 'openly' one of their first decisions was to ban the Press from their meetings. They did agree to issue regular Press statements.

****

However when covering all these bodies you had to rely a lot on the officials. I was fortunate in dealing with Murdo Macleod, the Town Clerk and later General Manager of the Harbour Commission, as well as D M (Safety) Smith, the Factor of the Stornoway Trust, as well as various Council officials. Their successors -- and their secretaries - were very helpful too. There were also court officials, lawyers, and Norman Macarthur of Stornoway Shipping Services.

I also became invoved in SNP politics and was Campaign Manager for Donnie Stewart when he was elected as MP for the Western Isles after the seat had been held by M K Macmillan for Labour for the previous 35 years. Donnie became a highly respected Parliamentarian and became a Privy Councillor.

When Donald and his wife Chrissie arrived in Glasgow from the island after his victory -- he was to be the only Scottish Nationalist in the government -- the celebrations at Glasgow Central Station were so great that instead of putting them on the London train they put them on the wrong one!

He held the seat for 17 years until his retiral when it was regained by Calum Macdonald for Labour. However the SNP now have an MP for Western Isles again - Angus MacNeil as well as an MSP Dr Alasdair Allan.

I also became hon. secretary of the Bethesda Nursing Home and Hospice in Stornoway. It is undergoing an extension and any profits from the sale of this book will be going to them. In 1998 I was made a Life Member of the National Union of Journalists.

After hilarious times playing for Stornoway Rugby Club in my younger years. for recreation I amused myself on the golf course - the clubs were my handicap -- and also became chairman of the Stornoway Sea Angling Club which at that time was able to attract the European Championships twice to the town. They were amongst the best organised championships anywhere because of the dedication of a great bunch of lads. I have a membership card dated 1794 but I'm not as old as that - it was a misprint!

The Rotary Club also beckoned and I served as secretary and as Junior Vice President as well as producing a newsletter for them.

However there came a change in my lifestyle and I now try to serve the Lord as an office-bearer in the Free Church of Scotland and that too has been a very fulfilling and happy time for me.

Bethesda Care Home and Hospice before extension

An old friend, the Rt Hon George Reid, MSP, the Presiding Officer at the Scottish Parliament, presented me with the Barron Trophy at the Highland Media Awards in 2005. It recognised a lifetime achievement in journalism and for outstanding service to the community. The panel were also kind enough to say that I 'had commanded the respect of the community and newsdesks throughout the land with my informed reporting.'

A chiel's amang ye takin' notes, an' faith he'll prent it -- Burns

Shalom aleikhem